Whole Earth

Ann E. Davis

Whole Earth

Beyond the Entitlement of the Property Owner

Springer

Ann E. Davis
School of Management
Marist College
Poughkeepsie, NY, USA

ISBN 978-3-031-01933-3 ISBN 978-3-031-01934-0 (eBook)
https://doi.org/10.1007/978-3-031-01934-0

This Springer imprint is published by the registered company Springer Nature Switzerland AG
The registered company address is: Gewerbestrasse 11, 6330 Cham, Switzerland

To Bob and our family

Preface

The purpose of this book is to explore the property relation and its environmental implications. My contention is that this concept provides the owner with the authority to command other people and the Earth. This notion of property is a form of knowledge, which is also enacted and defended by experts and the state. By treating other people as objects, there is a form of behavior which is expected and enforced, a form of compliance. This normative role then removes the agency of the actor, who must follow the script. The entire capitalist system is then a process of enactments which are beyond the control of the participants.

Property is a term which is widely known in the general public, as well as the subject of scholarly debate in philosophy, political science, economics, and history. This term structures daily life, and is understood to aid in life chances, although its operation undermines ecology and personal independence, in my view. While property is presumably an object, it is also a social relationship, capable of affecting personal identity and political affiliation.

Knowledge of the system is important in all its manifestations, including key terms, institutions, expertise, and debates, which requires the study of social and natural sciences, as well as philosophy and history. There is a world view and value system which can be explored, and possible alternatives articulated.

Chapter 1, "Beyond Reification: Envisioning the Earth," explores the concepts by which daily life can ignore the requirements of life, such as air, water, and stable temperature.

Chapter 2, "The Modern Institution of Science," explores the natural science which enables control of Earth processes, without specifying the purpose.

Chapter 3, "History of Political Economy," reviews the social sciences as well as political economy, and the divergence from natural science.

Chapter 4, "Fictitious Capital: Money, the Symbol, and the State," reviews Marx's insights into property and money, and how they are understood and enacted in the capitalist system.

Chapter 5, "The Public Private Divide," reviews the institutional divisions experienced as the "public" and "private," even though the system operates as a whole.

Chapter 6, "Abstraction and Reification," further explores how real abstractions and reifications permit the system to operate like a machine, with passive participants instead of collective agents.

Chapter 7, "Proletarianization and Commodification," reviews the long-term history of the USA, and the processes of commodification of the land and proletarianization of the population, with the impact on culture and politics.

Chapter 8, "Regional Ecological Communities," provides an alternative organization, regional ecological communities, which places priority on Earth and human capacity, providing a system for human agency and collaborative stewardship.

Chapter 9, "Conclusions," reviews the remaining questions and further explorations.

Poughkeepsie, NY, USA Ann E. Davis

Acknowledgments

I would like to thank Mona Ali, Gary Dymski, Paddy Quick, Al Campbell, Kirstin Munro, Chris O'Kane, and Paul Cooney for helpful discussions, as well as Jason Moore, Diana Gildea, John Antenucci, Robert McAulay, Jeff McAulay, Lucy Johnson, Leathem Mehaffey III, Mark Cladis, Edith Kuiper, and Hendrik Hartog.

Marist College students and colleagues have been very helpful, especially Helen Rothberg, Zion Klos. Caroline Rider, Richard Feldman, James Snyder, Jessica Boscarino, Steve Sansola, and Michael O'Sullivan.

All remaining errors and omissions are entirely my own.

Contents

Part I
Basic Framework

Chapter 1
Introduction: Beyond Reification: Envisioning the Earth

> *"And the time will come when you see we are all one*
> *And life flows on within you and without you"*
> *George Harrison, Beatles 1967*
>
> *"Within You Without You"*

The awareness of "society" emerged in the nineteenth century with the establishment of the labor market and the occurrence of the "social problem" related to unemployment and the increasing ranks of the poor (Polanyi 1944). That is, "society" was an emergent category (Poovey 2002).

Similarly, in the twenty-first century, the "Anthropocene" is an emergent category, with the disruption of normal weather patterns, and evidence of the accumulation of CO_2 in the atmosphere and its correlation with increasing surface temperatures.

Even with the new term and the new category, it is still a question as to how to proceed. Like others (Baucom 2020; Moore 2015), we search for an adequate method.

In the work that follows, we will build on previous explorations in historical institutionalism (Davis 2015, 2017, 2020a), which focuses on key terms like property and money, related institutions, and expertise. But in what follows, we will focus on the flip side of reification, the processes that go one without awareness, which are taken for granted, treated as stable "objects." We will describe the long-term co-evolution of humans and the earth, the development of human language, and, ultimately, the key institutions of capitalism. As shown in Fig. 1.1, a key term such as "property" can represent a specific relationship between a person and an object. That key term then signifies that relationship in other contexts, in which it is reinforced and taken for granted, or reified, as shown in Fig. 1.2. Ultimately with the emergence of capitalism, those specific institutions are integrated by money and finance, as shown in Fig. 1.3. These terms and institutions do not reveal the interdependence with the earth's ecology. With the Anthropocene, these previously assumed phenomena are disrupted, less predictable, and deserving of direct study and exploration.

A. E. Davis, *Whole Earth*, https://doi.org/10.1007/978-3-031-01934-0_1

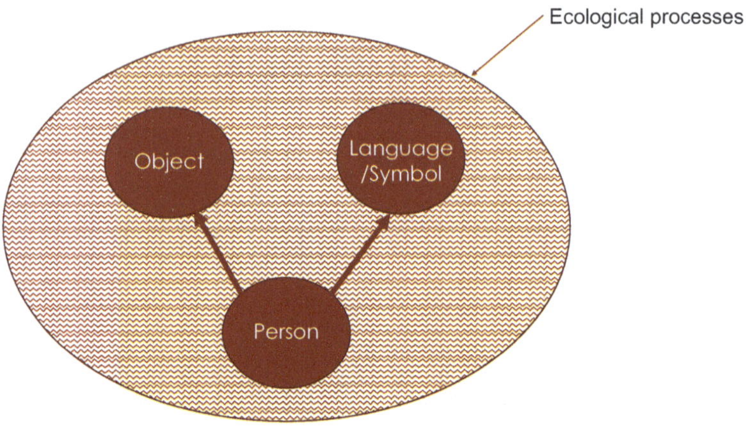

Fig. 1.1 Daily experience

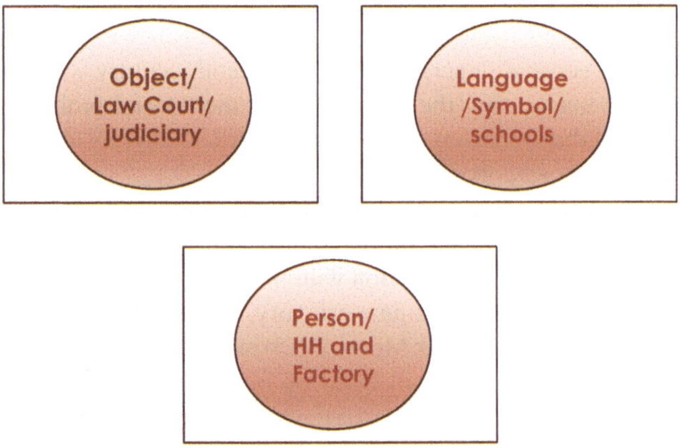

Fig. 1.2 Separate institutions to stabilize and reproduce key functions

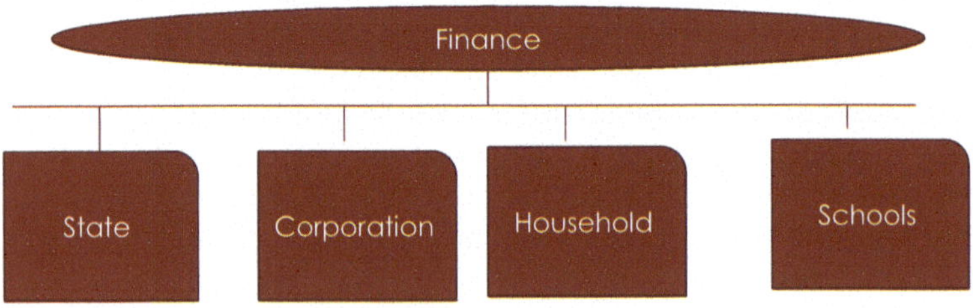

Fig. 1.3 Integration by finance

1 Summary of Project

The interface between humans and nature is still an issue in the development of methodology (Latour 1993; Moore 2015; Malm 2018). That is, are we still "modern," which generally means accepting a divide between humans and nature, as well as social and natural science. A starting place in this work is to continue the study of property (Davis 2015) and the "paradigm of property." In earlier work, we have stated that property is inherently social, although the "paradigm of property" proposes that property is individual, a discreet parcel of the earth which can be separated and traded on a market, distinct from other parcels. According to this view, human personality is developed by ownership and improvement of property, a deeply held incentive for economic activity.

By contrast, in this work, we hold that property is inherently social. Further, property in land, the paradigmatic metaphor, incorporates "nature" and also reifies it. Any parcel of land contributes to and is influenced by biogeochemical cycles which are global. Yet property is defined by a set of institutions, legal and economic, which enable its definition and enforcement without reference to these global ecological cycles. This omission is systemic, based on concepts which omit any reference to "nature." Rather, property is defined as if the earth were an abstract homogeneous geographical plane, defined by boundaries and standard metrics. The distinguishing features of property in land are location, such as GPS coordinates, and structures built by humans, such as the urban business center. That is, "space" is constructed. Various contributors have challenged this view, without widespread impact to date.

The goal of this work is to incorporate "nature" into economics, to overcome this "modern constitution" (Latour 1993). Land use is a key feature of the human interface with the atmosphere and the oceans, which is documented historically. The science of ecology has developed tools and metrics which facilitate direct measurement and modeling of changes in land use and the effect on global biogeochemical cycles. Rather than consider these effects a mere "externality," like an afterthought, it is now possible and necessary to integrate these global processes with the economy. In fact, humans encounter and incorporate "nature" at every scale, at every moment in time, with every breath and every meal, with every drink of water and disposal of wastes. These interfaces have become invisible and below conscious awareness, with the technological advances of modernity and urban infrastructures.

The founding framework of Lockean political economy enables this worldview. Locke's worldview is like placing a mantle over the entire earth and declaring it designed solely for human purposes. There is a presumed entitlement to the earth, given by God, for human survival and enjoyment. Parcelization and individualization of property ownership is presumed to be more productive of economic commodities, which contribute to Smith's goal of the "Wealth of Nations." The extension of markets is the objective of public and private spheres alike and the use of money to facilitate transactions (Davis 2017). The accumulation of money enables property owners to avoid Locke's "spoilage limit" and to apparently exceed ecological constraints.

For Locke, money is a precious metal which can be stored indefinitely, represent wealth, and trade for commodities in the future. The money object, such as gold, is considered valuable in itself and so can represent value. The role of money as a symbol, meaningful to other participants in the market system, is not explored. In this period, the focus was on the material composition of coin, to increase confidence in the market system, and the establishment of trade. Yet this symbolic dimension may increase its liquidity and durability, since the idea of sound money is reinforced with every trade, which then enhances its convertibility for coin and commodity in more places and circumstances. Confidence in the currency reinforces Smith's "extension of the market."

Even though Locke and Smith endorsed the labor theory of value, it was Marx who discussed reification. That is, the human energy embodied in the production of commodities is represented by money. Then money, as the abstract representation of "value," is convertible to raw materials extracted from "nature," the physical transformation of the production process with wage labor, and the distribution of commodities through the financial circuit, with that value to be accumulated ultimately as surplus. The recognition of money as a symbol of value is relative to a specific human community (Davis 2020b), whose existence becomes invisible, nonetheless, relative to that valuable object.

Property, money, and value are reifying abstractions. Such abstractions "seem as real as material entities…as a consequence of the general acceptance of what Thomas Nagel calls a 'view from nowhere'…. It has become possible to think about social structures, relationships, and processes as entities, as relatively autonomous, and as sufficiently systematic to warrant scientific descriptions" (Poovey 2002, 125). For example, an entity called "the economy" emerged in seventeenth-century England (Poovey 2002, 136), further delineated by Smith's work in the eighteenth century.

Modernity may be characterized by such abstractions, like value. Once labor has been performed on an object which is not owned by that worker, it takes on its own movements, driven by the need by the employer to earn cash proceeds to repay money borrowed to initiate production. This financial circuit then has its own dynamic and appears to be an "automaton," where money is loaned at a given rate of interest on financial markets. Given the visibility of financial circuits and the relative invisibility of the labor process, the technique of studying the performance of "the economy" can appear as amenable to the objective techniques of scientific management, to achieve "growth" (Mitchell 2014). The expenditure of human energy disappears into the "value" of the commodity, which can be apparently replaced by other energy sources like water, work animals, and fossil fuels. Energy is ubiquitous, characteristic of all living beings, but in modern discourse seems only to refer to fossil fuels which are essential to the industrial economy. The worker seems expendable, and the human foundation of the entire objective "economy" is not apparent. Another abstraction, "the market," becomes an impersonal "steering mechanism" for the entire process of production and consumption (Polanyi 1944), characterized by the new science of economics.

Is this foundation of contemporary political economy on Lockean premises based on such egregious omissions that a paradigm shift is the likely outcome, constituting phenomena like "counterperformativity" (MacKenzie 2007) or "systemic fallouts" (Searle 2010) or "counter-finality" (Baucom 2020, 32, 93–94)? Are these abstract entities like money and property stable foundations for life? Are the assumptions regarding time and space, as well as ecology, so profoundly limited as to require the development of new methods and worldviews? Contrary to the instantaneous time of modernity, "time does not pass, it accumulates" (Baucom 2020, 79–90; Malm 2018), a notion intrinsic to the delineation of stratigraphic markers of the Anthropocene.

We will proceed by reviewing the literature and considering alternative frameworks.

2 Review of the Literature

There are many dichotomies in the literature.

1. Reason/emotion
   (Damasio 1994; Kandel 2018, 176–197)
2. How can the relationship between humans and nature best be understood?
   (Hornborg 2019; Malm 2018; Moore 2015; Latour 1993; Baucom 2020; Chakrabarty 2018, 166–173; Merchant 1980, 2003)
3. What can humans know? There are issues related to ontology, epistemology, and phenomenology.
   (Jasanoff 2004; MacKenzie 2007; Callon 2007; Morton 2013)
4. Is economics performative?
   (MacKenzie 2007; Mitchell 2007, 2014)
5. There are dichotomies such as material/ideal as well as subject/object
   (consider new materialisms such as Bennett 2010; Coole and Frost 2010; Alaimo and Hekman 2008; Haraway 2016)
6. Individual/social (Tomasello 2019); self/other; consciousness

With new understanding of the human mind, the "self," and consciousness, we can overcome many of these dichotomies (Damasio 2010; Gazzaniga 2018; Kandel 2006, 2012; Johnston and Malabou 2013).

The human brain is fused with the body, a single unit, with feedback loops which aid awareness, survival, and life management. The brain forms images of these various states, including internal body homeostasis indicators, as well as sensory perceptions from outside the body. The information from inside the body and from outside sensory perceptions are both stored in the brain as images and memories. These images seem "ideal," not real, because they can be stored as symbols and words, and communicated to other humans with language and art. The "self" is based on perceptions and memories of one's own body during one's own lifetime. Yet these are stored as images in the brain, resulting from bodily states and experiences interacting with others and with objects. The "mind" appears above the body, qualitatively different, disassociated by its capacity to process chemical and electrical impulses, without necessarily being associated with concrete observable actions. Yet the contents of the mind can be communicated to others and form the basis of shared beliefs and meanings, which are apparently intangible (Searle 2010; Damasio 2010; Kandel 2006, 2012). The self is an object to itself, composed of processes connecting various brain regions, integrated for purposes related to survival and flourishing.

These dichotomies have been the source of perpetual debate and dialogue. Yet these dichotomies establish distinctions and definitions that enable the formation of stable objects for management and governance systems. To successfully challenge and resolve them may require new systems of governance, and knowledge frameworks.

3 Life Processes

The capitalist system operates by naming ongoing processes and relationships as discrete objects, like value, money, and property. By hijacking the reproduction methods of living plants and animals, human economic systems can obtain food, such as seeds, fruits, milk, and eggs, can produce commodities, and can expand "value" for humans, and "grow." Yet the capacity for growth is attributed to the system itself and to money, not these living systems.

To get beyond such reification (Davis 2020a), we study the following typically stable, invisible processes:

1. First, we typically assume that the autonomic systems of the human body proceed without the need for direct attention or awareness (Damasio 1999, 2010; Kandel 2006, 2012, 2018).
2. Second, we typically assume that the biogeochemical cycles of the earth are in equilibrium, providing air, water, and stable climate (Turner 2018), as well as cosmology.
3. Third, we typically assume population growth and reproduction, without inquiry into the conditions or requirements of demographic patterns, or evolution in the longer term. In fact, economics was founded on the assumption that there will be excess population growth and consequently scarcity, from the early writings of Malthus and Hardin.
4. Based on these three ongoing processes, we assume steady economic growth, with the consistent incentives provided by the capitalist system and property ownership (Nordhaus 2019).
5. Language provides the means of communication, knowledge retention, and enforcement of normative behavior to assure the smooth reproduction of key institutions. Language facilitates reference to "real world" objects, as well as provides means of expression and communication. That is, language can record the legacy of culture and science accumulated from past generations (Taylor 2016; Tomasello 2019).

Table 1.1 Framework of analysis

Type of structure	Entity (physical, social, ideal)	Requisites
Biophysical	1. Human body	Health; reproduction; nutrition
	2. Resilient biogeochemical cycles	Earth systems
	3. Population growth	Basic resources; net primary production; pair bonding
Social/cultural	4. Economic growth	Technology; production; credit
	5. Language and institutions; science; culture; history	Educational institutions
	6. Social groups; nations	Stable societies; peace; governance

6. Since humans are social creatures, language provides a means for the cohesion of human groups (Zunshine 2012), a means of affiliation, as well as intrapersonal reflection and cognition, or "consciousness" (Damasio 2010; Gazzaniga 2018). The use of language also maintains and reinforces stable institutions (Searle 2010).

Specific economic systems and cultural forms are often brought together in a "paradigm", a common set of assumptions and meanings which apply to a given place and period of history, or "narratives". The perceptions of participants in a given period are in turn influenced by the dominant worldview or paradigm of that specific period, like a Gestalt field.

To summarize, there are three basic natural/biological systems, autonomic biological systems, biogeochemical cycles, and population growth, and three cultural systems, economic form, language, and group affiliation. The summaries of key personae, norms, and worldviews tend to be persistent and resilient for a given population and place, known as paradigms or narratives (Table 1.1).

The operation of capitalism itself tends to focus on outputs and products rather than processes and relations, with a tendency towards reification (Davis 2020a). For example, the production of "value" is mysterious, behind the locked gates of the factory and the private household, hiding the instrumental use of human labor, represented by money and the value of commodities.

Because these normal biophysical cycles are potentially disrupted by the Anthropocene, the first three points, it is possible that the second three will be challenged in significant ways. The same science that facilitated and enabled human impact on the earth in significant ways is available for use in analyzing this impact.

Yet it is possible that this same structure of science will not be useful in measuring and modifying the human impact on the globe (Jasanoff and Kim 2015; Chakrabarty 2018; Latour 2017). Such distinctions in normal science as subjective/objective, reason/emotion, necessity/freedom, ideal/material, human/natural, and positive/normative may prevent the use of science in new ways appropriate to the Anthropocene. Dialectical methods and various materialisms may be more useful in this regard (Baucom 2020).

Economics in particular is not structured in a way to advance the analysis of the Anthropocene. First, the foundation is "the individual" and exclusionary, bounded private property (Davis 2015, 2017, 2020a). The modern liberal state is based on an infinite financial market, and money as a circular flow medium which is widely understood to be valuable in itself. Consumerism is assumed to be exogenous and innate, while also influenced by "conspicuous consumption" and "identity". Based on the assumption of continuous population growth, scarcity is assumed and "more is better". There is an assumption of zero cost of disposal, rather than limits to waste absorption in the earth's ecosystems, and externalities which are marginal, rather than system-disrupting pollution and climate change.

Economics assumes that it has no effect on ecology, history, or culture and that the system is separable and automatic, instead of emergent and path dependent. That is, the assumption of ceteris paribus allows the economist to isolate individual variables, assuming that the system as a whole remains unchanged. Economics assumes continuous homogeneous time, rather than historical institutional change or geological time. Technological change is likewise assumed to be autonomous and neutral (Nordhaus 2019).

Formal natural science typically assumes a separation between knowledge and the knower, science and the scientist (Daston and Galison 2007). This may be justified as articulate verifiable knowledge is only possible with humans, which is separate from nonhuman nature. Since the Enlightenment studies by Kant, there has been a question of how reliably humans can know "reality" outside their own direct experience. But with advances in neuroscience and evolution, it is clear that the structure of the human brain has much in common with other mammals and living species, with consciousness (Gazzaniga 2018; Damasio 1999), along with cells (respiration and reproduction) and other structures. Rather than a human/nonhuman dichotomy, it is now conceivable to identify the interactions of all species with global biogeochemical cycles in the processes of life, symbiotic and collaborative, as well as competitive.

Humans remain the only species whose knowledge of the world is also capable of intentionally (and unintentionally) changing the world, nonetheless, creating a built environment which changes the surface of the globe, as well as atmosphere and ocean.

In the case of economics, this assumption of separation of knower and known may be particularly untrue, as the study of economics affects norms and human behavior. In the case of quantum mechanics as well as the Anthropocene, the assumptions and studies of science may also affect the objects of inquiry, on a variety of scales. For example, the goal of ever-increasing productivity and speed of turnover, of science aligned with capitalism, can lead to outcomes and altered processes which subvert those goals, affecting the operation of the earth system as a whole, as in Nordhaus' image of the "Colossus" (Nordhaus 2019).

The split between nature and culture has been explored by Latour (1993), in his so-called "modern constitution". This split tends to privilege the human condition and the pursuit of happiness and wealth. With the advance of scientific knowledge and the aims of "consilience", we now know that there is no such necessary separation. There is nature within humans, and nature outside humans, an interdependence which determines their health, habitat, and life chances at every scale and time period (Falkowski 2015). The modern disciplines of natural science, social science, and the humanities could well be recast to be based on a common core of biological processes of life and death, in the context of large-scale geological evolution.

Like the paradigm shift between Ptolemy and Copernicus, there is now a shift in process from anthropocentric view of the world to planetary processes. I would suggest a focus on "life on earth" rather than the human species or the human individual. Life processes require energy flows across living and nonliving entities, in interactions which are conscious and not conscious, given Gazzaniga's (2018) expanded definition of consciousness.

In Table 1.1 above, the second three aspects noted above depend on the first three, which are below the horizon of visibility, conscious awareness. Yet the normal functioning of the human political institutions and the economy put the first three at risk. A new conceptual paradigm is necessary to integrate all six and to remove dichotomies for an integrated perspective.

According to the idiom of "co-production," "scientific knowledge, in particular, is not a transcendent mirror of reality. It both embeds and is embedded in social practices, identities, norms, conventions, discourses, instruments, and institutions" (Jasanoff 2004, 3). According to the Edinburgh School of Science Studies, "questions of epistemology are also questions of social order" (quoted in Latour 1993, 15–16). One can see, in this context, how the assumption that economics, and "the economy," is separable from the ecology can serve to protect the goals of growth and wealth creation. The message of the Anthropocene is now that this separation is no longer possible (Chakrabarty 2018; Morton 2013; Moore 2015).

4 Techniques of Reification

To get beyond reification, we need to examine the language and symbol system that makes the "real world" disappear, even as we claim to know it.

4.1 Property

The rights of property, to separate a parcel of earth for exclusive use in production, is a result of the historical development of markets.

Land was used first for direct production of human use values, and then for extraction of the resources necessary for the production of commodities, for profit for sale, the value of which was represented in money (Moore 2015, 189).

With property rights in means of production and means of subsistence, the right to survival for humans was based on access to money, to purchase necessities. The financial circuit then sets up an "alternate reality," where the "cash nexus" dominates life. Survival was based on the successful search for employment, for participation in the wage labor force (Polanyi 1944).

Then money itself was used to produce more money, in the development of capital markets from the late seventeenth century, to provide "safe assets" for wealth holders.

4.2 Money

The financial circuits are the process of using a given amount of money, M, to create more money, M', by means of the process of production. The capacity to add value to the inputs and raw materials, C, depends on the exploitation of labor, to reward only the necessities for human daily reproduction, not the full value produced in a given working day. The sales price of the commodity produced, M', includes that expanded, unpaid, surplus labor.

This financial circuit, M-C-M', translates a given amount of money into more money. Yet, ironically, each term of the circuit, both money and commodities, has both material and symbolic form. Money itself has a material substrate while representing value. The material commodity produced, although having material use value, is also a form of representation of the abstract value based on socially necessary labor time.

Money is entirely anthropocentric, but appears to be "objective." Value appears to be intrinsic to the object, while it is a human projection. As a representation of pleasure to humans, it also serves as a motivation and disciplinary device (Polanyi 1944).

That is, "value" has an objective reality, in material form, yet also has symbolic of value in the financial circuit. In this way, a material artifact serves as a social hieroglyph, according to the "fetishism of money" (Marx 1967). The material substrate of money makes it seem "real" and material, while also being a method of accumulation of an abstraction called "value." Value is a human project represented in material form, both money and commodities (Davis 2017).

Money is a human construction, which operates in a set of "automatic" processes, which seems to make money beyond human control. In this way, "the economy" seems nonhuman and capable of coercing humans to relinquish control of much of their energy and lifetimes. Money and markets are a form of global governance which seems to represent "freedom".

With his focus on "cheap natures," Moore (2015) is still wedded to value and price, human projections which blind us to ecological processes. His "cheap natures" and "cheap labor" can be better explained by the operation of property, in my view (see Chap. 4).

Hornborg is critical of general-purpose money, but does not examine how it is used to support the operations of the capitalist system (see Chap. 4). He also discusses uneven ecological exchange, which can be better explained by the use of property by Locke, to justify empire.

Foster and Malm see "ecological rift," but do not examine how the circuits of property and money obscure the contribution of natural and human life, in the financial circuits which appear to operate automatically. Malm views the distinction between human and nature as important to make more evident the impact of humans on the environment (Malm 2018).

4.3 *Ecosystems Services*

Because money is a representation of value to humans, there is no method of valuing ecological functioning per se. Nature itself has no value; it is a "free gift," according to Marx (Marx 1967, Vol. I, Ch. 7 and Ch. 15).

The use of money to value the ecology by "ecosystems services" is consequently doubly ironic. It is property and money that result in the degradation of the environment to produce value at an increasing rate, to accelerate the rate of accumulation.

As a result, the recommendation of this work is to measure the ecology directly, by means of biogeochemical and human development indicators, instead of money and markets.

4.4 *Public/Private Divide*

The public/private divide was a foundation of ancient Greek philosophy and democracy (Brewer 1995; Davis 2015).

The separation of workers from the means of production requires that they become part of the financial circuits, a form of coercion. Then "value" becomes the abstract reification of human energy and can ultimately determine life and death (Polanyi 1944).

The divisions of property prevent holistic vision of humans in nature and nature in humans, what Moore calls "double internalization" (Moore 2015).

4.5 *Modern Science*

Modern science has been an aid to capitalism (Marx 1967) as well as contributor to growth. The techniques of science have been adapted to social science (Daston and Galison 2007). The foundation on "objectivity" may also serve to reify the object of science, whether nature or human activities, and to facilitate their separation, transformation, and reintegration. Natural sciences constitute one of the "leading productive forces of modernity" (Callon 2007, 345).

Yet findings from modern science are confounding the stability of traditional governance entities, such as the individual, private property, and the state.

5 Governance Systems

The basic entities of modern governance, the individual, private property, and the state, seem incoherent, with the insights from ecology, neuroscience, and political economy. What seemed to be stable objects are in fact complex processes, contingent and interconnected in time.

We seem overwhelmed by "hyperobjects" (Morton 2013) or Colossus (Nordhaus 2019).

One response has been to reinforce those basic entities, such as the free market, to insist on their relevance, and to deny any challenges in the face of traditional verities. A second is to delineate a new "object" of study, such as ecology, to examine in isolation with specific disciplinary techniques, and to develop a new expertise. A third response is to redesign the vehicle while driving, a notable challenge, with new objects, expertise, and governing methods.

6 Freedom and Recognition

New definitions beyond individual private property are needed, towards integrated vision (Baucom 2020, 33–34, 110–117).

Re-enlivening nature is necessary, beyond reification, to understand interconnections and to achieve integration, as in the literature on "new materialisms."

It is important to clarify human purposes, to consider alternatives beyond money and wealth accumulation, which reorganize but also degrade earth's living processes.

To see beyond reification will require understanding the human species as a whole (Baucom 2020; Chakrabarty 2018). In the "division of labor" necessary to make instrumental use of humans, by skill and by class, there is also a perspective of the domination of nature to accomplish human purposes (Merchant 1980, 2003). The unification of the concept of the whole of earth will also require the unification of the view of the human species. A goal of human capability will also help to achieve the restoration of the earth's ecosystems.

Recognition is possible beyond the master/slave struggle to the death. The slave makes use of the earth as object, to fulfill the master's desire, and to achieve his own independence, in Hegel's narrative. At the same time, both the slave and the earth are objectified. To understand the life common to the slave and the earth is to view their unity on a new scale, by means of processes of interaction and interdependence. The master's authority as subject is at stake, and the techniques by which he objectifies both the slave and the earth.

Scholars are seeking new methodologies which integrate humans and nature, such as *Oikeios* (Moore 2015), *biogeocoenosis* (Foster 2015), and new forms of kinship (Haraway 2016). An alternative strategy may be to unify humankind, as a species (Chakrabarty, 2018, 180–184), instead of the internal divisions of capitalism. That is, instead of utilizing humans as sources of work, for part of the day, or identifying some segment of the human population as "workers," which process is then rendered invisible as "value," it is possible to unify humankind as a collective subject. This may be a new meaning of democracy, without the divisions of civil society (Marx 1978).

> Human emancipation will only be complete when the real, individual man has absorbed into himself the abstract citizen; when as an individual man, in his everyday life, in his work, and in his relationships, he has become a *species-being*; and when he has recognized and organized his own powers (*forces propres*) as *social* powers so that he no longer separates this social power from himself as *political* power. (Marx 1978, 46; italics in original)

That is, to solve the crisis of climate change, it may be important to unify humanity.

Bibliography

Alaimo, Stacy and Susan Hekman (eds.). *Material Feminisms*. Bloomington, IN: Indiana University Press, 2008.

Baucom, Ian. *History 4 degrees Celsius: Search for a Method in the Age of the Anthropocene*. Durham, North Carolina, Duke University Press, 2020.

Bennett, Jane. *Vibrant Matter: A Political Ecology of Things*. Durham, NC: Duke University Press, 2010.

Brewer, John. "This, That, and the Other: Public, Social and Private in the Seventeenth and Eighteenth Centuries," in Dario Castiglione and Lesley Sharpe (eds.). *Shifting the Boundaries: Transformation of the Languages of Public and Private in the Eighteenth Century*. Exeter, UK: University of Exeter Press, 1995.

Callon, Michel. "What Does it Mean to Say That Economics is Performative?" in MacKenzie, Donald A., Fabian Muniesa, and Lucia Siu (eds.). *Do Economists Make Markets? On the Performativity of Economics*. Princeton, NJ: Princeton University Press, 2007, 311-357.

Chakrabarty, Dipesh. *The Crises of Civilization: Exploring Global and Planetary Histories*. New York: Oxford University Press, 2018.

Coole, Diana and Samantha Frost (eds.). *New Materialisms: Ontology Agency, and Politics*. Durham, NC: Duke University Press, 2010.

Damasio, Antonio R. *Descartes' Error: Emotion, Reason, and the Human Brain*. New York: G.P. Putnam, 1994.

Damasio, Antonio R. *The Feeling of What Happens: Body and Emotion in the Making of Consciousness*. New York: Harcourt Brace, 1999.

Damasio, Antonio R. *Self Comes to Mind: Constructing the Conscious Brain*. New York: Random House, 2010.

Daston, Lorraine and Peter Galison. *Objectivity*. New York: Zone, 2007.

Davis, Ann E. *The Evolution of the Property Relation: Understanding Paradigms, Debates, Prospects*. New York: Routledge, 2015.

Davis, Ann E. *Money as a Social institution: The Institutional Development of Capitalism*. New York: Routledge, 2017.

Davis, Ann E. *The End of Individualism and the Economy: Emerging Paradigms of Connection and Community*. New York: Routledge, 2020a

Davis, Ann E. "Money as a Social Institution: Its Historical Emergence and Political Implications." Steven Pressman (ed.). *How Social Forces Impact the Economy*. New York: Routledge, 81-96, 2020b.

Falkowski, Paul G. *Life's Engines: How Microbes Made Earth Habitable*. Princeton, NJ: Princeton University Press, 2015.

Foster, John Bellamy. *Marx's Ecology: Materialism and Nature*. New York: Monthly Review Press, 2000.
Foster, John Bellamy. "Marxism and Ecology: Common Fonts of a Great Transition," Great Transition Initiative: Toward a Transformative Vision and Praxis. https://greattransition.org/publication/marxism-and-ecology, 2015.
Foster, John Bellamy and Paul Burkett. *Marx and the Earth: An Anti-Critique*. Leiden: Brill, 2016.
Friedman, Milton. *Capitalism and Freedom*. Chicago: University of Chicago Press, 1962.
Gazzaniga, Michael S. *The Consciousness Instinct*. New York: Farrar, Straus, and Giroux, 2018.
Haraway, Donna J. *Staying with the Trouble: Making Kin in the Chthulucene*. Durham: Duke University Press, 2016.
Harrison, George. "Within you Without You." Beatles, London: 1967.
Hegel, G.W.F. *The Phenomenology of Spirit*. New York: Oxford University Press, 1977.
Hornborg, Alf. *Nature, Society, and Justice in the Anthropocene: Unravelling the Money-Energy-Technology Complex*. New York: Cambridge University Press, 2019.
Jasanoff, Sheila (ed.). *States of Knowledge: The Co-Production of Science and Social Order*. New York: Routledge, 2004.
Jasanoff, Sheila and Sang-Hyun Kim (eds.). *Dreamscapes of Modernity: Sociotechnical Imaginaries and the Fabrication of Power*. Chicago: University of Chicago Press, 2015.
Johnston, Adrian and Catherine Malabou. *Self and Emotional Life: Philosophy, Psychoanalysis, and Neuroscience*. New York: Columbia University Press, 2013.
Kandel, Eric R. *In Search of Memory: The Emergence of a New Science of Mind*. New York: W. W. Norton, 2006.
Kandel, Eric R. *The Age of Insight: The Quest to Understand the Unconscious in Art, Mind, and Brain*. New York: Random House, 2012.
Kandel, Eric R. *The Disordered Mind: What Unusual Brains Tell Us About Ourselves*. New York: Farrar, Straus and Giroux, 2018.
Latour, Bruno. *We Have Never Been Modern*. Cambridge, MA: Harvard University Press, 1993.
Latour, Bruno. *Down to Earth: Politics in the New Climatic Regime*. Cambridge, UK: Polity, 2017.
Latour, Bruno and Peter Weibel (eds.). *Critical Zones: the Science and Politics of Landing on Earth*. Cambridge, MA: MIT Press, 2020
MacKenzie, Donald A., Fabian Muniesa, and Lucia Siu (eds.). *Do Economists Make Markets? On the Performativity of Economics*. Princeton, NJ: Princeton University Press, 2007.
Malm, Andreas. *Fossil Capital: The Rise of Steam Power and the Roots of Global Warming*. London: Verso, 2016.
Malm, Andreas. *The Progress of this Storm: Nature and Society in a Warming World*. London: Verso, 2018.
Marx, Karl. *Capital*. New York: International Publishers, 1967.
Marx, Karl. "On the Jewish Question." In Robert C. Tucker (ed.). *The Marx-Engels Reader*. 2nd ed. New York: W.W. Norton, 1978, 26-52.
Merchant, Carolyn. *The Death of Nature: Women, Ecology, and the Scientific Revolution*. New York: Harper & Row, 1980.
Merchant, Carolyn. *Reinventing Eden: The Fate of Nature in Western Culture*. New York: Routledge, 2003.
Mitchell, Timothy. "Economentality: How the Future Entered Government." *Critical Inquiry*. Vol. 40, No. 4, 2014, 479-507.
Mitchell, Timothy. "The Properties of Markets." In MacKenzie, Donald A., Fabian Muniesa, and Lucia Siu (eds.). *Do Economists Make Markets? On the Performativity of Economics*. Princeton, NJ: Princeton University Press, 2007, 244-275.
Moore, Jason W. *Capitalism in the Web of Life: Ecology and the Accumulation of Capital*. London: Verso, 2015.
Morton, Timothy. *Hyperobjects: Philosophy and Ecology after the End of the World*. Minneapolis: University of Minnesota Press, 2013.

Nordhaus, William. "Climate Change: The Ultimate Challenge for Economics." *American Economic Review*, Vol. 109, No. 6, June 2019, 1991-2014.

Poovey, Mary. "The Liberal Civil Subject and the Social in Eighteenth-Century British Moral Philosophy," *Public Culture*, Vol. 14, No. 1, 125–145, 2002.

Polanyi, Karl. *The Great Transformation*. Boston: Beacon Press, 1944.

Scott, Joan W. and Debra Keates (eds.). *Going Public: Feminism and the Shifting Boundaries of the Private Sphere*. Urbana: University of Illinois Press, 2004.

Searle, John R. *Making the Social World: The Structure of Human Civilization*. New York: Oxford University Press, 2010.

Taylor, Charles. *The Language Animal: The Human Linguistic Capacity*. Cambridge, MA: Harvard University Press, 2016.

Tomasello, Michael. *Becoming Human: A Theory of Ontogeny*. Cambridge, MA: Harvard University Press, 2019.

Turner, David P. *The Green Marble: Earth System Science and Global Sustainability*. New York: Columbia University Press, 2018.

Wu, Tim. *The Attention Merchants: The Epic Scramble to get Inside Our Heads*. New York: Alfred A. Knopf, 2016.

Yadav, Shristi. "Kuhn, Economics, and the Scientific Revolutions: A Critique." Paper presented at the Eastern Economic Association meetings, March 1, 2020, Boston, MA.

Zuboff, Shoshana. *Surveillance Capitalism:The Fight for a Human Future at the New Frontier of Power*. New York: Public Affairs, 2020..

Zunshine, Lisa (ed.). *Introduction to Cognitive Cultural Studies*. Baltimore: Johns Hopkins University Press, 2010.

Zunshine, Lisa. *What Cognitive Science Can Tell Us About Popular Culture*. Baltimore: Johns Hopkins University Press, 2012.

Chapter 2
The Modern Institution of Science

The human species evolved from the earth, constituting its "deep history." The earth itself changed significantly before human life became feasible in its current form, *Homo sapiens* (Falkowski 2015). The evolution of humans themselves has been affected by its own forms of knowledge, from the discovery of fire, the invention of tools, the capacity for language and writing. The capacity for accumulation of knowledge outside on an individual person's memory has enabled the species to develop cognitively, as well as technologically (Tomasello 2008; Kandel 2018). That is, human science has been able to influence human evolution.

Forms of knowledge consisted of magic and religion for many centuries. The development of formal science became a specific aim at least in seventeenth-century Europe. Even as objective science has been the hallmark of modernity, there are questions of "reality" which still bedevil scientific claims. Can modern science produce "truth," or is it possible that there are biases and distortions which are still possible? Does the history of science bely its claims to infallibility?

1 History of Science

Science was originally based on Aristotelian approaches, prior to adoption Bacon's experimental methods (Wennerlind 2011, 54–61; Mokyr 2016; Poovey 1998). Aristotle viewed nature as the source of order and the true essence of objects and the source of certain causal knowledge (Daston 2019, 10–14, 24). Key features of Bacon's experimental approach were claims to objectivity and disinterestedness (Daston and Galison 2007), the role of expert witnesses, and the replicability of the results under controlled circumstances (Shapin and Schaffer 1985). Robert Boyle and the Royal Society were classic examples, with the "laboratory" as an enclosed space where experiments could be conducted without need to consider political or partisan implications (Latour 1993). At the same time, the notion of politics and the

A. E. Davis, *Whole Earth*, https://doi.org/10.1007/978-3-031-01934-0_2

social contract were developed by Hobbes, and the norm of the calculating, self-interested citizen, represented by the Leviathan. These institutions, science and political economy, were conceived as separated domains and later developed into distinct academic disciplines. The distinctive methods of the scientist, the separate community of researchers, as well as the specialized instruments of observation and measurement made the scientists the only authoritative interpreters of nature, where ostensibly the "facts speak for themselves" (Daston and Galison 2007, 260).

The search for universal natural laws emerged in the seventeenth century, modeled on Newton's laws of mechanics (Daston 2019, 23–31). The willingness to consider nature as the source of materials for human betterment and the progress of knowledge was an important cultural element in this enterprise (Mokyr 2016, 16–17; Merchant 1980), as well as the belief in "improvement."

The division of humans and nonhuman others can be considered arbitrary, when compared with other cultures (Daston 2019, 57–59).

> Only from a parochial human point of view does it make any sense to divide up all that exists into our species on one side and everything else, from microbes to pulsars, on the other…And only once such a division is posited is it possible to identify anthropomorphic projections from the tiny province of the human onto the vast realm of the universe… (Daston 2019, 58)

That is, considered historically and comparatively, Western science is idiosyncratic, although the "rise of the West" (Mokyr 2016) is widely attributed to its advance.

2 Dichotomies

Objectivity is the common understanding of the delineation of modern science, in spite of its changing meanings historically (Daston and Galison 2007, 372–382). There are a series of dichotomies which result, including subject/object, mind/body, mind/world, reason/emotion, ideal/real, and individual/social. These dichotomies are concerned with what can be known by the human mind, producing reliable knowledge of the outside world, compared with imagination and fantasy, which, although compelling, are not "true." The criteria of "truth" then became replicable, communicable, predictable, capable of representation and documentation, relevant to technology in a practical setting.

One use of the term "subjective" can refer to contents of the mind (Searle 2010, 17–18). While mental objects have a sense of qualitatively different reality, mental contents can be physically represented, in biological manifestations, which can be observed (Table 2.1).

In this sense, mental contents are not less "real" than material objects and can be represented and communicated. In fact, social institutions have a "reality" because of common understandings which are recorded in the brain. A common language facilitates cognition inside the brain and can communicate and coordinate behavior outside the brain in practical social settings. That is, language is both subjective and

Table 2.1 Mind/world and individual/social

Representations		Representing: Subjective feelings (internal reality)	Representing: Perceptions, sensations (external reality)
Material form	Inside brain	Neurons (internal body processes); neurotransmitters; preconscious and subconscious awareness	Images; ideas; mental objects; conscious memory; cognition (in language)
	Outside brain (intersubjective)	Cultural forms (literature, art, music, dance)	Technology, science, culture, scientific instruments; computers; information; communication (in language)

objective, individual and social, inside the brain and outside the brain in oral and written communication and documents.

One way to resolve these dichotomies is to emphasize process and relation, rather than objects. That is, contents in the brain can be documented, communicated, and then observed by the person's behavior. Then the experience which results from that behavior can amend mental contents. A person embedded in social institutions will include learning by doing, as well as social norms and incentives. History can then record the changes in understandings and institutions over time. More broadly, this is related to a historical/institutional methodology (Davis 2015), where "truth" can refer to human knowledge, understanding, and behavior at a specific period and geography. To admit historical change is not equivalent to relativism (Daston and Galison 2007, 376–379) or untruth.

The composition of the scientific community, its methods, its aims, its sources of support, and its claims to truth are issues which are debated in the present (Oreskes 2019).

3 Standpoint

The development of formal science was coincident with the exploration and expansion of world trade. The objective point of view was important for epistemology and for trust in observations by merchants (Wennerlind 2011, 83–92; Leng 2014; Wennerlind 2014).

The discipline of the scientist as "objective" emerged in the mid-nineteenth century, in contrast with the artistic self (Daston and Galison 2007, 36–39, 246–251). The norm of objectivity required the development of the standard scientific object, as the common focus of the scientific community (Daston and Galison 2007, 19–27, 368–371), and the scientific self, characterized by specific norms and practices. As a result, science could produce "truth," without examining the relationship between the observed and the observer, which became invisible. Nature revealed her secrets, to the dedicated practitioner (Daston and Galison 2007, 202, 243–245; Merchant 1980, 186–191).

Yet the "scientific" observer was an unstable combination of passive observer and active experimenter (Daston and Galison 2007, 250), the discrete "self" was the result of the presumed natural laws of "human nature" (Poovey 2002, 134–140), and the scientific object was assumed discrete and separable from other natural phenomena. The daily intimate interface between humans and the environment, including air, food, water, and waste disposal, became removed from view and assigned to management by modern expert systems. The interaction among scientific objects was assumed constant, for the sake of the focus of any specific experiment. There is a presumed superiority between rational moderns and so-called primitive or traditional communities (Latour 1993, 97–100; Harding 2008).

The "view from nowhere" (Nagel 1986) is consistent with the perspective of Smith's "impartial spectator," which encompasses the merchant's point of view (Davis 2020, 145–151). Poovey mentions that the dichotomy between subject and object was a mode of reasoning institutionalized in the fifteenth and sixteenth centuries by Italian merchants and adopted by scientists in the Royal Society in the seventeenth century. As a result, these dichotomies, between subject and object, seem natural, rather than the result of a particular way of a society understanding and organizing itself (Poovey 2002, 131–133). Patel and Moore discuss "real abstractions" resulting from Cartesian dualism (Patel and Moore 2017, 51–58) or mind/body dualism.

Modernity is characterized by these "reifying abstractions" (Poovey 2002), like markets and the state, which seem like real entities (Patel and Moore 2017, 45–47) by which these objective, nonparticipant observers are able to make claims and propose policies, as if they were themselves not involved in the contexts they are observing. As experts and advisors, these "objective observers" may also claim greater authority than those who are being observed and analyzed.

The norm of the pursuit of pure knowledge for its own sake can then permit a lack of examination of the institutions of science in relation to other aspects of modern political economy, such as the state, the family (Harding 2008, 11), or the environment. The composition of the scientific community, its norms, and its objectives are then beyond examination and evolve as a separate institution. The lay citizen is reliant on the scientific expert in matters of growth and competition with other nations.

Support by the state for the military provides a public purpose, the classic "public good." Military competition can then provide for the "rise of the West" (Mokyr 2016; Hoffman 2015), along with the modern culture of improvement, progress, and growth (Slack 2015). And the military mission can distort the findings of science (Oreskes 2021).

4 Relations

The "objective" method of science presumably has no relation of subject and object. It is on this divide that the credibility of science is based. There are other observers who offer that "objectivity" itself is a relationship, which can be characterized.

4.1 *History of Science*

Historians of science have developed a concept of "paradigm," which studies the ways in which a scientist brings certain ways of knowing to the scientific project. A paradigm constitutes "normal science," which defines the object, the type of evidence, and the credible observer (Kuhn 1987). In this way, the composition of the scientific community can be specified in a certain place and time, with the acknowledgment that "facts" do not speak for themselves, but are represented (Latour 1993, 27–29). Both inductive and deductive methods may be involved, in order to frame experiments and to evaluate empirical results (Poovey 1998). Rather than the "view from nowhere," Latour feels that it is important to situate the scientific observers as located on earth. Rather than universal Galilean objects (Latour 2018, 67–75), and instead of nonparticipant observers in the laboratory discerning universal laws, it is important to recognize that the scientists are embodied persons located in time and place.

4.2 *Feminist Critics of Science*

Feminist scholars of the history of science raise the issues of relationship between knower and knowledge production (Harding 2008; Hrdy 1999, 2009; Keller 1983, 2010), which are obscured by the assumption of "objectivity" as a method to produce reliable knowledge, as well as the boundaries of the scientific community. The conception of nature as mechanical instead of organic also contributed to the notion of discrete parts, each of which could be examined and transformed separately. Feminists point out that the early modern scientists clearly articulated notions of the "domination" of nature, citing Francis Bacon in particular (Merchant 1980).

4.3 *Marxists*

Like feminists, Marxists criticize the relation of humans and nature as implicitly conceptualized in modern science. The distinction between nature and society is considered misleading (Patel and Moore 2017, 51–62). Marxists examine the systematic exploitation of nature by capitalism, historically and at present (Foster and Clark 2020). Some see the origin of this "rift" between nature and society in Descartes (Moore 2015, 18–21), or seventeenth-century science, such as Hobbes and Locke (Latour 1993), while others see the origins with Giambattista Vico (Foster et al. 2010, 217). Hornborg (2019) sees the undervaluation of nature as the result of general-purpose money and abstract technology. Malm (2016) sees the use of fossil fuels in the industrial revolution as determined by the pressure of capitalism to increase the rate of production and the productivity of labor, or Postone's "treadmill" (Postone 1996).

Malm recommends that the distinction between nature and society is important to retain, to analyze the influence of capitalism on nature, at least (Malm 2018, 177–190). Moore offers a World Ecology Research strategy, instead, to bring analysis of nature along with the analysis of capitalism in an integrated way. Latour's concept of "hybrids" would suggest that nature is always involved with every human action, in spite of the conceptual separation which divides them, which he calls the "modern constitution" (Latour 1993). Malm (2018, 157–168, 216–247) and Foster, Clark, and York (2010, 216–247) suggest that a more promising approach is Marx's dialectic of humans and nature.

5 Modern Sciences

Instead of supporting the model of the discrete object and the bounded self, modern science has shifted its focus to interrelations and interconnections, towards processes and long-term transformations. From the perspective of "deep history," both the scientist and the world have evolved over millennia, to some extent co-evolving. From the perspective of rational control and optimization, modern sciences are now more likely to consider chaos and complexity sciences.

5.1 Co-evolution

The findings of Darwin challenged the time frame of biblical history, from 5000 years of human life and the creation of earth to a much longer time frame, from 5 to 7 millennia in terms of the evolution of hominins (Smail 2008, 194–195; Gamble 2021).

One example of major shifts in earth's evolution is the Great Oxygenation Event of 2.4 billion years ago (Falkowski 2015, 74–89; Turner 2018, 35–40). As a result of microbial respiration, the earth's atmospheric composition changed from a level of 1% to a level of 20% oxygen, affecting the subsequent evolution of living things. Because all living cells utilize the same mechanism of energy production, evolutionarily conserved from microbes, it can be said that all life on earth is derived from a single microbial organism (Falkowski 2015, 37–39, 117–123).

According to some interpretations, the "Little Ice Age" was partially caused by the impact of European exploration on the indigenous populations of the Americas (Campbell 2016; Koch 2019). The resulting decline in population led to the fallowing of agricultural land, which absorbed sufficient carbon dioxide to reduce global temperatures, and to disrupt food production with widespread political and economic impacts (Degroot 2018). This explanation is a relatively rare example of historians taking into account in a substantive way the interaction of socioeconomic and environmental variables (Diamond 2005; Maslin 2017).

5.2 Human Exceptionalism

There have been major thresholds in human evolution, such as upright posture, the discovery of fire, and the invention of tools. Language was arguably another aspect of human evolution, that became part of an evolved brain capacity, which further influenced human social and technological changes (Schoenemann 2018).

The use of symbols and language capacity differentiate humans from our closest evolutionary relatives, the primates (Tomasello 2019; Friederici 2017; Shryock and Smail 2011, 229–234). Comparisons reveal different capacities and brain structures across species (phylogeny), as well as different developmental sequences according to maturation (ontogeny). Language is one example of an evolved capacity, which is located in a specific part in the brain, Broca's and Wernicke's areas, discovered in the nineteenth century. Recent research has identified the importance of connections among brain regions (Przezdzik et al. 2019), in the complex interrelated functions of comprehension and communication. Specific genes have been associated with the capacity for language (Vernes 2019) as well. There is an ongoing debate regarding whether particular languages can affect types of behavior (Ginsburgh and Weber 2020). With the evolution of language, the resulting increase in capacity for cognition and communication then expanded the human capacities for innovation and adaptation, in cultural productions. That is, evolution affected human biology, the capacity for language in the structure of the human brain, which could then further influence evolution.

There is evidence of a positive dynamic feedback loop (Schoenemann 2018, 339–341) in human evolution. Approximately 2– 3 million years ago, the brain size of hominins increased relative to primates, along with evidence of tool use. There was greater specialization of brain areas with greater size and increased capacity for processing of complexity. This capacity for complex processing could then enable the development of language, which would increase social interaction, which would in turn further increase brain size and the capacity for complex cognition and communication. That is, although primates are social, with similar brain regions such as mirror neurons and Broca's area, the increasing size and specialization increased the capacity for complex processing for humans (Dunbar 2014, 43–50). The role of religion and material culture is further hypothesized to increase cohesion and the size of manageable groups (Dunbar 2014, 277–301, 323–329; Davis 2020, 5–8; Coward and Gamble 2014).

The increasing size of the hominin brain and the constraint of the pelvic region resulted in birth of human infants before they are capable of self-care, the "obstetric dilemma" (Dunbar 2014, 244–248). These altricial infants then rely on their mother and other adults for survival. This social context for early development, in a period of rapid wiring of the brain, can lead to learning of symbolic communication, where wishes and random utterances result in need fulfillment (Barbieri 2015, 2020). The intimate interaction of mother and infant can induce imitation, modeling, as well as attempts to endear oneself with the caregivers (Hrdy 1999, 2009). The large brain, intense sociality, and utter dependency of the infant are the conditions for learning language, a cognitive system of communication unique to humans (Keller 2010). In such a context, the role of childhood in learning and cultural transmission is very important, even though this category is "almost invisible" in archaeology (Coward and Gamble 2014, 465). "The mother-child dyad, along with adult pair bonding, is one of the principal units in the construction of hominid social life," leading to the introduction of the concept of "childscape" (Coward and Gamble 2014, 466–467). The predominance of female figurines may be partially explained by this increasing importance of the mother in kin networks of migrant hominins (Gaudzinski-Windheuser and Joris 2015).

"Language presupposes that individuals share a significant degree of overlap in their conceptual understanding of the world" (Schoenemann 2018, 337), to make symbolic reference possible and to make communication useful. Once having developed the capacity for language, the opportunity for further conceptual development was increased, stimulating further expansion of brain size.

Arguably, a form of consciousness is present in other living beings, even if only related to the search for food and for mating (Gazzaniga 2018; Graziano 2019). In humans, consciousness is more complex, with the experience of volition as well as requirements of homeostasis. There are differentiated brain structures which control autonomic nervous systems, like heartbeat and digestion (brain stem), which are separate from the brain regions which process conscious cognition (prefrontal cerebral cortex). It is possible, nonetheless, that an awareness of usually subconscious bodily functions can be represented in conscious thought as a separable, conscious "self," compared with the body (Damasio 2010). This mind/body dualism is an outcome of this differentiation of brain regions, while the human body is in fact a single biological organism, made of living cells of various types interconnected in a holistic system. That is, there are representations of the body in the brain, and these representations or maps then coordinate internal body states with external perceptions for conscious processing to determine actions (Ramachandran 2011). The "self" is a process rather than an object (Damasio 2010, 8), a result of the interactions of millions of neurons among specialized regions of the brain.

The view of oneself as an object is characteristic of "consciousness." The dependent infant may well perceive the mother as an "object" for fulfillment of its intense needs (Bass 2018). Such dependence may be increased in the modern forms of the nuclear family, compared with extended families in the medieval period. This insight has been developed in the "object relations" school of psychology, based on the work of Melanie Klein and Donald Winnicott. The child, especially female children, may then have subsequent difficulty separating themselves from their mothers, according to the work of Nancy Chodorow, while males become "separable" and struggle to become differentiated from their mothers to achieve masculinity, an analysis developed by Paula England.

5.3 *Potential Bias to Science*

In spite of the emphasis on neutral objectivity, there is a potential bias to the development of science. As emphasized by Marx in Chapter 15 of Volume I on "Machinery," science has been an aid to capital. There has been a direction to innovation, to replace human labor and intelligence, and to recruit the consumer. The result has been automation and AI in the history of technology, and simulation and virtualization in communication, rather than direct relation and deliberation on the Internet.

5.4 *Anthropocene*

To a large extent, the future of the only place where life is known to exist is being determined by the actions of humans. Yet the power that humans wield is unlike any other force of nature, because it is reflexive and therefore can be used, withdrawn, or modified. More widespread recognition that human actions are driving far-reaching changes to the life-supporting infrastructure of earth may well have increasing philosophical, social, economic, and political implications over the coming decades (Lewis and Maslin 2015, 178).

6 New Collective

Is membership in the scientific community privileged? Is it only for humans of the highest intelligence, however measured, selected on the basis of competitive, meritocratic criteria? Does this role establish a hierarchy and commanding role in political economy? What is the relationship to a given society or nation? How does it affect nonhumans?

The relationship between knowledge and social order has been posed by historians of science (Shapin and Schaffer 1985, 15, 332, 339, 342; Jasanoff 2004). The separation and isolation of the laboratory and its privileged production of reliable knowledge of "natural laws" was presumably unrelated to human affairs (Latour 1993). The scientists were separable from the state, a separate "domain" or space (Poovey 1998, 31; Shapin and Schaffer 1985, 332–336), but could support the mission of the state, at the discretion of the political leaders. The claim that scientists formed a separate, autonomous, rule-governed community enabled their activities to escape challenges from other sources of knowledge in seventeenth-century England, a period of religious civil wars based on competing claims to sacred authority. The political and economic impacts of scientific inquiry, such as military technology and automation, were outcomes whose intention was deniable. Matters of pure "fact" could be separable from values and norms, according to "positivism," and hence escape moral condemnation. The notion that society could be separated into distinct domains, such as public and private, science and the state, had political implications, nonetheless. The presumed separation of natural and human sciences poses challenges for the integration of ecology in the twenty-first century.

The expert scientist is a nonparticipant observer, as if she were not also a member of the community, or object of study. This "objective" stance or standpoint may inhibit achievement of the highest potential of modern science, a long-term perspective on the human species, and the achievements of science and human knowledge. An awareness of human exceptionalism may not necessarily convey superiority, when recognizing the "cognition" of other life forms and the reactivity of nonlife forms (Hutchins 1995). Allowing full species membership in the study of humankind may also provide a new collective standpoint, or "collective intentionality," with promise of wider distribution of the collective benefits of the achievements of modern science (Harding 2008).

In recent literature, there has been a proliferation of envisioning of new agencies and communities. For example, consider the literature cited: "terrestrials" (Latour 2018); "multitude" (Hardt and Negri 2005); new political agent, the "swarm" (Connolly 2017); "assemblage" (Connolly 2019); cosmopolitans (Benhabib 2008; Appiah 2007); vibrant matter (Bennett 1993); kinship with other species (Haraway 2016); partnership (Merchant 2003); double internality (Moore 2015); integration of all humans as a species, building on the insights of Darwin and Marx.

Instead of the typical subject/object dichotomy, reifying abstractions, and third person objectivity, it is possible to envision a collective second person plural as self-aware human agent, with history, knowledge, and collective self-determination. Such a human community could be a knowledge and scientific community, sharing insights and best practices, for common values and purposes, as well as kinship and common residence in the earth.

7 The Limits of Modernity

The institutions of modernity are based on separable "domains," like the initial assumptions of modern science, including science itself, as well as the economy, the state, and the church. That is, according to the concept of "co-production," modern science and society reflect common principles (Jasanoff 2004), that the parts are separable and can operate independently, like a machine (Merchant 1980). These separate institutions allow for competing claims to truth (Oreskes and Conway 2010; Michaels 2008), which permit tolerance but can jeopardize the integration of the society along any particular worldview or value system. The integrative insights of modern science, like ecology, are then difficult to implement in practice.

Darwin's insights initiated the "time revolution of 1859" (Gamble 2021), which may make humanity shrink in significance, evolving 50,000 years ago (Maslin 2017, 14–40; Dunbar 2016, 8–17) in relation to the 4.8 billion years of the earth's evolution. On the other hand, the awareness of the Anthropocene may focus attention more directly on the impact of humanity on its own and on the earth's future (Maslin 2017, 190–191). The possibility of a new ecological revolution is discussed further below.

Appendix: Consideration of Other Topics and Issues

1. Garden of Eden as origin story (Merchant 2003; Bennett 1993).
2. Implicit standpoint or perspective for modern natural science; objectivity; modern fact (Nagel 1986; Daston and Galison 2007; Poovey 1998; Harding 2008).
3. Performativity and "social construction" of social institutions (Searle 2010; MacKenzie 2006; Goede 2005); reflexivity.
4. Knowledge and power (Hobbes in Latour 1993); ideology and paradigms (Kuhn 1987).
5. There is a history of science, and a complex relationship with capitalism; science itself as an object, a reifying abstraction (Postone 1993, 2020; Poovey 2002).
6. Consciousness; emergence of "self" as process, not object (Damasio 2010; Gazzaniga 2018; Bass 2018; Graziano 2019; Dennett 2017); perceived as "object."
7. There is a literature on the role of language in social life of humans (Tomasello 2008; Shryock and Smail 2011; Przezdzik et. al. 2019). Arguably, language is a MOS and MOP, a special form of communication and coordination among humans that is rarely examined, without which the social capacity of humans could not have expanded. A MOC of means of communication, culture, and control. Possible role for the "linguistic turn," which seems to be ideal, not material. Terms, institutions, expertise (historical institutionalism). Role of "objective" perspective.
8. Ancient Greece; Renaissance; Enlightenment (Jonathan Israel); humanism (Grafton in NYRB); liberal governmentality based on natural philosophy (Poovey 1998).
9. History of science and technology (Mokyr 2016; Malm 2018; Shapin and Shaffer 1985; Oreskes 2019; Kuhn 1987).
10. Scientific revolution, probabilistic revolution, and financial revolution (Levenson 2020; Poovey 1998, 2008; Kaye; Kuhn 1987); emergence of "liberal governmentality" and political economy.
11. Dominance of "nature" (Merchant 1980, 2003, 2020; Harding 2008; Haraway 2000, 2016); objective method. Earth as object, observational, optimizing, controlling (Edwards 2010).
12. Fetishism and control of the object (Bass 2018).
13. Information as a new category of science and knowledge, from trade, finance, and value production (Gleick 2011; Postone 1993, 2017, 2019, 2020; Blair et al. 2021); market prices as superior to human intelligence and information technology and AI as a new "division of learning," superior to human intelligence

(Zuboff 2019); evolution of smart machines as control technologies (Edwards); technology as "inevitable"; autonomous force vs. commercial imperative (Zuboff 2019, 14–17, 180–192); DNA coding.

14. Second person plural: the new "we." Not just "actants" (Latour 1993) or "vibrant matter" (Bennett 1993) or "cyborgs" (Haraway 2000, 2016) but co-agents in the evolution of the earth; "partners" (Merchant 2003). Relinquishing special status of humanity in creation, based on Cartesian privilege to consciousness, it is more feasible to see a unity with all living things (Schwagerl 2014, 169).
15. Co-production of science and social life (Jasanoff 2004); rational, discrete parcels, capable of independent examination and experimentation, management; cet. paribus.
16. Deskilling and automation; scientific management; HR and advertising; entertainment and persuasion; the information and information technology; AI; "surveillance capitalism" (Zuboff 2019).
17. Free gifts from nature and science (Marx, Vol. I, Chap. 15; Mokyr 2016).
18. The idea and history of climate science (Hulme 2009).
19. Anthropocene or Capitalocene (Moore 2015; Schwagerl 2014); ecological rift.
20. Denial and resistance (Mooney 2006, 2008; Oreskes and Conway 2010).
21. Political conflict based on new visions, new governance mechanisms.
22. Science and governance (vs. religion).
23. Ontology and epistemology; to what extent does what we know affect reality, what is, and vice versa.

Bibliography

Barbieri, Marcello. *Code Biology: A New Science of Life*. The Netherlands: Spring, 2015.

Barbieri, Marcello. "The Semantic Theory of Language," *Biosystems*. Vol. 190, 2020.

Bass, Alan. *Fetishism, Psychoanalysis, and Philosophy: The Iridescent Thing*. New York: Routledge, 2018.

Bennett, Jane. "Primate Visions and Alter-Tales" in Bennett, Jane and William Chaloupka (eds.). *In the Nature of Things: Language, Politics, and the Environment*. Minneapolis: University of Minnesota Press, 1993, 250-265.

Bennett, Jane and William Chaloupka (eds.). *In the Nature of Things: Language, Politics, and the Environment*. Minneapolis: University of Minnesota Press, 1993.

Bittman, Mark. *Animal, Vegetable, Junk: A History of Food, from Sustainable to Suicidal*. New York: Houghton Mifflin Harcourt, 2021.

Blair, Ann, Paul Duguid, Anja-Silvia Goeing, and Anthony Grafton. *Information: A Historical Companion*. Princeton, NJ: Princeton University Press, 2021.

Campbell, Bruce M.S. *The Great Transition: Climate, Disease and Society in the Late Medieval World*. New York: Cambridge University Press, 2016.

Clark, Brett and Stefano B. Longo. "Marxism and Ecology," in David M. Brennan, David Kristjanson-Gural, Catherine P. Mulder and Erik K. Olsen (eds.). *Routledge Handbook of Marxian Economics*. New York: Routledge, 399-408.

Connolly, William E. *Facing the Planetary: Entangled Humanism and the Politics of Swarming*. Durham: Duke University Press, 2017.

Connolly, William E. *Climate Machines Fascist Drives and Truth*. Durham: Duke University Press, 2019.

Coward, Fiona and Clive Gamble. "Big Brains, Small Worlds: Material Culture and the Evolution of Mind" in R.I.M. Dunbar, Clive Gamble, and J.A.J. Gowlett (eds.). *Lucy to Language: The Bench Mark Papers*. New York: Oxford University Press, 461-480, 2014.

Coward, Fiona and Clive Gamble. "Big Brains, Small Worlds: Material Culture and the Evolution of Mind" in R.I.M. Dunbar, Clive Gamble, and J.A.J. Gowlett (eds.). Lucy to Language: The Bench Mark Papers. New York: Oxford University Press, 2014, 461-480.

Daston, Lorraine J. *Against Nature*. Cambridge, MA: MIT Press, 2019.

Daston and Galison. *Objectivity*. New York: Zone Books, 2007.

Damasio, Antonio. *Self Comes to Mind: Constructing the Conscious Brain*. New York: Random House, 2010.

Davis, Ann E. *The Evolution of the Property Relation: Understanding Paradigms, Debates, Prospects*. New York: Palgrave MacMillan, 2015.

Davis, Ann E. *The End of Individualism and the Economy: Emerging Paradigms of Connection and Community*. New York: Routledge, 2020.

Degroot, Dagomar. *The Frigid Golden Age: Climate Change, the Little ice Age, and the Dutch Republic, 1560-1720*. New York: Cambridge University Press, 2018.

Dennett, Daniel C. *From Bacteria to Bach and Back: The Evolution of Minds*. New York: W.W.Norton, 2017.

Diamond, Jared. *Collapse: How Societies Choose to Fail or Succeed*. New York: Viking, 2005.

Dunbar, Robin. *Human Evolution: Our Brains and Behavior*. New York: Oxford University Press, 2016.

Edwards, Paul N. *A Vast Machine: Computer Models, Climate Data, and the Politics of Global Warming*. Cambridge, MA: MIT Press, 2010.

Falkowski, Paul G. *Life's Engines: How Microbes Made Earth Habitable*. Princeton, NJ: Princeton University Press, 2015.

Foster, John Bellamy, Brett Clark, and Richard York. *The Ecological Rift: Capitalism's War on the Earth*. New York: Monthly Review Press, 2010.

Foster, John Bellamy and Brett Clark. *The Robbery of Nature: Capitalism and the Ecological Rift*. New York: Monthly Review Press, 2010.

Friederici, Angela D. *Language in Our Brain: The Origins of a Uniquely Human Capacity*. Cambridge, MA: MIT Press, 2017.

Gamble, Clive. *Making Deep History: Zeal, Perseverance, and the Time Revolution of 1859*. New York: Oxford University Press, 2021.

Gamble, Clive, John Gowlett and Robin Dunbar. Thinking Big: How the Evolution of Social Life Shaped the Human Mind. London: Thames and Hudson, 2014.

Gaudzinski-Windheuser, Sabine and Olaf Joris. "Contextualizing the Female Image – Symbols for Common ideas and Communal identity in Upper Paleolithic societies," in Fiona Coward, Robert Hosfield, Matt Pope, and Francis Wenban-Smith (eds.). *Settlement, Society and Cognition in Human Evolution: Landscapes in Mind*, New York: Cambridge University Press, 2015, 288-314.

Gazzaniga, Michael S. *The Consciousness Instinct: Unraveling the Mystery of How the Brain Makes the Mind*. New York: Farrar, Straus, Giroux, 2018.

Ginsburgh, Victor and Shlomo Weber. "The Economics of Language" in *Journal of Economic Literature*, Vol. 58, No. 2, 2020, 348-404.

Gleick, James. *The Information: A History, A Theory, A Flood*. New York: Pantheon, 2011.

Goede, Marieke De. *Virtue, Fortune, and Faith: A Genealogy of Finance*. Minneapolis: University of Minnesota Press, 2005.

Graziano, Michael S.A. *Rethinking Consciousness: A Scientific Theory of Subjective Experience*. New York: W. W. Norton, 2019.

Haraway, Donna J. *How Like a Leaf*. New York: Routledge, 2000.

Haraway, Donna J. "Staying with the Trouble: Anthropocene, Capitalocene, Chthulucene," in Jason W. Moore (ed.). *Anthropocene or Capitalocene? Nature, History, and the Crisis of Capitalism*. Oakland, CA: Kairos PM Press, 2016, 34-76.

Harding, Sandra. *Sciences from Below: Feminisms, Postcolonialities, and Modernities*. Durham: Duke University Press, 2008.

Hoffman, Philip T. *Why Did Europe Conquer the World?* Princeton, NJ: Princeton University Press, 2015.

Hornborg, Alf. *Nature, Society, and Justice in the Anthropocene: Unravelling the Money-Energy-Technology Complex*. New York: Cambridge University Press, 2019.

Hrdy, Sarah Blaffer. *Mother Nature: Maternal Instincts and How They Shape the Human Species*. New York: Ballantine, 1999.

Hrdy, Sarah Blaffer. *Mothers and Others: The Evolutionary Origins of Mutual Understanding*. Cambridge, MA: Harvard University Press, 2009.

Hrdy, Sarah Blaffer and Judith M. Burkart. "The Emergence of Emotionally Modern Humans: Implications for Language and Learning." *Philosophical Transactions of the Royal Society B*. Vol. 375, 2020, 1 – 11.

Hulme, Mike. *Why We Disagree About Climate Change: Understanding Controversy, Inaction, and Opportunity*. New York: Cambridge University Press, 2009.

Hutchins, Edwin. *Cognition in the Wild*. Cambridge, MA: MIT Press, 1995.

Jasanoff, Sheila (ed.). *States of Knowledge: The Co-Production of Science and Social Order*. New York: Routledge, 2004.

Kandel, Eric R. *The Disordered Mind: What Unusual Brains tell us about Ourselves*. New York: Farrar, Straus, and Giroux, 2018.

Keller, Evelyn Fox. *A Feeling for the Organism: The Life and Work of Barbara McClintock*. San Francisco: W.H. Freeman, 1983.

Keller, Evelyn Fox. *The Mirage of a Space Between Nature and Nurture*. Durham, NC: Duke University Pres, 2010.

Koch, Alexander, Chris Brierley, Mark M. Maslin, Simon L. Lewis, "Earth System Impacts of the European Arrival and Great Dying in the Americas After 1492," in *Quaternary Science Reviews*, 207, (2019) 13–36.

Kruger, Lorenz, Lorraine J. Daston, and Michael Heidelberger (eds.). *The Probabilistic Revolution: Volume I: Ideas in History*.

Kuhn, Thomas S. "What Are Scientific Revolutions?" in in Kruger, Lorenz, Lorraine J. Daston, and Michael Heidelberger (eds.). *The Probabilistic Revolution: Volume I: Ideas in History*, 1987, 7-22

Latour, Bruno. *We Have Never Been Modern*. Cambridge, MA: Harvard University Press, 1993.

Latour, Bruno. *Down to Earth: Politics in the New Climatic Regime*. Cambridge, UK: Polity, 2018.

Leng, Thomas. "Epistemology: Expertise and Knowledge in the World of Commerce." In Philip J. Stern and Carl Wennerlind (eds.). Mercantilism Reimagined: Political Economy in Early Modern Britain and Its Empire. New York: Oxford University Press, 2014, 97-116.

Lewis, Simon L. and Mark A. Maslin. "Defining the Anthropocene" in *Nature*, Vol. 519, March 12, 2015, 171-180.

Levenson, Thomas. *Money for Nothing: The Scientists, Fraudsters, and Corrupt Politicians Who Reinvented Money, panicked a Nation, and Made the World Rich*. New York: Random House, 2020.

MacKenzie, Donald A. *An Engine, Not a Camera: How Financial Models Shape Markets*. Cambridge, MA: MIT Press, 2006.

Malm, Andreas. *Fossil Capital: The Rise of Steam Power and the Roots of Global Warming*. London: Verso, 2016.

Malm, Andreas. *The Progress of this Storm: Nature and Society in a Warming World*. London: Verso, 2018.

Maslin, Mark. *The Cradle of Humanity: How the Changing Landscape of Africa Made Us So Smart*. New York: Oxford University Press, 2017.

Merchant, Carolyn. *The Death of Nature: Women, Ecology, and the Scientific Revolution*. New York: Harper & Row publishers, 1980.

Merchant, Carolyn. *Reinventing Eden: The Fate of Nature in Western Civilization*. New York: Routledge, 2003.

Merchant, Carolyn. *The Anthropocene and the Humanities: From Climate Change to a New Age of Sustainability*. New Haven: Yale University Press, 2020.

Michaels, David. *Doubt is Their Product: How Industry's Assault on Science Threatens Your Health*. New York: Oxford University Press, 2008.

Mokyr, Joel. *A Culture of Growth: The Origins of the Modern Economy*. Princeton, NJ: Princeton University Press, 2016.

Mooney, Chris C. *The Republican War on Science*. New York: Basic, 2006.

Mooney, Chris C. *Storm World: Hurricanes, Politics, and the Battle Over Global Warming*. San Diego: Harcourt, 2008.

Moore, Jason W. *Capitalism in the Web of Life: Ecology and the Accumulation of Capital*. London: Verso, 2015.

Nagel, Thomas. *The View from Nowhere*. New York: Oxford University Press, 1986.

Nagel, Thomas. *Mind and Cosmos: Why the Materialist Neo-Darwinian Conception of Nature is Almost Certainly False*. New York: Oxford University Press, 2012.

O'Mara, Margaret. *The Code: Silicon Valley and the Remaking of America*. New York: Penguin, 2019.

Oreskes, Naomi. *Why Trust Science*. Princeton, NJ: Princeton University Press, 2019.

Oreskes, Naomi and Erik M. Conway. *Merchants of Doubt: How a Handful of Scientists Obscured the Truth on Issues from Tobacco Smoke to Global Warming*. New York: Bloomsbury, 2010.

Oreskes, Naomi. *Science on a Mission: How Military Funding Shaped What We Do and Don't Know About the Ocean*. Chicago: University of Chicago Press, 2021.

Patel, Raj and Jason W. Moore. *A History of the World in Seven Cheap Things: A Guide to Capitalism, Nature, and the Future of the Planet*. Oakland: University of California Press, 2017.

Poovey, Mary. *A History of the Modern Fact: Problems of Knowledge in the Sciences of Wealth and Society*. Chicago: University of Chicago Press, 1998.

Poovey, Mary. "The Liberal Civil Subject and the Social in Eighteenth-Century British Moral Philosophy," in *Public Culture*, Vol. 14, No. 1, 125-145, 2002.

Poovey, Mary. *Genres of the Credit Economy: Mediating Value in Eighteenth- and Nineteenth-Century Britain*. Chicago: University of Chicago Press, 2008.

Postone, Moishe. *Time, Labor, and Social domination: A Reinterpretation of Marx's Critical Theory*. Cambridge, UK: Cambridge University Press, 1993.

Postone, Moishe. *Time, Labor, and Social Domination: A Reinterpretation of Marx's Critical Theory*. Cambridge, UK: Cambridge University Press, 1996.

Postone, Moishe. "The Current Crisis and the Anachronism of Value: A Marxian Reading." *Continental Thought and Theory*. Vol. 1, No. 4, October 1, 2017, 38-54.

Postone, Moishe. "The Current Crisis and the Anachronism of Value" in Marcello Musto (ed.). Marx's Capital After 150 Years: Critique and Alternative to Capitalism. New York: Routledge, 2019, 94-107.

Postone, Moishe. "Capital and Temporality" in Marcello Musto (ed.). *The Marx Revival: Concepts and New Critical Interpretations*. New York: Cambridge University Press, 2020, 157-176.

Przezdzik, Izabela, Koen V. Haak, Christian F. Beckmann, and Andreas Bartsch. "The Human Language Connectome." In Peter Hagoort (Editor in Chief.) *Human Language: From Genes and Brains to Behavior*. Cambridge, MA: MIT Press, 2019, 467-480.

Ramachandran, V.S. The Tell-Tale Brain: A Neuroscientist's Quest for What Makes Us Human. New York: W. W. Norton, 2011.

Searle, John R. *Making the Social World: The Structure of Human Civilization*. New York: Oxford University Press, 2010.

Schabas, Margaret. *The Natural Origin of Economics*. Chicago: University of Chicago Press, 2005

Schoenemann, P. Thomas. "The Evolution of Enhanced Conceptual Complexity and of Broca's Area: Language Preadaptation," *Interaction Studies*, Vol. 19, No. 1, 2018, 336-351.
Schwagerl, Christian. *The Anthropocene: The Human Era and How It Shapes Our Planet*. London, Synergetic Press, 2014.
Searle, John R. *Making the Social World: The Structure of Human Civilization*. New YOrk: Oxford University Press, 2010.
Shapin, Steven and Simon Schaffer. *Leviathan and the Air-Pump: Hobbes, Boyle, and the Experimental Life*. Princeton, NJ.: Princeton University Press, 1985.
Slack, Paul. *The Invention of Improvement: Information and Material Progress in Seventeenth-Century England*. New York: Oxford University Press, 2015.
Shryock, Andrew and Smail, Daniel Lord. *Deep History: The Architecture of Past and Present*. Berkeley: University of California Press, 2011.
Smail, Daniel Lord. *On Deep History and the Brain*. Berkeley: University of California Press, 2008.
Spang, Rebecca L. *Stuff and Money in the Time of the French Revolution*. Cambridge, MA: Harvard University press, 2015.
Tomasello, Michael. Origins of Human Communication. Cambridge, MA: MIT Press, 2008.
Tomasello, Michael. *Becoming Human: A Theory of Ontogeny*. Cambridge, MA: Harvard University Press, 2019.
Turner, David P. *The Green Marble: Earth System Science and Global Sustainability*. New York: Columia University Press, 2018.
Vernes, Sonja C. "Neuromolecular Approaches to the Study of Languages" Peter Hagoort (Editor in Chief.) *Human Language: From Genes and Brains to Behavior*. Cambridge, MA: MIT Press, 2019, 577-593.
Wennerlind, Carl. *Casualties of Credit: The English Financial Revolution, 1620-1720*. Cambridge, MA: Harvard University Press, 2011.
Wennerlind, Carl. "Money: Hartlibian Political Economy and the New Culture of Credit." In Philip J. Stern and Carl Wennerlind (eds.). Mercantilism Reimagined: Political Economy in Early Modern Britain and Its Empire. New York: Oxford University Press, 2014, 74-93.
Zuboff, Shoshana. *The Age of Surveillance Capitalism: The Fight for a Human Future at the New Frontier of Power*. New York: Public Affairs, 2019.

Chapter 3
History of Political Economy

1 Introduction

The purpose of this chapter is to explore the role of ideas which then affect human behavior, which in turn can alter ideas. Further, there is a tendency in capitalist modernity to have a series of abstractions which presume to objectively describe human behavior, but which also structure it. The effect of these abstractions is to remove agency, because behavior is circumscribed in a series of discrete institutions which are established and performed by these concepts, such as work and home, and the public/private divide. Finally, these concepts do not describe the effect of human behavior on the environment, and so any such interactions are invisible. An examination of these ideas and institutions can help increase awareness of the essential interaction of humans and earth. In fact, these interactions can affect the "means of life," such as air, water, and regular temperature.

2 Evolution of Language

Humans are unique among primates for a developed articulate language, more complex than animal communication (Tomasello 2008). Language has been important in group formation, cohesion (Dunbar), and socialization. Like jewelry and clothes, language can be a semiotic carrier of membership and belonging (Smail, Stiner, and Earle 2011, 219–241).

Language is a symbol system, which can be studied for its objective structure building on the work of Noam Chomsky, Ferdinand de Saussure, and Charles Peirce. Language is also a method of coordination, preservation of technology, and expression of group identity.

Language can also be studied in social context, in pragmatic situations of daily use. Williams is critical of the "privileged" position of the experts, which they do

A. E. Davis, *Whole Earth*, https://doi.org/10.1007/978-3-031-01934-0_3

not acknowledge, who study language as if they were not also themselves speakers. Language is constitutive of humans and is involved in life process. "Language, then, is not a medium; it is a constitutive element of material social practice...Language is in fact a special kind of material practice: that of human sociality" (Williams 1977, 165, 168). That is, Williams would not consider production, communication, cognition, expression, and subject formation in isolation, but in a holistic social context.

In spite of its importance in human evolution and social cohesion, language has been controversial as a tool in social science and history (Surkis 2012; Spiegel 2009), even while the "problematic of representation" has been acknowledged in literary studies (Poovey 1998). Language has been considered crucial in the social construction of institutions (Searle 2010), the formation of rules and law (North, Wallis, Weingast 2009; Pistor 2019), and the "social imaginary" of nation-states. Language is clearly social, even while particular ideologies can stress "the individual" (Davis 2020). Language can be a tool of deliberation and mutual understanding (Wessler 2018), as well as distortion and delusion, poetic expression, or objective science (Taylor 2016).

There is a long-standing and ongoing philosophical debate regarding the "reality" of human community and its cultural expressions and norms, compared with "reality" outside the human brain (Gordon 2010). That is, are symbols any less "real" for having been produced by the human mind? Linguistic philosopher John Searle notes that humans can create "institutional facts," which are human institutions based on common understandings and regular human behavior (Searle 2010, 93–98). The participants in these institutions have a shared "collective intentionality" and cooperate to achieve certain ends, by coordinated behavior. These institutions have "real" effects in the outcomes of this coordinated behavior, whether consisting of feelings, ideas, or work products. Because feelings and ideas are recorded in the human brain, by patterns of neurons, they are no less real than material objects, and can affect human behavior in the world, with material effects (see Table 2.1 in Chap. 2).

Language can be used in two distinct ways, according to Searle. One is simply the reference function, pointing to an object and providing an associated name. Searle calls this world to word "direction of fit." The object exists in the world prior to the naming by the language. The other is the word to world direction of fit, whereby the naming in language is associated with norms and behavior, which is understood by human actors and which changes the world by their coordinated actions (Searle 2010, 38–41). Institutions like money, property, and corporations are human creations by associating words with distinctive behaviors, which often involve the particular way to make use of objects, called "status function declaration" (Searle 2010, 10–14, 84–86, 100–106). Language is part of the human capacity for "collective intentionality," which can cause changes in the world.

Searle discusses the "deontology" associated with status function declarations (Searle 2010, 80–86). Once a person has performed an utterance, there is an obligation to use the term according to conventional meanings and to enact according to social standards. In this sense, the statement is an act by an individual with volition, but the meaning is guided by expectations of the listeners for the common understanding of the terms. In this sense, language and action are decided by individuals, but the social expectations have a conforming effect. A person making statements without such conformance risks ostracism, a threat which exerts pressure on the individual. That is, language is both individual and social, and meaning is inside each person and also maintained by social performance.

Contributors to the debate regarding the social production of science recognize that science is a social endeavor, with knowledge created by the human mind. According to Bhaskar, science is a social endeavor, producing knowledge of a "real" world which exists outside of that production and outside of humans (Bhaskar 1978). According to Hacking, the claim of "social construction" can be used to provide a critique of the status quo, which is often taken for granted but can be altered (Hacking 1999, 6–14). Hacking too differentiates social phenomena, like money and the economy, as socially constructed, compared with "quarks" which are "natural" (Hacking 1999, 12–14, 30, 68–70), even though the "idea" of quarks is socially constructed, as is the science which defined them as an experimental object. That is, products of the human mind can be used to refer to natural phenomena, which build a scientific knowledge which can serve as a produced "means of production" (Bhaskar 1978, 17, 185–199). That knowledge can refer to both nature and humans, but is expressed in a language that is only understood by humans. There is always a "problematic of representation," by which science can use metaphors to communicate certain ideas, always imperfectly and always in flux, in the process of refinement and clarification.

In past work, I have approached the issue of language from a "historical institutional" perspective. That is, historical institutionalism provides a method for long-term historical analysis (Davis 2015, 2017, 2020), tracing the changing meanings of such key terms as "corporation" and "property." Language is important as a method for coordinating and disciplining human behavior. Institutions channel that behavior based on these key terms, and expertise aids in the authoritative interpretation and enforcement, the meaning of which may tend to become modified over time (Banner 2011; Pistor 2019). Those changing meanings can be studied and documented, to provide a greater understanding of the process of institutional change. Rather than take the meaning of such key terms as a simple referent, or "self-evident," one can analyze the "problematic of representation" (Poovey 1998), by which meanings can be challenged, and the necessity for disciplinary and enforcement mechanisms, or "incentives." Once a particular concept becomes familiar, its extension can provide acceptance and continuity, even as the meanings change, such as a "corporate body." In this approach, meanings are expressed in language and manifested in behavior, which is then observed and can change authoritative meanings. Where stability can reinforce authority, the documentation of changing institutions can provide the opportunity for reflection and critique. When the structure of institutions is based on key ideas, like property and money, these institutions structure experience and so influence beliefs, which tend to reaffirm the institutional structure.

The term "nature" has many meanings and can provide a rationale for certain types of behavior and values. Those meanings of "nature" can include (1) outside of human influence, (2) essential, (3) God-given, (4) unchanging, and (5) objective and material. Human institutions are not "natural," according to the first four meanings, because they exist by explicit statements of authoritative sources, which are enacted, interpreted, and enforced by humans. But human institutions are objective and material, the fifth meaning, because human performances involve behavior by living creatures, which exist in bodily manifestations and involve the earth for their existence and action.

3 Co-evolution of Nature and Culture

The observation that human knowledge accumulates in language and can be represented in durable forms available to historians has been formulated in the concept of "noosphere" by Vernadsky (Worster 2016, 191–192; Turner 2018, 9–11, 253). That is, human knowledge can exist outside human brains in forms of representation which can include natural science and other forms of human creation such as humanities and social sciences. These forms of human knowledge can affect consciousness and self-awareness, as well as human behavior and consequently the earth, like another "sphere" distinct from the biosphere and the atmosphere in material form.

It is possible to propose periodization of the forms of human knowledge and to identify the associated distinctive types of human impacts on the earth. Further, these impacts may then influence human knowledge and behavior, in a mutually interactive system of co-evolution. Worster proposes major "revolutions" in human worldviews as including (1) Copernican, which affected the role of religion; (2) the European explorations (which were associated with political revolutions, the industrial revolution, and the emergence of capitalism); (3) the discovery of human evolution by Darwin; and (4) the discovery of climate change and other limits of the earth (Worster 2016). The concept of these cumulative impacts on the earth by human knowledge and behavior has recently been called the "Anthropocene," and may affect the writing of human history, and broader questions of the relationship between humans and the earth.

> The very idea of history is, with fits and starts, going through a metamorphosis. The history we write in the future may start not with the rise of human civilizations, but with the deeper origins of the universe, putting off until late in the story the appearance of a tiny mammal on a tiny planet that thought itself supremely important....[These humans] discovered the sobering truth that they face many limits. The universe, while infinite, is not infinite for them. (Worster 2016, 225).

The idea that nature and culture have co-evolved is expressed by Worster (2016, 24), but is not widely accepted. Rather, the typical history of political economy and economics proceeds in linear fashion, without considering the influences of history and ecology that may have shaped it. Worster himself has proposed a new academic discipline to study the interaction of nature and culture, called environmental history. The assumptions of such a field would include that (1) humans are subject to natural constraints, (2) humans are not a separate and uniquely special species, and (3) the environmental consequences of past human actions cannot be ignored (Worster 1990).

Further, a history of human knowledge could also make note of changing "paradigms" and their effects (Kuhn 1957, 1970). That is, human knowledge, even of natural science, has taken distinct forms and frameworks, which in turn influence views of human nature, social organization, and values. In observing major shifts in human relation to nature, Worster proposes that the emergence of capitalism has had an effect on the earth's ecosystems as significant as the Neolithic revolution and the development of settled agriculture (Worster 1990, 1097–1100), which is akin to a "reorganization of nature."

Like philosophy and anthropology, history can provide a perspective for humans of their own long-term development. The shifts that Worster observes may be underway: instead of celebrating European civilization and its superiority, there is a movement now for "provincializing Europe" (Chakrabarty 2000) and celebrating indigenous methods of relation to the earth (Graeber and Wengrow 2021), rather than the modern.

4 Emergence of History, Political Economy, and Time

In the Anthropocene, it is important to seek longer-term understanding of the place of humans in relation to ecology. An analysis of "deep history" reveals human/ecological co-evolution, rather than human exceptionalism and the separation of humans from nature. Human self-awareness as a species may be important for such a task (Chakrabarty 2018; Baucom 2020). This new perspective on the relation of humans to the evolution of the earth presents a challenge to all social and natural sciences and their disciplinary divides (Merchant 2020).

Peter Gordon explores the "broader and more perplexing phenomenon of philosophical memory, the complicated and overdetermined process whereby philosophy comes to understand itself by telling itself stories about where it has been" (Gordon 2010, 2). This analysis can be applied to history as well, whereby the history profession, and writers who complete scholarly perspectives on a given period, attempts to account for itself in a reflexive manner, designed to share insights into trends and lessons to be learned. In this way, history and philosophy are forms of collective self-awareness of humanity and the human community, and its continuity over time. Yet such works are not uncontroversial and offer methodologies and claims that can be contested. Ideally, the categories of the analysis are derived from the analysis of history itself.

There is a view of history itself as influenced by dominant worldview. For example, there are interpretations of history as teleological, origin of religions, nations, scientific progress, and formation of imagined communities (Hartog 2005; Clark 2019; Baucom 2020; Marx 1967; Postone 1993). History can also have many shapes and patterns, such as Christian eschatology (Clark 2019, 13); working class as agent of history (Marx 1967); accumulation of time with climate change (Baucom 2020, 19, 79–81); return to previous greatness (Clark 2019, 16–18); and decline and fall (Pocock 1975).

There is an irony of capitalism: time is a factor of production, with speedup of lifestyles and longer life expectancy; but the dynamics of history are absorbed within "the category of capital," an apparently objective, static entity which reproduces itself by temporal domination (Postone 1993; Davis 2022). Capitalism is also subject to "stages of development," according to Marx, and represents a distinct mode of production in comparison with feudalism and communism. That is, capitalism is also a period in history, subject to historical forces.

There are also varieties of methods of historical analysis, such as neutral and objective, realist (Bhaskar 1978), subject to influence by dominant paradigms (Kuhn 1957, 1970; Postone 1993) or world views (Foucault 1972; Surkis 2012). The awareness of history can also provide a challenge to "eternal truth," which claims to be universal and invariant. That is, awareness of history can be an implicit challenge to the verity of any given paradigm, a form of "relativism."

There is also a history of the various conceptions of the human relation to nature (Merchant 2020; Latour 1993), including animism, religion, science, technology, "modernity," and mutualism. Implicit in the concept of "property" is the use of nature for human utility.

5 Separation of Natural from Social Science and Economics from History

The Enlightenment separation between nature and culture is reflected in the structure of modern sciences and the academic division between natural and social sciences (Latour 1993; Chakrabarty 2018). The implication is that natural sciences exist outside of human influence and are unchanging, in contrast with social sciences which can be modified by research and rational deliberation. This "modern constitution" can be misleading, nonetheless, because all living beings involve interaction with the earth, in terms of metabolism and production. Second, facts are "represented" by scientific constructions, whether metaphors, images, or equations, as well as political science, in which citizens are "represented." Third, the existence of the human species, and its growth and distribution over the globe, has affected the earth's ecological and evolutionary processes (Lewis and Maslin 2015). In turn, human evolution has been affected by the earth's evolution (Falkowski 2015).

In "modern societies," nonetheless, the role of "nature" is invisible. Technological "progress" has made understanding nature unnecessary, as many operations in modern economies are automatic, easy, and fast. Concepts such as the "social" are presumably only applicable to interaction of humans with each other in a given context. The social interaction occurs in a built environment, supplied with air and water and waste disposal, connected by transportation and communication with other locations. Provisions are available for three meals per day plus snacks and other forms of refreshments. The source of food and its implications are not well understood (Bittman 2021). The wildlife which may have once resided there, as well as previous settlers or civilizations, are not relevant. The clothes and furnishings may have been produced in near or far locations, with technologies only vaguely understood by the participants, available from international trade. The task of a comprehensive identification of the ecological interfaces of a given human "social" interaction is complex, revealing the infrastructure and institutions which are part of the "background." The very fact of "modernity" enables this disappearance of the ecological.

5.1 Property

The definition of "property" (Piketty 2014, 2020) provides owners with rights for instrumental use of natural beings, both human and the earth (Shryock and Smail 2011; Ostrom 1990; Pistor 2019; Banner 2011; Merchant 2020), to be combined, transformed in the priviled space of the factory into commodities which have "value" reflected in money, a social abstraction. Money is a "hybrid" according to Latour, consisting of both human and natural elements (Latour 1993).

Property can include land, inventions, social arrangements, technologies (Banner 2011), as well as "human capital." The allocation of property to its "highest" use (highest market value) can legitimate the command of earth's ecosystems, without accounting for any impact on those ecosystems. The only metric is market value, which is based on human utility and economic costs of production.

The constitutional protections of property can in fact impede any retrospective accounting for the impact of property and markets on ecosystems, in what can be known as "takings". Such "externalities" have been considered as "marginal" to the operation of the economy (Medema 2020).

The trope of "property" enables this disappearance. The individual parcel on which any particular building is located is assumed to come equipped with adequate air and water and typical temperature. The global cycles which influence that availability are invisible, not well understood, and presumably managed by the state as part of the public infrastructure. Yet the very operation of a capitalist economic system presumes that any given parcel will be managed to increase its market value, expressed in an abstract medium of money, rather than contribute to or deflect global cycles. The global scheme of economic governance ignores the ecological cycles, which until recently were not even studied.

See Fig. 3.1 with distinct bands of types of existence, with the middle band depicting the social, the upper the realm of ideas, and the lower the realm of production. Figure 3.2 repeats these three bands with more explicit direct interaction with nature. For example, ideas are recorded in material substances, and production requires materials and technologies. Figure 3.3 expresses the notion that accumulating experience and history can affect changing relations with nature.

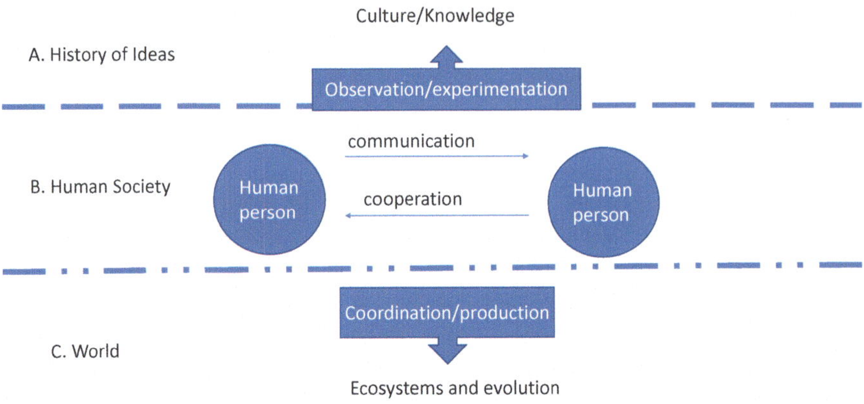

Fig. 3.1 Human social relations

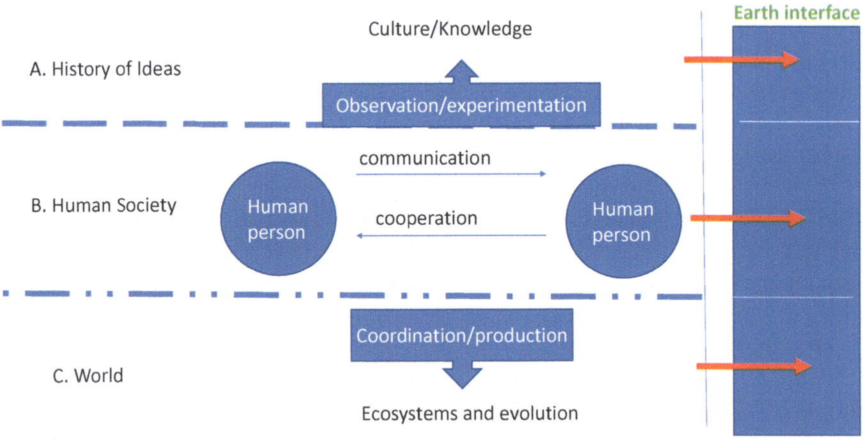

Fig. 3.2 Human social relations with environmental interface

Modern categories like money, property, and corporations are "institutional facts" which are created by linguistic "status function declarations" and the associated behavior (Searle 2010). But these concepts are not only linguistic. These concepts are similar to Poovey's "reifying abstractions," which have real effects (Poovey 2002), or Habermas's "real abstractions" (Habermas 1987, 336, 374–375). That is, ideas which humans believe and enact affect behavior on the earth which can potentially disturb ecological processes. The belief that "property" is real entitles the "owner" to make use of a parcel of earth to increase its market value, which may destabilize global ecosystems and affect other property values negatively. What are considered "externalities" by economists (Caldwell 2020) can destabilize global climate systems. In terms of its effects, social science is no less "real" than natural science, and the categorical separation can lead to oversights and errors in both.

The contradictions of this global economic governance system are becoming more visible on a daily basis. For example, public electricity provided by Pacific

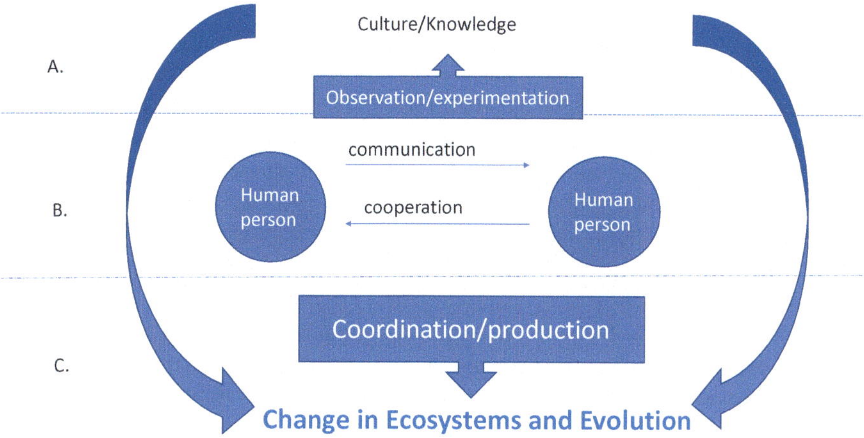

Fig. 3.3 Dynamic interrelationships of human and ecological systems

Gas and Electric has contributed to forest fires. As a result, blackouts occur during heat waves, making air conditioning unavailable. The residential homes near fire-prone districts cannot obtain home insurance. The wild fire season now extends to winter. As several have noted, California is particularly prone to contradictions (Worster 1985). The provision of water was primarily the role of the federal government, yet California politics has been the home of the modern conservative movement (Worster 1985, 260). California has been the beneficiary of federal defense spending, which helped provide the locus for "Silicon Valley", yet preserves the culture of fantasy and individualism.

As Worster points out, understanding the history of a region can help elucidate the present issues. What he calls a "hydraulic society" is necessarily centralized due to the need to manage water in an arid climate. Yet the issue of who organizes that system remains, whether imperial bureaucracy as in ancient India and China or the "capitalist state" of the modern era. In the example of California, developers and investors were able to call upon the support of the federal government to develop a regional water system, while not allowing citizen participation or without taking into account the limits noted by the initial surveyors. A drought emergency in the Colorado River in August 2021 (Huth and Umlauf 2021) did not cause the ringing of alarm bells, because so much economic development depends on the model of business as usual.

5.2 *Corporation*

The corporate form is another way in which the environment becomes invisible. As documented in Davis (2015, 64–74, 103–106), the corporation may have evolved from medieval communes and city-states, as well as the church. Long-distance trade was another stimulus, in providing a form for capital accumulation and sharing risks and rewards from shipping ventures. The private business corporation evolved from the state-chartered merchant monopoly corporations, which had delegated governance and military powers. What Harris calls the "organizational revolution" of the early 1600s may have been responsible for the "rise of the West" (Harris 2020, 369, 375–376). The corporation also helped to solve the question of time. With a perpetual form with rotating membership, which is reliant on no single member for its continuity, the perpetual corporation can support the perpetual state and provide the basis for finance. In turn, the state can benefit from its exploration, trade, and innovation.

One example of a type of corporation with global environmental impact is the fossil fuel corporation. Standard Oil, the trust organized by John D. Rockefeller, was one of the "world's very first and largest multinational enterprises" (Yergin 1991, 13), associated with the rise of capitalism. Because this industry was essential for the provision of energy, to substitute for hydro, animal, and human, it was strategic for industrialization (Malm 2016). That is, by substituting for human labor, the pace of production was increased, the commodity price reduced, and extension of scale was feasible. The private business corporation was allowed to develop by administrative procedure, with general incorporation laws in the early nineteenth century in the United States. The expansion of scale and the merger wave of the late nineteenth century resulted in the formation of oligopolies in key industries, such as oil. In the United States, oil was discovered in Titusville, Pennsylvania, in 1859. The first antitrust case was against Standard Oil, the Rockefeller combination, which was split into 38 separate companies, which later were able to recombine into the "majors" (Sampson 1975, 32–51; Yergin 2011, 88–107).

Oil was discovered in the region around the Caspian Sea in the early nineteenth century, when it was part of the Russian Empire, although the seepages had been observed for centuries. European investors like the Rothschilds and the Nobels were able to found oil companies to extract and transport to markets by means of pipelines (Yergin 1991, 57–62). There was a geopolitical competition for control of oil, with discoveries in Central and Latin America, as well as the Middle East. The conversion of the British Navy to oil had military as well as commercial impact, in the run-up to World War I (Yergin 1991, 151–173). Later, Vladimir Putin recognized the fossil fuels as a continuing source of strategic power and source of export earnings for Russia, after the collapse of the USSR (Yergin 2011, 37–64).

Because of the strategic importance of this industry, these firms have received subsidies, exemptions from antitrust, and military support for the control of oil. The development of internal combustion automobiles as well as the distribution of gasoline stations across the country helped to support the American love affair with the automobile. The real estate industry also thrived from the greater mobility, and mortgage debt became a major financial asset. With technological innovation, petroleum became the stock for the development of synthetic textiles, pharmaceuticals, and plastics. The Iranian Revolution, and the formation of the Organization of the Petroleum Exporting Countries in the 1970s, associated with rising prices of gasoline, had major impacts on the US economy. Part of the motivation for the Iraq War of 2003 was to secure additional supplies of petroleum, constituting another entry of the US into the political economy of the Middle East.

Even though the implications of fossil fuel combustion were known in the nineteenth century (Yergin 2011, 423–474), the development of the industry was not disturbed. In the current global context, oil corporations have been nationalized and privatized, alternately, depending on the strategic importance and desire for control. At present, the petroleum industry is a global oligopoly, consisting of both private, investor-owned companies and state-owned companies. Financial assets consisting of petroleum reserves may end up as "stranded assets," which cannot be sold due to concern about climate change, and may affect the market value of these corporations. Activist investors have been urging the development of transitional business plans, to varying success, while part of the corporate strategy has been to finance climate denial and free market think tanks to resist regulation.

The notion that a basic necessity, such as gasoline, could cause climate change is far from the direct experience of the typical US consumer. The operation of these particular corporations, and their production of regular profits, has made these companies familiar logos, favorite investments, with satisfied consumers. The environmental impact has been invisible until recent decades, depending on the level of education and concern. There is no requirement to date of environmental impact reporting to the Securities and Exchange Commission, although recently this type of requirement has been considered, along with standard reporting protocols.

The corporations manage the concrete characteristics of the commodity, such as its various uses, and the locations in which it can be drilled and transported by hiring geologists and engineers, as well as the sale of the product for money for profit, managed by marketing and distribution specialists. These fossil fuel corporations also have a complex relation to time. On the one hand, they are perpetual, and can outlast any absolute scarcity of oil, with substitute investments and technological innovations. On the other hand, they must make the quarterly earnings reports and provide short-term returns to satisfy shareholders. Further, they are arbitraging the wager regarding the speed of climate change and the impact on a global market for fossil fuels: how fast will tipping points occur, destabilizing the global economy and ecology, compared with extracting profits from the remaining oil reserves? These large corporations are leading players in this human/ecological drama.

5.3 *Money, Finance, and Contradictions*

The goal of the capitalist system, more money, has led to "financialization" in which the value of any investment is subject to bubbles and bursts. A global system of balance of payments in key currencies requires emerging countries to export cash crops, even while risking ecology and human development. The use of refrigerants to maintain comfortable temperatures in rising numbers of warming events can cause destruction of the ozone layer, leading to more global warming. Modern technologies such as computer chips and batteries rely on rare earths like cobalt and lithium, while the production process requires much water. Global communication and information technology rely on an increasing number of orbiting satellites and are subject to cyberattacks. Consumerism motivated by relative status has led to global increases in inequality.

6 Modernity and Capitalist Institutionalism

There is a challenge for writing the history of capitalism (Neal and Williamson 2015; special issue of the *Busines History Review*, Vol. 94, No. 1, Spring 2020; Harris 2020; Arrighi 1994). There are contrasting methods and assumptions, as well as a long sweep of history. The History of Capitalism workshop at Harvard University, led by Sven Beckert and Christine Desan, has sponsored workshops and graduate students, with notable recent publications. Some of the issues involve the assumptions of positive vs. normative, voluntary vs. coercive markets, optimal vs. evolutionary, universal vs. particular, idealized vs. critical (Habermas 1985, 374–403).

There are different roles for the historian, whether observer or participant in the system, and whether dominated by "steering media" of the life world, or aimed at achieving mutual understanding. Foucault's "gaze" created an object of study for each individual and for the population as a whole (Habermas 1987, 294–301); and there was a shift in perspective with Adam Smith's "impartial spectator," even when viewing oneself.

Habermas studies language and communication in social context of capitalist modernity. Habermas notes the shifting perspective of the observer and the participant in his analysis of the structure of modernity (Habermas 1987, 244–248). The sociologist as observer, such as Durkheim or Parsons, sees the systemic dimension of human communication, and such "steering media" as money and political power. By contrast, the participant sees the "lifeworld," in which daily activities such as food, clothing, and shelter as well as social relationships are experienced. Modernity is characterized by these two systems, which are not always in harmonious relationship (Habermas 1984, 1985, 153–197). For example, the need to obtain employment for a wage may drive behavior that is not compatible with supportive social relationships. There is a similar dichotomy between forms of communication, in which rational instrumental action is oriented towards the steering media, in contrast to the motive of mutual understanding, which is located in the "lifeworld." The monetization of labor is one method of integration among the two elements (Habermas 1985, 332–373), which is subject nonetheless to the vagaries of the business cycle and the drive for productivity in competing capitalist firms.

This tendency in modern social science to the objective perspective of the outside observer is associated with the labor market and the monetization of labor (Habermas 1985, 332–343). Even while self-consciousness is a feature of evolved human capacities, the labor contract presumes that the worker is willing to follow the price signals of the product market and the labor market and submit to the direction of the employer and his manager. This is a form of "abstract" labor, which is indifferent to its skills, technologies, and products, or personality of the worker. To Habermas, the wage is the formal link between the worker's life context and the employer's competition in labor and product markets, for the purposes of making profit. The wage is the transformation between two types of language, the worker's concrete existence, the "lifeworld," and the employer's management of abstract "steering media," of money and markets. The worker is willing to objectify himself, to sell himself as a worker, and the firm is willing to participate in markets which only judge the product by criteria of price and quantity. There is a tenuous connection between lifeworld and steering media, sometimes contradictory, which is managed by the manager and the worker. The primacy of the profit motive in capitalism means that the "steering media" of money and markets will be dominant, and the worker's "lifeworld" will comply and adjust. The observers can monitor the "steering media," the economists, and the government officials, whose perspective as outsiders is reflected in the abstract concepts of social science.

The steering media of money is arguably more powerful than the bureaucracy, although Habermas sees these two forms of "steering media" as coequal. The influence of money becomes greater due to the needs of financing the state, for war and for extension of the market. Global capital markets become influential for government policy because of the reliance by government financing on the issue of debt. Money issued by the state is essential for disciplining labor and product markets, supporting credit markets, as well as funding the state with tax revenue. Corporations become the dominant institution because of their access to credit, as well as production of commodities for revenue and profit. By projecting financial markets into the future, the state was able to assure its own continuity, by means of perpetual corporations issuing stock and bonds, and providing liquidity for investors in public and private assets. Money is the survival constraint for firms and for households and links all components of the system. Money is the means of the logic of calculation and rationality, so famously analyzed by Weber. The historical evolution of financial markets is the subject of a large literature (Atack and Neal 2009; Neal 1990).

Habermas sees mechanisms within the state, such as mass democracy and the welfare state, as modifying and managing the conflicts between the steering media and the lifeworld. To the extent that these state-based features are the responsibility of social science professionals with an "objective" worldview, nonetheless, the potential for direct deliberation among citizens is not fulfilled, along with other imperfections in the mass media (Wessler 2018). Brown (2019) sees pressure on both mass democracy and the welfare state by the turn to "neoliberalism" after the 1980s in the United States and the United Kingdom.

While Habermas ultimately eschews Marx's value theory, Postone applies Marx's value framework to the dialectic between value and wealth. For Postone, the competitive pressures among firms to increase productivity lead to competitive success, but reductions in value per unit, even as physical wealth increases. That is, there is an increasing mass of products, representing wealth, but less value per unit. The limits in value production then intensify the technological imperatives to increase labor productivity even further. This pressure is manifest in the modern perception of time, which seems to increase its pace at an ever greater speed, which seems to be a characteristic of modernity, rather than capitalism. As a result, there is an ever-increasing focus on the present, and the "present discounted value" of any future event.

There have been various methods to deal with abstractions. Marx begins his major work "Capital" with an exploration of the "commodity." This is a concrete object, but has intrinsic to it two forms of value, use value and exchange value. That is, the object is material, but "value" is abstract. Whether from production by living labor, as in the labor theory of value, or from utility, as in modern economics, or simply "supply and demand," value is not visible to the human eye. Smith uses the metaphor of the "invisible hand," and economics textbooks refer to "economic forces." Hayek stresses the price as the outcome of the unfettered market, producing a superior kind of knowledge. These are various methods to communicate a concept which is abstract, yet drives the capitalist system. "Value" is reflected in market price, in money terms, but money itself is abstract, and prices are variable.

A particularly important aspect of abstraction from Marx's method is the reversal of living and dead, by means of "fetishism." First, the commodity has "value" only because of its production by living labor and its use by humans for their survival, even though it is a simple material object. The value of the commodity is expressed by price in money terms, another object. Money itself, in capitalism, seems to reproduce itself, literally, with reference to human reproduction drawing from Aristotle. Money's "laws of motion" derive from the property rights of lenders and commodity purchasers, the actions of humans, enforced by law. The value of capital also results from being a product of labor and increasing the productivity of labor. That is, "the economy" seems to be an object, but consists of human relationships, masked by apparently self-animating "flows" of money and products. Abstraction also results from the discipline of labor in labor markets, of firms in commodity markets, and financiers in capital markets. The results are consistent "socially necessary labor time" and average rate of profit (Davis 2022).

Standpoint may be another complexity with respect to abstract concepts. These modern abstractions may require a "view from nowhere" (Nagel 1986) or a disinterested observer. Yet to the extent that these abstractions involve human participants, the observer is also a participant. Such a participant must be able to take various points of view, both subjective and objective. Smith refers to the "impartial spectator," which is a stance which one must assume to be an effective participant in a market economy. The market is considered like an abstract machine, with automatic self-regulation features, while also consisting of humans. That is, any given person must be both an observer and a participant, like an amphibian alternatively occupying both worlds. An "entrepreneur" is a person who can perceive the potential for commodification, a type of worldview which can see any object or idea with its potential for profit, even oneself (Davis 2020, 146–148).

Such abstractions may require different types of writing or genres (Poovey 2008). On the one hand, fictional narratives, such as novels, may enable market participants to imagine life in diverse circumstances. On the other hand, formal narratives, like economic theory, may allow a person to understand the market as a system, with various interacting components. The economics discipline, established in universities, then can claim the status of a modern science or at least a "social science."

Abstractions may be conveyed by personifications. For example, the abstract concept of sovereignty is personified by the "king's two bodies" (Whalen 2020); Marx discusses the character "moneybags" (Wolff 1988) and popularizers of the financial markets used the character "Lady Credit" (Poovey 2008; Staheli 2013; Murphy 2019) or the goddess "Fortuna" (Pocock 1975). Smith uses the "invisible hand". Modern financial markets are populated by characters like "Gordon Gekko" who seem real and who make statements that are quoted to help understand the system, like "greed is good" (Samman 2019).

Concepts like "the market" are made observable by the use of numbers (Poovey 1998), to validate the concept which is entirely socially constructed, while presumably grounded in natural philosophy (Schabas 2005) and natural science. Concepts like "property" are also considered simple objects, like land, or alternatively social laws, formal institutions, and rights recognized among people (Banner 2011; Searle 2010; Pistor 2019).

Once theorized and institutionalized, these "reifying abstractions" (Poovey 2002) appear to have agency, like credit, corporations, markets, and even Habermas's "steering media." The abstractions are managed by "experts" who are equipped with a modern worldview, to view oneself and others as objects. These abstractions are clearly "hybrids," consisting of both human and natural elements (Latour 1993), but their operation does not reveal these foundations, which are analyzed based on universal axioms grounded in economic theory. The economics vocabulary consists of inputs, production functions, productivity, technology, prices, quantities, incomes, and GDP, without reference to human or ecological particulars.

7 Varieties within Economics Discipline

Historians of economic thought have identified changing relation of economics to nature, from once unified to now divided (Schabas 2005; Merchant 2020; Worster 1977). Economics as a consistent discipline is usually described as beginning in ancient Greece, with Xenophon and Aristotle, and the study of the *oikos* (Schabas and Marchi 2003, 4). In this case, there is a direct relation of humans to the land, and notions of effective household management and stewardship. Carl Linnaeus built on this foundation to develop a taxonomy of species and to analyze their interrelationships to maintain ecological balance (Schabas 2005, 29–32). Linnaeus saw the relation of humans as "seamlessly joined to the economy of nature, an exchange system among animals, plants, minerals, and the atmosphere" (Schabas 2005, 40). The physiocrats, particularly Francois Quesnay, saw agriculture as the source of wealth (Schabas 2005, 45–50). The three key sectors, landowners, artisans, and farmers, each followed natural laws which could be managed to encourage the production of surplus. Malthus, Ricardo, and Smith all analyzed natural features for use in the creation of economic wealth, at a time when economics was still considered part of natural philosophy. Malthus and Ricardo were particularly concerned with the limits to land and the possibility of declining fertility. Hume and Ricardo both believed in natural balance of trade based on laws of reason (Schabas 2005, 105–120; Schabas and Wennerlind 2011).

Smith, Turgot, and Ferguson developed a method of analyzing economics, making use of distinctive relations of humans to the means of subsistence as a way to understand historical change, called "stages." There was an implicit view of progress, from primitive forms of property to more advanced ones, as society evolved from hunter-gatherers and shepherds to settled agriculture and commerce (Schabas 2005, 53, 152). It is possible to find in these ideas a form of a "materialist conception of history," where the search for subsistence leads to development of technology and society, which may have been a precursor to Marx (Meek 1971). Like these classical economists, Marx also had a view of stages of development, ultimately resulting in Communism (Worster 1985, 24–27).

Neoclassical economics diverged from the classical school in important ways. Their analysis was conducted in terms of individuals, subject to universal laws of utility maximization, instead of classes with specific relation to the land (Schabas 2005, 125–141). The material limits of nature were dissolved in the possibility of continuous innovation in technology and in the infinite substitution possibilities in both production and consumption. Both production and consumption functions have the same general form, with abstract inputs and commodities, subject to diminishing returns. Neoclassical economics was also ahistorical and apolitical (Schabas 2005, 150–151), building on objective empirical data, and eschewing normative dimensions. In this discipline, the economy is a distinct entity with no necessary connection to any other discipline. The possible exception is psychology, which has provided a foundation for innovations in behavioral economics, building on an earlier affinity (Schabas 2005, 139).

Recent moves to behavioral economics have incorporated imperfectly rational economic behavior and costs of information and greater use of probabilistic models like game theory vs. irrationality of capitalism.

Innovations in complexity economics have incorporated a different view of the system, from stable and separable to unstable, nonlinear and interdependent (Kruger 1987; Arthur 2015).

The idea of the unity of living things on earth was developed in the science of ecology, named first by Ernst Haeckel in 1866, drawing on Humboldt and Darwin as well as Lyell (Worster 1977, 191–204). Rather than individualism, there was a view of symbiosis as prominent in nature.

Unlike neoclassical economics, Marxist economists have retained the notion of the ecology as integrally related to the economy (Moore 2015; Malm 2018; Foster, Clark, and York 2010; Foster and Clark 2020) and use this connection to provide a critique of capitalism. For Marxist analysis, "property" is not an indicator of the progress of civilization, but rather one basis for the separation of workers from the means of production. Property is a general term, which can refer to any means of production from which workers can be excluded. Marx also stresses the role of science and technology in the development of capitalism, in the competitive drive for accumulation of profits. Marx makes note in his writings of the tendency for capitalism to deplete the soil and to exhaust the workers, unless prevented by reformers and workers' organizations. Science is primarily an aid to capital, to break the resistance of workers, and to increase automation and unemployment at will. Property enforced by the military power of the state enabled the domination of colonies and production of cash crops and commodities regardless of the environmental or social implications. Marxist economists are also more likely to include history and politics in their analysis.

There is a debate among some Marxists regarding whether there is a split between humans and nature. Malm (2018) argues that both humans and nature are composed of the same substance, such as minerals, water, and living cells. He maintains nonetheless that the social should remain differentiated from the natural, in order to identify the impact of certain social organizations, like capitalism, on the environment. In my view, identifying the role of language would be helpful. That is, humans can only refer to nature in a human language, communicated with other humans. Nature exists outside this communicative framework among humans. It is still possible to identify historically a distinction between various "modes of production," and their impacts on environmental degradation, even while understanding that these are all human institutions. It is also true that a term like "property" refers to both nature, such as a parcel of land, and human institutions, like law, with the same term. Such a usage makes the distinction between nature and social impossible to untangle, because it is both. The term "property" is a referent to a parcel of land which is used in a certain way depending on the history, culture, and laws of a certain period. In this sense, the term "property" is reified, a capacity of language (Davis 2015, 2017). Capitalism is a world system which has varied historically, with extensive "commodity frontiers" for producing cash crops (Moore 2015, 182–189). It is important nonetheless to identify the distinctive institutions by which it operates, their historical variation, along with the human and ecological impacts.

8 Re-envisioning the Human Relation to Nature

A critical theory of society would need to account for itself (Habermas 1985, 401–403) and its own context (Habermas 1987, 300–301). An ongoing study of historical institutionalism would improve understanding of social institutions and their long-term evolution. A careful study of language and institutions would elucidate the integral relation between knowledge and action, statements and behavior, and the ways in which "individual choices" are constrained by social meanings and expectations. A new awareness of the relationship of humans to the earth and a critique of existing institutions would allow for the development of new concepts and institutions. New academic disciplines can help recover a deeper understanding of the integral human relation to nature, such as environmental history as exemplified by Donald Worster and William Cronon, and new sciences such as ecology.

New ways of understanding human relation to nature could be disseminated to the public and would constitute a new environmental literacy (Orr 1992). This new framework would be as basic as human health and collaboration in environmental stewardship. New ways of sustaining ecology would provide new forms of political institutions, rather than protection of independent private property and the owner's expected returns. There would be new forms of solidarity based on common residence in a given ecosystem and then generalized to the interconnections among other parts of the earth. Citizens would become more knowledgeable and active in protecting their means of life, water, air, and climate, which they share with all other living species.

Rather than assuming ecology as an unchanging context for human actions, new awareness regarding the human relation to nature would be reflected in new institutions and ways of organizing human societies, such as regional ecological communities, discussed more in Chapter 8 below.

Bibliography

Abbate, Janet. *Inventing the Internet*. Cambridge, MA: MIT Press, 1999.

Abdelal, Rawi. *Capital Rules: The Construction of Global Finance*. Cambridge, MA: Harvard University Press, 2007.

Abu-Lughod, Janet. *Before European Hegemony*. New York: Oxford University Press, 1989.

Arrighi, Giovanni. *The Long Twentieth Century: Money, Power, and the Origins of Our Times*. London: Verso, 1994.

Atack, Jeremy and Larry Neal. *The Origins and Development of Financial Markets and Institutions from the Seventeenth Century to the Present*. New York: Cambridge University Press, 2009.

Arthur, W. Brian. *Complexity and the Economy*. New York: Oxford University Press, 2015.

Banner, Stuart. *American Property: A History of How, Why and What We Own*. Cambridge, MA: Harvard University Press, 2011.

Baucom, Ian. *History 4^0 Celsius: Search for a Method in the Age of the Anthropocene*. Durham: Duke University Press, 2020.

Bernstein, Peter L. *Capital Ideas: The Improbable Origins of Modern Wall Street*. New York: Free Press, 1992.

Bernstein, Peter L. *Against the Gods: The Remarkable Story of Risk*. New York: John Wiley & Sons. 1996.

Bhaskar, Roy. *A Realist Theory of Science*. Sussex: Harvester Press, 1978.

Bittman, Mark. *Animal, Vegetable, Junk: A History of Food, from Sustainable to Suicidal*. New York: Houghton Mifflin Harcourt, 2021.

Brown, Wendy. *In the Ruins of Neoliberalism: The Rise of Antidemocratic Politics in the West*. New York: Columbia University Press, 2019.

Chakrabarty, Depesh. *Provincializing Europe: Postcolonial Thought and Historical Difference*. Princeton, NJ: Princeton University Press, 2000.

Chakrabarty, Depesh. "The Climate of History: Four Theses" in *The Crises of Civilization: Exploring Global and Planetary Histories*. New York: Oxford University Press, 2018, 161-190.

Clark, Christopher. *Time and Power: Visions of History in German Politics, From the Thirty Years' War to the Third Reich*. Princeton, NJ: Princeton University Press, 2019.

Connolly, William E. *Facing the Planetary: Entangled Humanism and the Politics of Swarming*. Durham: Duke University Press, 2017.

Connolly, William E. *Climate Machines Fascist Drives and Truth*. Durham: Duke University Press, 2019.
Daston, Lorraine. *Against Nature*. Cambridge, MA: MIT Press, 2019.
Davis, Ann E. *The Evolution of the Property Relation: Understanding Paradigms, Debates, Prospects*. Palgrave MacMillan, 2015.
Davis, Ann E. *Money as a Social Institution: The Institutional Development of Capitalism*. New York: Routledge, 2017.
Davis, Ann E. *The End of Individualism and the Economy: Emerging Paradigms of Connection and Community*. New York: Routledge, 2020.
Davis, Ann E. "Postone's Legacy: Capitalism and Time." *Critical Historical Studies*, Spring, 2022, Vol. 9, No. 1, 1-34.
Devigne, Robert. *Recasting Conservatism: Oakeshott, Strauss, and the Response to Postmodernism*. New Haven: Yale University Press, 1994.
Dourish, Paul. *The Stuff of Bits: An Essay on the Materialities of Information*. Cambridge, MA: MIT Press, 2017.
Falkowski, Paul G. *Life's Engines: How Microbes Made Earth Habitable*. Princeton, NJ: Princeton University Press, 2015.
Foucault, Michel. *Archaeology of Knowledge*. London: Tavistock. 1972.
Foster, John Bellamy, Brett Clark, and Richard York. *The Ecological Rift: Capitalism's War on the Earth*. New York: Monthly Review Press, 2010.
Foster, John Bellamy and Brett Clark. *The Robbery of Nature: Capitalism and the Ecological Rift*. New York: Monthly Review Press, 2020.
Gamble, Clive, John Gowlett, and Robin Dunbar. *Thinking Big: How the Evolution of Social Life Shaped the Human Mind*. New York: Thames and Hudson, 2014.
Garland, David. *The Welfare State: A Very Short Introduction*. New York: Oxford University Press, 2016.
Giedion, Sigfried. *Mechanization Takes Command: A Contribution to Anonymous History*. New York: Oxford, 1948.
Gleick, James. *The Information: A History, A Theory, A Flood*. New York: Pantheon, 2011.
Gordon, Peter E. *Continental Divide: Heidegger, Cassirer, Davos*. Cambridge, MA: Harvard University Press, 2010.
Graeber, David and David Wengrow. *The Dawn of Everything: A New History of Humanity*. New York: Farrar, Straus, and Giroux, 2021.
Habermas, Jurgen. *Theory of Communicative Action: Volume One*. Reason and the Rationalization of Society. Boston: Beacon Press, 1984.
Habermas, Jurgen. *Theory of Communicative Action: Volume Two*. Lifeworld and System: A Critique of Functionalist Reason. Boston: Beacon Press, 1985.
Habermas, Jurgen. *The Philosophical Discourse of Modernity: Twelve Lectures*. Cambridge MA: MIT Press, 1987.
Hacking, Ian. "Was There a Probabilistic Revolution 1800-1930?" in Kruger, Lorenz, Lorraine J. Daston, and Michael Heidelberger (eds.). *The Probabilistic Revolution: Volume I: Ideas in History*, 1987, 45-55.
Hacking, Ian. *The Social Construction of What?* Cambridge: Harvard University Press, 1999.
Harris, Ron. *Going the Distance: Eurasian Trade and the Rise of the Business Corporation, 1400-1700*. Princeton, NJ: Princeton University Press, 2020.
Hayek, Friedrich A. Von. *The Road to Serfdom*. Chicago: University of Chicago Press,1945.
Hartog, Francois. *Regimes of Historicity: Presentism and Experiences of Time*. New York: Columbia University Press, 2015.
Hopkin, Jonathan. *Anti-System Politics: The Crisis of Market Liberalism in Rich Democracies*. New York: Oxford University Press, 2020.
Horkheimer, Max and Theodor W. Adorno. *Dialectic of Enlightenment*. New York: Seabury Press, 1944.
Hunt, Lynn. *Writing History in the Global Era*. New York: W. W. Norton, 2014.

Huth, Lindsay and Taylor Umlauf. "Severe Drought Could Threaten Power Supply in West for Years to Come." *Wall Street Journal*, August 14, 2021.
Katz, Richard S. and Peter Mair. *Democracy and the Cartelization of Political Parties*. New York: Oxford University Press, 2018.
Kloppenberg, James T. *Toward Democracy: The Struggle for Self-Rule in European and American Thought*. New York: Oxford University Press, 2016.
Koselleck, Reinhart. *Sediments of Time: On Possible Histories*. Stanford: Stanford University Press, 2018.
Kruger, Lorenz. "The Slow Rise of Probabilism: Philosophical Arguments in the Nineteenth Century," in Kruger, Lorenz, Lorraine J. Daston, and Michael Heidelberger (eds.). *The Probabilistic Revolution: Volume I: Ideas in History,* 1987, 59-89.
Kuhn, Thomas S. *The Copernican Revolution*. Cambridge, MA: Harvard University Press, 1957.
Kuhn, Thomas S. *The Structure of Scientific Revolutions*. 2nd ed. Chicago: University of Chicago Press, 1970.
Latour, Bruno. *We Have Never Been Modern*. Cambridge, MA: Harvard University Press, 1993.
Latour, Bruno. *Down to Earth: Politics in the New Climatic Regime*. Cambridge, UK: Polity, 2019.
Lewis, Simon L. and Mark A. Maslin. "Defining the Anthropocene" *Nature*, Vol. 519, March 12, 2015, 171-180.
Malm, Andreas. *Fossil Capital: The Rise of Steam Power and the Roots of Global Warming*. London: Verso, 2016.
Malm, Andreas. *The Progress of this Storm: Nature and Society in a Warming World*. London: Verso, 2018.
Mann, Thomas E. and Norman J. Ornstein. *It's Even Worse than it Looks: How the American Constitutional System Collided with the New Politics of Extremism*. New York: Basic Books, 2012.
Marx, Karl. *Capital*. New York: International Publishers, 1967.
Medema, Stephen G. "The Coase Theorem at Sixty." *Journal of Economic Literature*. December 2020, Volume 58, No. 4, 1045-1128.
Meek, Ronald L. "Smith, Turgot, and the 'Four Stages' Theory." *History of Political Economy*. 1971. Vol. 3, No. 1, 9 – 27.
Merchant, Carolyn. *The Anthropocene and the Humanities; From Climate Change to a New Age of Sustainability*. New Haven: Yale University Press, 2020.
Moore, Jason W. *Capitalism in the Web of Life: Ecology and the Accumulation of Capital*. London: Verso, 2015.
Muller, Jan-Werner. *Contesting Democracy: Political Ideas in Twentieth-Century Europe*. New Haven: Yale University Press, 2011.
Murphy, Anne L. "Performing Public Credit at the Eighteenth-Century Bank of England." *Journal of British Studies*, January, 2019, Vol. 58 58-78.
Nagel, Thomas. *The View from Nowhere*.New York: Oxford University Press, 1986.
Neal, Larry. *The Rise of Financial Capitalism: International Capital Markets in the Age of Reason*. New York: Cambridge University Press, 1990.
Neal, Larry and Jeffrey G. Williamson (eds.).*The Cambridge History of Capitalism*. Volume I. The Rise of Capitalism: From Ancient Origins to 1848. Cambridge, UK: Cambridge University Press, 2015.
North, Douglass, Wallis, Weingast
North, Douglass C., John Joseph Wallis, and Barry R. Weingast. *Violence and Social Orders: A Conceptual Framework for Interpreting Recorded Human History*. Cambridge, UK; Cambridge University Press, 2009.
Orr, David W. "Environmental Literacy: Education as if the Earth Mattered." Stockbridge MA: Schumacher Center Lecture, 1992.
Ostrom, Elinor. *Governing the Commons: The Evolution of Institutions of Collective Action*. Cambridge, UK: Cambridge University Press, 1990.

Piketty, Thomas. *Capital in the Twenty-First Century*. Cambridge, MA: Harvard University Press, 2014.

Piketty, Thomas. *Capital and Ideology*. Cambridge, MA: Harvard University Press, 2020.

Pistor, Katharina. *The Code of Capital: How the Law Creates Wealth and Inequality*. Princeton, NJ: Princeton University Press, 2019.

Pocock, J.G.A. *The Machiavellian Moment: Florentine Political Thought and the Atlantic Republican Tradition*. Princeton, NJ: Princeton University Press, 1975.

Polanyi, Karl. *The Great Transformation*. Boston: Beacon Press, 1944.

Poovey, Mary. *A History of the Modern Fact: Problems of Knowledge in the Sciences of Wealth and Society*. Chicago: University of Chicago Press, 1998.

Poovey, Mary. "The Liberal Civil Subject and the Social in Eighteenth-Century British Moral Philosophy," *Public Culture*, Vol. 14, No. 1, 2002, 125-145.

Poovey, Mary. *Genres of the Credit Economy: Mediating Value in Eighteenth- and Nineteenth-Century Britain*. Chicago: University of Chicago Press, 2008.

Postone, Moishe. *Time, Labor, and Social Domination: A Reinterpretation of Marx's Critical Theory*. Cambridge, UK: Cambridge University Press, 1993.

Reinert, Erik S. *How Rich Countries Got Rich and Why Poor Countries Stay Poor*. New York: Public Affairs, 2007.

Samman, Amin. *History in Financial Times*. Stanford: Stanford University Press, 2019

Sampson, Anthony: *The Seven Sisters: The Great Oil companies and the World they Shaped*. New York: Penguin, 1975.

Schabas, Margaret and Neil De Marchi. "Introduction to Oeconomics in the Age of Newton." History of Political Economy. Vol. 35 Annual Supplement 2003, 1-13.

Schabas, Margaret. *The Natural Origin of Economics*. Chicago: University of Chicago Press, 2005.

Schabas, Margaret and Carl Wennerlind. "Hume on Money, Commerce, and the Science of Economics," *Journal of Economic Perspectives*, Vol. 25, No. 3, Summer 2011, 217-230.

Searle, John R. *Making the Social World: The Structure of Human Civilization*. New York: Oxford University Press, 2010

Shapiro, Carl and Hal R. Varian. *Information Rules: A Strategic Guide to the Network Economy*. Boston: Harvard Business School Press, 1999.

Shiller, Robert. *Narrative Economics: How Stories Go Viral and Drive Major Economic Events*. Princeton, NJ: Princeton University Press, 2019.

Shryock, Andrew and Daniel Lord Smail. *Deep History: The Architecture of Past and Present*, Berkeley, CA: University of California, 2011.

Smail, Daniel Lord and Andrew Shryock. AHR Forum: "History and the 'Pre'". *American Historical Review*, June, 2013, 709-737.

Smail, Daniel Lord, Mary C. Stiner, and Timothy Earle. "Goods" In Shryock, Andrew and Daniel Lord Smail. *Deep History: The Architecture of Past and Present*. Berkeley, CA: University of California, 2011, 219-241.

Spiegel, Gabrielle M. "The Task of the Historian," *American Historical Review*, Vol. 114, No. 1, February, 2009, 1 – 15.

Staheli, Urs. *Spectacular Speculation: Thrills, The Economy, and Popular Discourse*. Stanford: Stanford University Press, 2013.

Surkis, Judith. AHR Forum: "When Was the Linguistic Turn? A Genealogy." *American Historical Review*, June, 2012, 700-722.

Taylor, Charles. *The Language Animal: The Full Shape of Human Linguistic Capacity*. Cambridge, MA: Harvard University Press, 2016.

Tomasello, Michael. *Origins of Human Communication*. Cambridge, MA: MIT Press, 2008.

Toulmin, Stephen. *Cosmopolis: The Hidden Agenda of Modernity*. Chicago: University of Chicago Press, 1990.

Turner, David P. *The Green Marble: Earth System Science and Global Sustainability*. New York: Columbia University Press, 2018.

Wennerlind, Carl. Casualties of Credit. 2011.

Wessler, Hartmut. *Habermas and the Media*. Cambridge, UK: Polity, 2018.
Whalen, Brett Edward. "Political Theology and the Metamorphoses of *The King's Two Bodies*," *American Historical Review*, Vol. 125, No. 1, 2/2020, 132-145.
Williams, Raymond. *Marxism and Literature*. New York: Oxford University Press, 1977.
Williamson, Oliver E. *The Economic Institutions of Capitalism*. New York: Free Press, 1985.
Wolff, Robert Paul. *Money Bags Must Be So Lucky*. Amherst, MA: University of Massachusetts, 1988.
Worster, Donald. *Nature's Economy: A History of Ecological Ideas*. New York: Cambridge University Press, 1977.
Worster, David. *Rivers of Empire: Water, Aridity, and the Growth of the American West*. New York: Pantheon Books, 1985.
Worster, David. "Transformations of the Earth: Toward an Agroecological Perspective in History." *Journal of American History*, Vol. 76, No. 4, 1990, 1087-1106.
Worster, Donald. *Shrinking the Earth: The Rise and Decline of American Abundance*. New York: Oxford University Press, 2016.
Wright, Robert. *NonZero: The Logic of Human Destiny*. New York: Pantheon, 2000.
Yergin, Daniel. *The Prize: The Epic Quest for Oil, Money, and Power*. New York: Simon & Schuster, 1991.
Yergin, Daniel. *The Quest: Energy, Security, and the Remaking of the Modern World*. New York: Penguin, 2011.

Part II
Conceptual Development and Critique of Capitalism

Chapter 4
"Fictitious Capital": Money, the Symbol, and the State

1 Modernity and Reifying Abstractions

In this chapter, we will review Marx's concept of money and capital, as an illustration of the ways in which the meaning of a term includes the appropriate roles, norms, and actions. Actors can use money as a way to generate more money, following specific rules according to the logic of "capital." The meaning of these terms "money" and "capital" only exists by the regularity of these specific actions, which then are represented in the symbol of money. When money itself is reified, it stands for the actions of those participating in the capitalist system, with implications we will explore in a case study.

The definition of reification is when a word is understood as the thing itself or the elision of the word and the thing (Davis 2020, 30–36). According to Bass, there is a psychological dimension to reification (Bass 2018). There is a large literature on reification and the relation to capitalism (O'Kane 2021), but the usage in this context focuses on the linguistic dimension (Searle 2010).

When the word, such as property, stands for the object, such as land, there is an elision of the set of social relationships, such as legal and economic, that secure the object for the owner (Davis 2015, 2017a, 2020). In such a case, it is easier to naturalize these relationships, which then are represented and rendered invisible by the object itself. The term then refers to this institution and becomes a key category for social analysis and for social processing.

Drawing upon Peirce, in addition to the person and the object, there is a representation in language, a third term (Davis 2022). This third term is a symbol or term that relates the specific relationship to the larger set of norms and procedures for the particular society and economy (see Fig. 1.1 in Chap. 1). This third term relates the individual to the social. This use of language helps establish the meaning of the term and to enforce a consistent usage. It also assures the connection and the coordination of the individual with the social, even though meanings and enforcement mechanisms change historically.

A. E. Davis, *Whole Earth*, https://doi.org/10.1007/978-3-031-01934-0_4

As Graeber points out, Marx's analysis of fetishism is a type of social power in which the cumulative effects of the actions of the participants are attributed to an object, such as money (Graeber 2001, 60–69). It is the role of critical theory to explain these effects to participants and to provide space for alternative visions (Graeber 2001, 240–261).

2 Review Literature Defining "Money" and "Capital"

Capital is a term for the complex set of relationships, reified as a thing or object.

In spite of the large literature which addresses the definition of "capital," including Marx's magnum opus and the associated voluminous commentary, there remains considerable discussion and debate. This chapter will briefly sample this literature, explore the nature of the quandaries which make the definition of "capital" so difficult (Pistor 2019, 9–13; Karak 2021), and suggest an alternative approach. In Marx's own writings, even chapter titles from Vol. I suggest that this topic is "contradictory." Drawing from *Capital*, a proposed definition of capital includes the related terms of commodity, money, and value and their apparent capacity to expand value. The definition of "capital" and these related terms is illustrated in the long-term history of financial institutions, as well as the recent examples of financial market volatility and actions of the Federal Reserve Bank of the United States. Ultimately, the capacity of money as a symbol which can represent the whole system, yet appears to be a simple object of individual private property, is one important source of the contradictions of the capitalist system. We will show that the apparent capacity of money itself to expand automatically can lead to an intensification of the contradictions of capitalism.

This chapter will proceed first with a discussion of the multiple usages and meanings of "capital," followed by a synthesis of the term in Marx's most mature work, *Capital*. Using this term as the name of a complex evolving social system, whose workings were analyzed by Marx, we will apply this understanding to the evolution and operation of modern financial markets. A short case study of the "repo" market illustrates the dynamics and fragility of this system. Trust in the resilience of financial markets, and the treatment of private financial assets like "repos" as "safe," has increased the vulnerability of the system to bubbles and crises.

3 Multiple Usages of "Capital"

As is consistent with Marx's discussion in the *German Ideology* (Marx 1947, 39), the term "capital" refers to the dominant idea in the modern era (Moseley 2017). Max Weber refers to the "spirit of capitalism" (Weber 1958), and Moishe Postone sees the category of capital as similar to Hegel's Geist (Postone 1996, 76–83; Bellofiore 2018, 358, 364–365). The term "capital" is widely used in contemporary discourse, including "social capital," "human capital" (Adkins et al. 2020, 45, 57), and "natural capital" (Hawken and Lovins 1999; https://naturalcapitalproject.stanford.edu/), in metaphorical terms. It has been the subject of other disciplines, including anthropology (Graeber 2011, 345–346), history of economic thought (Cannan 1921), and history (Levy 2017). There is a large literature which addresses the definition of "capital" in economics as well. Among Austrian economists, the importance of time has been considered central, as well as risk and entrepreneurship. For leading institutionalists and Marxists, there are a variety of emphases as well. For Hodgson (2014), capital is a physical asset or a sum of money. The Cambridge controversy considered capital as a factor of production (Garegnani 2012; Hodgson 2015, 183, 202–203). For Piketty, capital includes "nonhuman assets which can be owned and exchanged on some market" (Piketty 2014, 46); further, capital is a store of value or a factor of production, excluding human capital (Piketty 2014, 47–48). For Kotz, the defining features of capitalism are "the ownership/control of enterprises by …the capitalists, who employ wage earners to produce products for sale in the market," for profit (Kotz 2015, 3). For Shaikh, "capital is a thing used in the process of making profit," part of the financial circuits M-C-M' (Shaikh 2016, 206). But it is not just the qualities of the thing, but "rather the process within which it operates that turns it into capital" (Shaikh 2016, 207).

> Capitalist relations add another dimension because within the grip of capital both the labor process and the commodity's price become means of realizing a profit. In the labor process, this gives rise to the drive to extend the length and intensity of the working day…This compulsion is the source of capitalism's historically revolutionary role in raising the productivity of labor to great heights…Whereas the tool is an instrument of labor in earlier modes of production, it is the laborer who becomes an instrument of the machine in capitalist production…. (Shaikh 2016, 207)

That is, for Piketty, capital is a nonhuman factor of production which generates income. For Shaikh, capital is an aid to producing profit within capitalist relations. The quote above from Shaikh emphasizes the "drive" and "compulsion" to increase the productivity of labor, like Postone's "treadmill" (Postone 1996).

Hodgson (2015) notes that for Marx, capital is a historically specific system, with the goal of expanding value, M-M'. Quoting Marx, he notes that "capital is not a thing, but a social relation between persons….the means of production monopolized by a particular section of society…" (Hodgson 2015, 177–178). In his definition of capitalism as a system later in the book (Hodgson 2015, 251–261), Hodgson places less emphasis on the goal of accumulation, but includes the wage labor market as a central feature. Neal and Williamson mention property rights and markets, but do not emphasize money and finance (Neal and Williamson 2015, 2–3). For Postone, "capital" is "the central, totalizing category of modern life" (Postone 1996, 352).

4 "Capital" Is the Name of a Complex Evolving Social System

The approach here is to recognize that "capital" is a term, the name of a complex evolving social system, with multiple interrelated characteristics. There is a typical reluctance among commentators to discuss the linguistic dimension, for fear of missing the "material" element. There is a hint of a linguistic dimension, nonetheless, in the multiple references to "fictitious commodities" (Polanyi 1944), "fetishism" of commodities and money in capitalism (Marx 1967), and "fictitious capital" (Smith 1994, 339–340; Marx 1967, Vol. III, Chap. 25, 401; Chap. 29, 465, 466, 469; Chap. 34, 541) and "fictional expectations" (Beckert 2016). As a social institution, capital operates as a set of rules, terms, meanings, and behavior encoded in language (Searle 2010). For example, Marx makes the analogy between "value" and language and emphasizes the symbolic dimensions of money (Marx 1967, Vol. I, Chap. 3, Sect. 2.c, 126–129; Poovey 2008, 25).

> Value, therefore, does not stalk about with a label describing what it is. It is value, rather, that converts every product into a social hieroglyphic....for to stamp an object of utility as a value, is just as much a social product as language. (Marx 1967, Vol. I, Chap. 1, Sect. 4, 74)

4.1 *Definition of Capital*

In Vol. III of *Capital*, Marx offers a definition of "capital" in Chapter 21, in the process of drawing together the implications of the treatment in the preceding two volumes.

> Capital exists as capital in actual movement, not in the process of circulation, but only in the process of production, in the process by which labour-power is exploited.... This relation to itself, in which capital presents itself when the capitalist production process is viewed as a whole and as a single unity...[is one] in which capital appears as money that begets money.... (Marx 1967, Vol. III, Chap. 21, 343, 345)

And later in the same chapter,

> Capital manifests itself as capital through self-expansion...The product of capital is profit.... (Marx 1967, Vol. III, Chap. 21, 354–355)

The implication of these quotes is that "capital" relies on the entire financial circuit and the capacity for exploitation of labor as described in Vol. I. The term "capital" refers to the system as a whole, and its capacity to extract surplus and produce profit, which "appears as money that begets money." This is similar to phrasing in Vol. I (Marx 1967, Vol. I, Chap. 4, 154–155), focusing on the mystery of money's apparent reproduction.

> Capital thus becomes a very mystic being since all of labour's social productive forces appear to be due to capital, rather than labour as such, and seem to issue from the womb of capital itself. (Marx 1967, Vol. III, Chap. 48, 827)

In these passages, Marx is using the metaphor of human reproduction to fathom the mystery of capital, and the associated capacity of money to "beget" more money, based on the Greek term for usury (Marx 1967, Vol. I, Chap. 5, pp. 164–165; Daston 2019, 12). An important implication is that money can be functionally separated from the production and expansion of value by the employment of labor power, but, without the whole system of social relations, money would lose its meaning and power to expand "automatically." To extend Marx's metaphor, money appears "pregnant" (Marx, Vol. III, Chap. 24, 393), but is actually barren without the specific social relations of capitalism. That is, "capital" is not just a unique social relationship, but a special capacity of money which appears to expand automatically.

4.2 Logical Development

There is a well-organized progression in the treatment of the mystery of "capital" in the three volumes by that title. The first definition of capital is the financial circuits, in Vol. I, Chapter 4, "the general formula for capital." In the financial circuits, money is the means by which the owner can purchase commodities, produce commodities for greater value, and expand value by M-C-M'. The financial circuit itself includes both abstract (money) and concrete (labor and commodities) elements in a process of transformation over time. Facilitated by the appearance of money as an independent form of value, the functional separation of industrial and finance capital became possible, as discussed in Vol. III, Chapter 23, and the foreshortened circuit, M-M', which becomes the focus of finance, in Chapter 24. This prepares the groundwork for "fictitious capital" in Chapter 25, where money may not actually be used in the production of commodities, but exist as claims to surplus and objects of speculation. The critique of credit culminates in Chapter 27, with "other people's money" and the appearance of the corporation, the "social means of production as private property" (Vol. III, Chapter 27, 440). The discussion of "fictitious capital" continues in Chapter 29, where the process of "capitalization" can reinforce the notion that money naturally grows on its own (Vol. III, Chap. 29, 466–472), applied to expectations of the future value of securities like corporate stock and public debt.

The specialization of finance capital as distinct from industrial capital can lead to economies of scale and the reduction of turnover time. As soon as the value of labor power is represented by money in an external form, nonetheless, there is the potential for crisis. In the capitalist system, money can be considered valuable in itself, outside these specific financial circuits, as an object of independent private property (Marx 1967, Vol. I, Chap. 3, Sect. 3.a, 132). This externalization and division of the value of the commodity into exchange value, represented by money, and use value can be a cause for crises (Marx 1967, Vol. I, Chap. 1, Sect. 2.a, 113–114; Vol. III, Chap. 32, 516–517).

To define "capital," it is important to trace the entire set of social relationships. Financial circuits represent the roles and relationships of the entire capitalist system, as performed in time. Money represents the exchange value of the commodity produced, but money also effectuates the extraction of surplus value. That is, the worker sells the use value of his commodity labor power in exchange for a wage, which represents the exchange value of necessities, C-M-C. The sale of the commodity for money then realizes that use value of the commodity labor power by representing the exchange value of the commodity. Money is able to expand, M-C-M', by the difference between the use value and the exchange value of the commodity labor power (Marx 1967, Vol. I, Chap. 1, Sect. 4, 80–81). The motive energy behind the interlocking financial circuits is the desire for the human person to acquire necessities, but it appears merely as the function of money as a means of circulation and a means of payment. These functions of money are reified, not revealing the human actions and relationships which accomplish the financial circuits.

5 Institutional Definition of Capital

This section further develops the definition of "capital," while also analyzing why the operation of the system is not transparent to its participants. Marx offers concepts such as "fetishism" to help explain why appearances can be misleading. It is possible to make use of these mystical appearances, nonetheless, to better understand the operation of the system. Ultimately, a system which seeks only to expand money is irrational (Harvey 2014), in spite of its ubiquitous, apparently rational, methods of calculation (Cook 2017).

The more complete definition offered here is that "capital" is a historically specific social system, consisting of key terms, institutions, and knowledge of its workings. An important aspect of Marx's contribution is the critique of the mainstream political economy of his time. This understanding of "capital" includes a set of market and state institutions, based on laws of individual private property, the goal of which is the expansion of value, M-M'. "Capital" refers to the right to purchase the commodity labor power on the market (Marx 1967, Vol. I, Chap. 6), a wage labor force without access to the means of production. The capitalist can then monetize human needs for profit, in a value system which promotes that arrangement. For example, "negative" rights of property protection are promoted over "positive" rights to meet human minimal necessities, a value system which serves to strengthen market discipline (Berlin 1969; Searle 2010, 184–187, 193–194). That is, there is an inextricable link between money as a store of value and the institutions of wage labor, where workers are employed in, but not in control of, the process of commodity production for profit. The centrality of wage labor makes possible and also requires the externalization of "value" in money (Marx 1967, Vol. I, Chap. 3, Sect. 3.b, 138) and enables the reification of the system of "capital."

There is a tendency for reification in the capitalist system, where an object stands for a relationship (Davis 2017b, 2020). For example, the "value" of commodities and capital appears to be a characteristic of the thing itself, whether money or factor of production. Yet the object or thing represents the relationships of the system, including a wage labor market constituted by workers, who are "free in a double sense," as well as monopoly over the means of production by firms, and financial markets which provide access to credit for interest (by loaning state money to creditworthy entrepreneurs). Money itself becomes a commodity when it represents the exchange value of the commodity by its market price (Marx 1967, Vol. I, Chap. 3, Sect. 2, p. 108). The exchange of commodities for money, including the worker as the commodity labor power and the purchase of necessities with his wages, "develops a whole network of social relations spontaneous in their growth and entirely beyond the control of the actors" (Marx 1967, Vol. I, Chap. 3, Sect. 2, p. 112).

The objective "thing," whether money, commodity, or factor of production, represents this specific human system of related institutions, what Marx called the "fetishism" of commodities and money (Marx 1967, Vol. I, Chap. 1, Sect. 4, 71–83; Vol. III, Chap. 24, 391–399).

5.1 *Consciousness, Roles, and Relations*

As a "social relation," the system of capital affects one's view of oneself and others. As human agents with discrete roles of "worker" and "capitalist," our actions appear as objective features of an abstract system beyond our individual control, even as we perform these roles ourselves.

According to Marx, the consciousness of the worker is an important part of this system of relations. As the owner of his own labor power as a commodity, the worker confronts the employer as "equal in the eyes of the law." The worker "must constantly look upon his labour-power as his own property, his own commodity, and this he can only do by placing it at the disposal of the buyer temporarily, for a definite period of time…For the conversion of his money into capital, therefore, the owner of money must meet in the market with the free labourer, free in the double sense…as a free man he can dispose of his labour-power as his own commodity, and…he has no other commodity for sale…" (Marx 1967, Vol. I, Chap. 6, 168–169).

> Otherwise with capital…It can spring into life, only when the owner of the means of production and subsistence meets in the market with the free labourer selling his labour-power. And this one historical condition comprises a world's history. Capital, therefore, announces from its first appearance a new epoch in the process of social production. (Marx 1967, Vol. I, Chap. 6, 170)

And Marx continues in a footnote, "The capitalist epoch is therefore characterized by this, that labour power takes in the eyes of the labourer himself the form of a commodity which is his property; his labour consequently becomes wage-labour. On the other hand, it is only from this moment that the produce of labour universally becomes a commodity." In these passages, Marx is emphasizing that the unique social relations of capitalism are both material and social; both capitalist and worker come to a certain realization about their distinctive roles, with a change in consciousness, and encoded in the laws of property.

As Marx explains further at the end of Chapter 6, "The Buying and Selling of Labour Power," the operation of the labor market is a "very Eden of the innate rights of man. There alone rule Freedom, Equality, Property and Bentham…" (Marx 1967, Vol. I, Chap. 6, 176). This equal labor is homogeneous labor in the abstract, measured by hours, a practice which still is found in the ubiquitous metric of labor productivity in macroeconomics (see the US Bureau of Labor Statistics; http://www.bls.gov).

The distinctive social relations affect the theorist as well. Marx notes that Aristotle was not able to analyze the value of commodities, because ancient Greece was a slave society, without the formation of the wage labor force as so-called "equal" commodities (Marx 1967, Vol. I, Chap. 1, Sect. 3 A.3, 59–60).

> The secret of the expression of value, namely, that all kinds of labour are equal and equivalent, because, and so far as they are human labour in general, cannot be deciphered, until the notion of human equality has already acquired the fixity of a popular prejudice. This, however, is possible only in a society in which the great mass of the produce of labour takes the form of commodities, in which, consequently, the dominant relation between man and man, is that of owners of commodities. (Marx 1967, Vol. I, Chap. 1, 60)

The capitalist also assumes a distinct role. Beginning in Vol. I, Marx describes the role of money as an abstract expression of the value of commodities and the self-expanding circuit, M-C-M'. With this self-expansion of value, the holder of money becomes a capitalist.

> As the conscious representative of this movement, the possessor of money becomes a capitalist. His person, or rather his pocket, is the point from which the money starts and to which it returns. (Marx 1967, Vol. I, Chap. 4, 152)

Later in the same chapter, Marx continues

> value therefore now becomes value in process, money in process, and, as such, capital… M – M', money which begets money, such is the description of Capital from the mouths of its first interpreters, the Mercantilists. (Marx 1967, Vol. I, Chap. 4, 154–155; capitalization as in original)

The personification of the capitalist, "our friend, Moneybags," is "only an embryo capitalist" (Vol. I, Chap. 5, 166) until he buys and sells labor power, further described in Chapter 6. It is only then that he "strides in front as a capitalist…with an air of importance, smirking, intent on business…" (Marx 1967, Vol. I, Chap. 6, 176).

On the one hand, capital is a produced means of production, equipment, and machine. On the other hand, the money holder can use money to hire labor power as an object and so become the subject, the agent of production, in the role of "capitalist" (Marx 1967, Vol. III, Chap. 22, 368). This active role as organizer of production, or the delegation of this role to subordinates, then allows the capitalist to claim a share of surplus, as owner. The value of production is objectified in the price of the commodity, and the "return to capital" is drawn from the price/wage differential, often called value-added, no longer considered the product of labor.

The use value of capital becomes its ability to expand in value by employing labor power in the process of production (Marx 1967, Vol. III, Chap. 21, 338–339,

343, 345). The role of industrial capitalist, with a claim to profit, can be differentiated from the role of moneylender, with a claim to interest. These two roles can be like two different personalities in the same person. The individual capitalist can choose between commodity production or moneylending at his discretion, but if the entire capitalist class chose moneylending, there would be a dramatic decline in the rate of profit (Marx 1967, Vol. III, Chap. 23, 375, 377–378). In such a circumstance, the production of value would be insufficient to validate the claims to surplus by the moneylenders.

When money is loaned as a legal claim to a share of future profits, but not used in the process of commodity production, Marx calls this "fictitious capital" (Marx 1967, Vol. III, Chap. 29, 465, 468–470). Marx includes the calculation of present discounted value as "fictitious," because "all connection with the actual expansion process of capital is thus completely lost, and the conception of capital as something with automatic self-expansion properties is thereby strengthened" (Marx 1967, Vol. III, Chap. 29, 466). For Marx, interest-bearing capital exemplifies the fetishism of money, as an "automaton" (Marx 1967, Vol. III, Chap. 24, 391, 395, 399).

> It becomes a property of money to generate value....which is a mystification of capital in its most flagrant form (Marx 1967, Vol. III, Chap. 24, 392).

For both Marx and mainstream economics, money serves as a store of value. Yet this pursuit of preservation of value is always contingent on the operation of the system as a whole (Marx 1967, Vol. III, Chap. 33, 34). Arguably, even Keynes viewed money as an object, with unique circumstances of production, with its "own rate of return," due to liquidity preference. That is, for Keynes, money was an object of value, traded on a market (which meets Piketty's definition of "capital"), the value of which was influenced by psychological tendencies, such as "liquidity preference." Somehow, in Keynes' analysis, such investor sentiment is projected onto the value of the object, the financial asset, possibly with some remote connection to the perceptions of the state of the system as a whole. For these reasons, Keynes was critical of the "liquidity fetish" (Davis 2017b, 128–130) and understood that hoarding of money would not expand value. He viewed the government as a more reliable agent for guiding the investment of the macroeconomy, while *rentiers* may be distracted by the fluctuations of the "casino" (Keynes 1964, 135–146, 222–236, 315–324).

5.2 Reification of Money

While "capital" as a system involves discrete roles and relationships, money represents that set of relations. Money is a representation of the relationship of labor power as a commodity, a central aspect of the institutions of capitalism, by the realization of the exchange value of the commodity when sold. As a representation of a relationship, money can take a symbolic and "imaginative" form (Searle 2010; Ivanova 2020, 139; Marx 1967, Vol. I, Chap. 3, Sects. 1 and 2.c).

> The independent existence of the exchange-value of a commodity is here a transient apparition, by means of which the commodity is immediately replaced by another commodity. Hence, in the process which continually makes money pass from hand to hand, the mere symbolical existence of money suffices.... Being a transient and objective reflex of the prices of commodities, it serves only as a symbol of itself, and is therefore capable of being replaced by a token....this token must have an objective social validity of its own, and this the paper symbol acquires by its forced currency [by] this compulsory action of the State.... (Marx 1967, Vol. I, Chap. 3, Sect. 2.c, 129)

Money is also an instrument, authorized by the state, available as credit for the entrepreneur through the regulated financial system (Marx 1967, Vol. III, Chap. 36, 600). Money can be transformed into "capital" as long as it is used to hire labor power, produce commodities, and realize surplus (Marx 1967, Vol. III, Chap. 21). Because money is loaned but not sold, it is a legal relationship between lender and borrower that does not reveal the actual use to which money is put (Marx 1967, Vol. III, Chap. 21, 347–349), but the lender can claim a pro rata rate of return regardless (Marx 1967, Vol. III, Chap. 21, 338–339). As Schumpeter emphasized, this capacity of credit enables the dynamic nature of the capitalist system, by innovation and development of new products and technologies. This access to credit enables the entrepreneur to hire labor, purchase raw materials, organize the production and sale of commodities, and repay lenders. The entrepreneur can produce surplus value, which is then shared with the lender in the repayment of interest.

Money can also be used to extract and distribute surplus from value already produced. The use value of money includes a legal claim to a share of future surplus (Marx 1967, Vol. III, Chap. 21, 338, 343, 347–348, 351–352, 355; Chap. 29, 468–469), in addition to other functions. What Marx called "fictitious capital" is now the routine calculation of expected returns, which then represents the return on investment (Cook 2017; Beckert 2016). As a legal relation, these returns can be claimed by the lender, even if the borrower did not succeed in the production and realization of surplus value. Bankruptcy provisions are legal means of dividing the remaining assets according to the priority of creditor claims.

As a focus only on M-M', financialization (Krippner 2011; Lapavitsas 2013; Kotz 2015, 32–35) can lead to excess issue of financial assets in the present, without generating the surplus to realize their expected returns in the future. Especially when money is assumed as valuable in itself, presumably generating an "automatic rate of return," the future claims related to this current issue of financial assets may lead to collapse in contemporary market valuations at the date of redemption, if unmet (Haldane et al. 2010).

Marx's theory of fetishism of commodities and money is often overlooked and misunderstood. Because the object represents a specific relationship, all the powers of that relationship are projected onto the object, whether commodity or money. For example, the commodity's price represents the cooperation of labor and the technology of production, for an object which has use value to the consumer. The value of money represents the entire system of production and the ability to aggregate social surplus and decide upon its allocation in terms of investment and distribution in terms of income. In this sense, money has "social" power, but can be owned by a single person, which seems somewhat mystical.

> But money itself is a commodity, an external object, capable of becoming the private property of any individual. Thus social power becomes the private power of private persons. (Marx 1967, Vol. I, Chap. 3, Sect. 3.a, 132)

This contradiction between individual and social is further emphasized in the discussion of credit, which makes use of "other people's money." Marx's critique of the corporate form has this in common with Smith (Smith 1994, Part III, Article 1, 789–818), although Marx also sees the role of credit in centralizing production and providing an incentive for the further development of the means of production (Marx 1967, Vol. III, Chap. 27, 435–441).

In summary, the definition of "capital" is the term which refers to this entire interrelated set of institutions, including ideas, relations, and concrete objects. Specific terms like "commodity," "worker," and "capitalist" refer to roles, with associated norms and rules, encoded in social and legal institutions. These institutions provide a scaffolding for the entire "capitalist" system, in ongoing evolution. Some authors emphasize the factor of production, some the sum of money, some the rate of return, some the time for roundabout methods of production, others the entrepreneurship and risk-taking, and incentives. The definitions are so fluid because some aspects are more visible in certain periods. But no one aspect would have "value" without the operation of this interrelated system of human institutions as a whole.

6 Institutional Shifts in Capital Markets

In *Capital*, Marx reviews the long-term historical institutional development of finance, including "merchant capital" and pre-capitalist relations (Vol. III, Chaps. 20 and 36). In Chapter 48, "The Trinity Formula," Marx reiterates that "capital is not a thing but rather a definite social production relation" (Vol. III, Chap. 48, 814).

As part of a complex evolving social system, capitalist institutions are in the process of constant change. Although not stressed by Marx, there is a connection between the understanding of money by recognized experts and the actual operations of financial institutions. In tracing the historical evolution of capitalist institutions, Marx quoted a variety of political economists, including Smith, Ricardo, Petty, and Locke, whose ideas were important in the operation of the system (Kotz 2015, 81–84).

6.1 Merchant Capital

Marx provides typologies for the early manifestations of capitalist institutions, such as "merchant capital." In reference to "usurers," Marx cites the changing views of the Catholic church, along with the destructive impact of their high interest charges on independent producers (Marx 1967, Vol. III, Chap. 36, 593–599, 610–613). The "credit system developed as a reaction against usury," building on the experience of the maritime republican city-states, and the ideas related to the formation of the Bank of Amsterdam and the Bank of England (Marx 1967, Vol. III, Chap. 36, 600–609). Marx notes the range of ideas regarding the formation of the Bank of England, as well as its transition over time from a private bank to a central bank which was empowered to issue legal tender, based on the gold supply of the nation (Marx 1967, Vol. III, Chap. 33, 541–545; Chap. 34, 546–564).

6.2 Central Banks

As the credit system became specialized, as distinct from industrial production, a new institution emerged to manage finance at the state level. The experience and role of merchants were important in developing bills of exchange, merchant monopoly corporations, and early capital markets in the low countries (Macaulay 2019; Zuijderduijn 2009), which provided lessons for the emergence of state finance in the industrial revolution. The United Kingdom, as the model for the liberal state, internalized taxes and provided funding for the standing military, by means of a central bank which monetized public debt (Davis 2017b).

The basic tenets of the liberal creed included the gold standard and was enforced by the British by means of the actions of central banks or gunboats, when the balance of payments did not adjust automatically (Polanyi 1944; Marx 1967, Vol. III, Chap. 35). The expectation of automatic adjustment of specie flow provided the model, in turn, for the United States as the next hegemonic power, and the post-World War II Bretton Woods agreement on the dollar/gold standard facilitated the role of the dollar as a global key currency.

The establishment of the central bank of the United States had a complex domestic political history, like the Bank of England, due to the mistrust of the corporate form. Only after the Civil War, with a brief experience in national banking, and after the late nineteenth-century economic crises was the Federal Reserve Bank established in 1913 (Eichengreen 2019; Brine and Poovey 2017). While unable to prevent the Great Depression, the Fed supported financing for US engagement in World War II.

6.3 The Extension of Markets

The market system became "naturalized" by the "liberal creed" in the 1820s, based on the gold standard, free trade, and the labor market. This market economy is contrasted with "society," which must then be protected against it. Townsend's writings authorized the focus on the animal nature of humans and the power of the prod of hunger as an incentive for work (Polanyi 1944, 111–116). The entire market system, a set of interlocking institutions, symbols, and meanings, is represented by terms like money and markets, which can then constitute an "automatic steering mechanism" (Polanyi 1944, 137–138). Polanyi too resorts to the language of religion to describe the market system (Polanyi 1944, 139; Block and Somers 2014).

> Economic liberalism was the organizing principle of a society engaged in creating a market system…It evolved into a veritable faith in man's secular salvation through a self-regulating market… The liberal creed assumed its evangelical fervor only in response to the needs of a fully deployed market economy. (Polanyi 1944, 135)

Marx did not expect that a paper currency could operate as universal money (Marx 1967, Vol. I, Chap. 3, Sect. 3.c), rather than a precious metal. Yet his theory of the fetishism of money (Marx 1967, Vol. I, Chap. 1, Sect. 4; Vol. III, Chap. 24) can help explain the role of the US dollar as a hegemonic currency. That is, the legal tender, declared by the state, managed by the central bank, and subject to rules of international trade, can represent the entire system, especially for a hegemonic country like Great Britain and later the United States.

The issue of the hegemonic currency provides the United States with "exorbitant privilege" (Eichengreen 2011), which then facilitates the extraction of value from global money circuits. That is, emerging countries must export commodities to acquire US dollars as international reserves, a form of forced savings which provides low cost credit to the US economy, and may have resulted in the "savings glut" and asset bubbles. Because other countries hold US dollars as reserve assets, the United States can maintain a negative net international investment position and is the world's largest debtor, contrary to the mainstream model prediction of capital flows from wealthy to poor countries.

6.4 Financial Markets

Treating money as a commodity like any other, it can be traded in specialized markets which can have the same characteristics as commodity markets, according to monetary theorists. The increasing differentiation of financial markets was one important component of neoliberalism (Kotz 2015, 41–43). The turn to primary securities dealers to manage the market for Treasury bonds after the Fed/Treasury Accord of 1951 then provided the experience for the increasingly market-based global system after the end of Bretton Woods in the early 1970s (D'Arista 2018; Brine and Poovey 2017, 359–370; Panitch and Gindin 2012). The allowance of floating exchange rates and global capital flows was supported by the new "Washington Consensus." IMF conditionality for indebted countries was intended to mimic the gold standard. Observers have called the emerging system the "Wall Street/Treasury complex" (Bhagwati 2004, 204–207; Harvey 2014, 162–163) or "state-finance nexus" (Harvey 2010, 48–57) or "the nexus of state and finance" (Vogl 2017, 155), to indicate the confluence of government and finance in the post-war era. Deregulation of banking from the 1980s allowed the growth of large complex financial institutions with global reach.

After 1980, with the neoliberal consensus of Thatcher and Reagan, the academic support for "perfect" financial markets was reinforced (Fama 1970). The trust in financial markets justified deregulation and facilitated the changing role of the IMF. The focus of the international financial system shifted towards the trading of "safe assets," resulting in increasing inequality, increasing ratio of financial assets to GDP, lower real interest rates, and lower rates of real investment (Krippner 2011; Mian 2019; Gourinchas et al. 2017; Adkins et al. 2020). The increasing frequency and scope of global financial crises left the financial system more concentrated and more subject to moral hazard with the doctrine of "too big to fail," especially after the Great Financial Crisis of 2008.

Recent research has focused on this long-term history of financial institutions to explain the impact of the changing performance of the financial markets. According to Philippon (2019, 207–222), the declining rate of real investment in the United States is due to financial deregulation and increasing concentration, influenced by lobbying and political power of the financial sector. Because of a belief in the efficacy of market completion and "financial deepening," the financial sector was allowed to expand relative to GDP in both the United States and the United Kingdom, along with leverage ratios and the "mispricing of risk" (Haldane et al. 2010).

In summary, the financial system has evolved continually, based on dominant ideas in each epoch. After the end of the Bretton Woods system, liquidity among an increasingly specialized range of financial assets was a substitute for redemption by, and convertibility to, precious metals, or the expansion of value by real investment.

7 Case: Repo Hiccup of 2019 and 2020

To summarize the analysis above, money can be a reified symbol which refers to the entire capitalist system. Yet money can be the property of an individual owner, who then gains a social power. Money can be used to extract and to transfer value. Money dealers can be distinguished from industrial capitalists, with specialized financial institutions, which focus only on the abbreviated circuit M-M'. The questions addressed in this section are the ways in which financial institutions have evolved further since Marx's analysis. In particular, (1) Can "capital" be created by legal coding (Pistor 2019)? (2) Can "safe" assets be created by the private sector (Gorton and Metrick 2013)? And (3) is the state always already involved as a backstop in financial markets? Drawing on the perspective of David Harvey (2014, 151–163), one could argue that there is no such thing as a "safe asset," only a temporary "fix" in the context of global flows of value and capital. We propose that reification is necessary for money to serve as the foundation of the "shadow banking system" which has emerged in recent years, with implications for stability and risk of crisis.

The definition of "safe assets" by Gorton and Metrick (2013, 45–47) reveals the ambiguities of the valuation of financial assets. At one point, a given asset is judged to be "safe," liquid, but subject to new information and changing sentiments; the value of that same asset can be subject to wild fluctuations. Further, while "safe assets" can be constructed by the private sector, they are never really as safe as public assets, backed by the government with its power to tax and to issue currency. As Pistor points out, the safety of the asset is a function of the transferability, durability, and recourse built into the legal definitions, which can be influenced by the financial sector itself, with its lobbying and political power (Pistor 2019, 77–79; Philippon 2019, 153–203).

7.1 Historical Context

Historically, the core institutions of finance have been created by the state. For example, because money is loaned, not sold, it is the subject of legal contracts, which do not reveal the manner in which value actually expands (Marx 1967, Vol. III, Chap. 21, 347–349). The Bank of England was created by law in 1694 and was allowed to circulate bank notes with the backing of founders' and government gold deposits, as well as its own corporate stock. Its bank notes gradually acquired the status of legal tender (Marx 1967, Vol. III, Chap. 33, 540–545; Poovey 1998, 44–49). The "component parts of bank capital" consist of assets such as cash, gold, or securities. In turn, securities can consist of private commercial paper and public securities, such as public debt. Liabilities consist of deposits which are "loans which the public makes to the bankers," as Adam Smith and Marx agree (Marx, Vol. III, Chap. 29, 472). Because ownership of state debt allows the owner to collect interest payments, these debts "appear to the banker as commodities" (Marx, Vol. III, Chap. 29, 464–465).

The existence of central banks revealed the fallacy of the self-regulating market based on the gold standard (Polanyi 1944, 192–200). The modern money supply is likewise backed by government debt and other key currencies, and central banks issue liabilities regarded as legal tender. The role of government debt as the backing of the currency has replaced the gold standard, which is managed based on the same principles as the gold specie flow mechanism. The role of government debt as the secure asset traded on secondary markets arose in early eighteenth-century England and might have given the impression that sovereignty was like a marketable asset (Poovey 1998, 150–151). In modern financial markets, the role of international investors as a form of discipline for government debt persists and now often managed by the International Monetary Fund.

7.2 *Shadow Banking*

While government debt was the ballast of the early financial markets trading corporate stock and bonds (Marx 1967, Vol. I, Chap. 31, 754–757), it is now the "safe asset" for unregulated global financial markets trading currencies and a variety of other securities. This so-called "shadow banking system" has emerged through regulatory arbitrage, to evade the post-Depression regulations of the insured commercial banking system, which were subsequently repealed. Supported by theoretical advances such as the "Efficient Market Hypothesis" (Fama 1970) and competitive deregulation (Tooze 2018), new types of financial organizations were allowed to offer access to credit by means of trading financial assets, cleared through the largest primary dealer banks, instead of by means of deposits and loans from the regulated banking system (Singh 2017).

One result of deregulation and trust in the financial markets has been the evolution of "shadow banking," a form of regulatory arbitrage. The term "shadow banks" was recently replaced by the phrase "monitoring universe of non-bank financial intermediation" (or MUNFI) in 2018 by the Financial Stability Board of the G20, perhaps indicating the intention of the FSB to shed light on these "shady" financial institutions. The size and share of MUNFIs, now nearly half of global financial assets, has continued to grow, nonetheless, relative to the regulated public financial institutions (see Fig. 4.1 below). One subcategory of MUNFIs, the "other financial intermediaries" (OFIs, excluding central banks, banks, or other public financial institutions, insurance corporations, pension funds, and financial auxiliaries), has increased to 30% of global financial assets, at $114.3 trillion, compared with a total of $378.9 trillion, and the fastest-growing segment since 2012. That is, these "other

Macro-mapping of the financial system

21+EA-Group

Exhibit 2-1

	Total global financial assets	Central banks	Banks	Public financial institu-tions	MUNFI	Insurance corpora-tions[1]	Pension funds	OFIs	Financial auxiliaries[2]
Size at end-2018 (USD trillion)	378.9	30.1	147.9	17.3	183.7	32.9	35.6	114.3	1.0
Share of total global financial assets (%)	100.0	7.9	39.0	4.6	48.5	8.7	9.4	30.2	0.3
Growth in 2018 (year-over-year, %)	1.4	2.5	2.8	3.2	-0.1	0.2	0.4	–0.4	8.8
Growth 2012-17 (annualised growth, %)	5.9	8.5	3.4	4.7	7.8	5.5	6.3	9.0	8.8

Fig. 4.1 Panel (A). [1]For some jurisdictions, data on insurance corporations include separate accounts. [2]Financial auxiliaries are institutional units principally engaged in serving financial markets, but do not take ownership of the financial assets and liabilities they handle (SNA 2008). The figures for financial auxiliaries excludes the euro area due to reporting constraints. (Sources: Jurisdictions' 2019 submissions (national sectoral balance sheet and other data); FSB calculations; FSB GMR 2020a)

private financial intermediaries" like hedge funds and money market mutual funds have almost overtaken regulated banks, which had a 39% share of total financial assets in 2018 (FSB GMR 2020a, 3–11).

The purpose of the shadow banking system was to provide safe liquid assets for large "cash pools," such as pension, money market, and hedge funds, whose primary goal was to increase yield in a low interest rate environment (Pozsar 2015, 12–13, 29–30). This goal was in contrast with that of the nineteenth century of funding real investment and trade, or the twentieth-century functions of underwriting war bonds, or financing the American suburbs. These cash pools are financed by emerging countries' foreign exchange reserves, corporate cash holdings, and rising inequality (Pozsar 2015, 5–6), increasing from over $2 trillion in 1997 to nearly $6 trillion in 2013 in the United States.

The shadow banking system is considered private, and its core asset is a "repo" (Baklanova et al. 2015). A repurchase agreement, or "repo," is the sale and commitment to repurchase a "safe," liquid asset, such as US Treasury bonds, for a specified price over a short time period of time. The market for repos emerged in the 1920s, but expanded after the Fed/Treasury Accord of 1951. Along with broader financial deregulation (Banner 2017, 232–240), exemptions from certain restrictions in bankruptcies made repos even more liquid after 1984 (Pistor 2019, 144–152). The use of Treasury bonds as collateral makes repos presumably safe, but still depends on the market value of those bonds at any given moment, and the extent to which a given piece of collateral is "rehypothecated" or resold to other participants (Gorton and Metrick 2010). Participants in the market for repos include the central bank, large primary securities dealers, money market funds, and hedge funds. A given Treasury bond, or "collateral," can be traded multiple times, seven times on average (Infante et al. 2020, 13), in a repo chain, leading to a type of credit "multiplier," as well as high leverage, and interconnectedness.

> The 'reuse' or rehypothecation of a security is somewhat analogous to the money creation that takes place in commercial banking through the process of accepting deposits and making loans (Singh 2017, 7),

but takes place by means of trades by primary dealer banks without the associated regulation and supervision by the central bank, and without the accurate data collection of its order of magnitude.

In this case, the object of value of a repurchase agreement is often the US Treasury bond, which represents the relationships of future tax payments of the US total economy, the trust among large financial institutions who are conducting these trades, and the confidence in financial market makers instead of government regulation, since the 1980s. The global liquidity of US Treasury bonds is a result of the role of the US dollar as key reserve currency since World War II and the relative size of the US market and military power.

The emergence of the "shadow banking system" was the outcome of several developments. First, with option price models, a variety of securities could be priced and exchanged on the market (Brine and Poovey 2017). Second, with the trend towards deregulation of financial markets, larger, complex bank holding companies and systemically important financial institutions (SIFIs) were allowed to consolidate. Third, the belief became more widespread that private markets were capable of producing "safe assets," by developing specialized assets for trading specific types of risk in specialized institutions (Mehrling et al. 2013, 7). A variety of securities were "coded" using long-standing legal strategies, and considered "safe," using ratings by reputable ratings agencies (Pistor 2019; Akerlof and Shiller 2015). The outcome was a new model of credit creation. Instead of deposits transformed into loans in the regulated commercial banking system, there was short-term "money market funding of capital market lending" (Mehrling et al. 2013, 2). In this context, "capital" is defined as the bank's own funds, an entry on the asset side of its balance sheet, against which leverage can be measured (Adrian et al. 2018, 3–7). "Capital markets" are the organized exchanges of a variety of assets, including repos, by "cash pools" to maintain safety and increase yield in a low interest rate environment. The core asset, US Treasury bonds, would certainly qualify as Marx's "fictitious capital," and evaluated by present discounted value and other models which are removed from the actual process of producing and realizing surplus.

Loss of confidence in the repo market was one cause of the Great Financial Crisis of 2008 (GFC). Securitized home mortgages (mortgage-backed securities, or MBS), widely traded as "safe assets," were losing value as home prices began to fall in the early 2000s. The repo trades based on MBS were losing value, and traders were unable to complete their promised repurchases. Forced to sell prematurely, there was a sudden deflation of their value, leading to a "run on repo," and an increase in the amount of securities which needed to be pledged as collateral to back a loan of a given size (or "haircut"). This loss of confidence, or "contagion," spread to other securities and other large traders. Banks which had backed these trades as "off balance sheet" transactions were forced to contribute capital. The interconnections of the financial system, high leverage, and the role of large "systemically important financial institutions" (SIFIs) led to the merging and the large bailouts of financial institutions like AIG in 2008 (Gorton 2010).

7.3 Crisis Indicator

With this history in mind, a spike which occurred in the secured overnight financing rate (SOFR) on repos on September 17, 2019 (Fig. 4.2), caused some alarm (Anbil et al. 2020). Some claimed that regulations after GFC reduced liquidity by raising capital requirements of banks. The Federal Reserve had also begun to reduce the size of its balance sheet, seeking to normalize monetary policy after the bouts of quantitative easing after 2008. An increase in US government budget deficits and a raising of the debt ceiling also drained liquidity out of the system by the purchase of larger quantities of these assets. There is evidence that the four largest investment banks, J.P. Morgan, Bank of America, Citigroup, and Wells Fargo, conduct the largest share of trades in the repo market (Avalos et al. 2019). This makes the operation of the financial markets subject to the profit motives of a few large private banks,

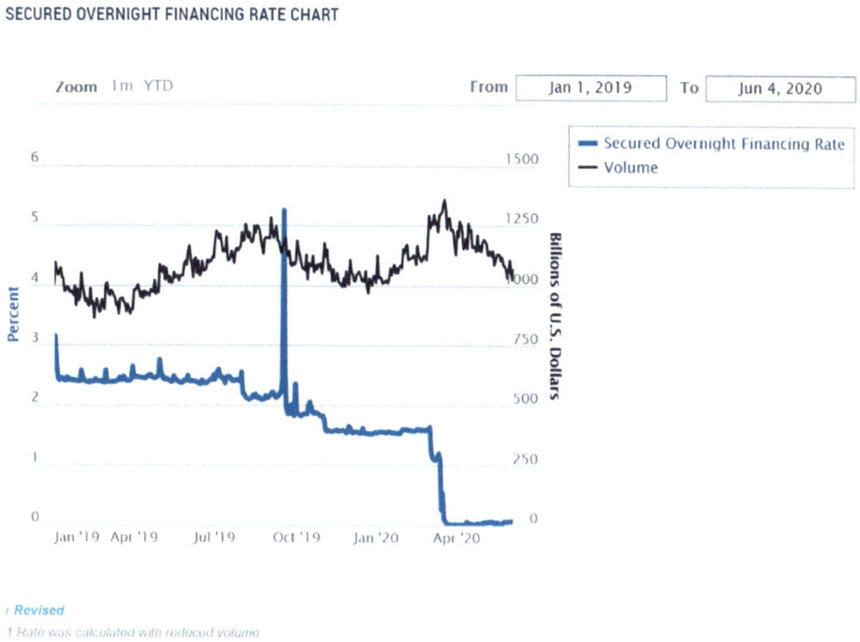

Fig. 4.2 Repo rates. (Source: https://apps.newyorkfed.org/markets/autorates/sofr)

rather than the systemic perspective of the nonprofit central bank, the Federal Reserve, or a normal probability distribution among many small independent market participants.

The Fed acted quickly in September 2019 to calm the markets by purchasing government securities, to add liquidity, even reversing its pledge to "normalize" its balance sheet and interest rates after the GFC. Market participants could then blame the post-GFC regulations for the crunch and the spike in interest rates on repo markets and seek to further undermine them. Given the Fed's reaction, it can be viewed as reentering the policy of quantitative easing, far in advance of any recession, potentially reducing its capacity in the event that such a recession occurs.

Even with the extended period of record low interest rates, real investment has remained below the norm (Gutierrez and Philippon 2017; Kotz 2019). Such Fed support of existing accumulation of nominal asset values calms the market, but prevents the correction of an apparent bubble in government securities, corporate bonds, and stock prices. That is, the discretionary actions by the central bank may increase the hold that large private banks have on the system, increasing their position as "too big to fail." Given the size of the repo markets, relative to the insured commercial banks, the role of managing its production of "safe" assets becomes more challenging. According to one estimate (Gorton and Metrick 2010, 507), the average daily trading volume in the repo market was about $7.11 trillion in 2008 and $1 trillion a day since 2017 (Anbil et al. 2020).

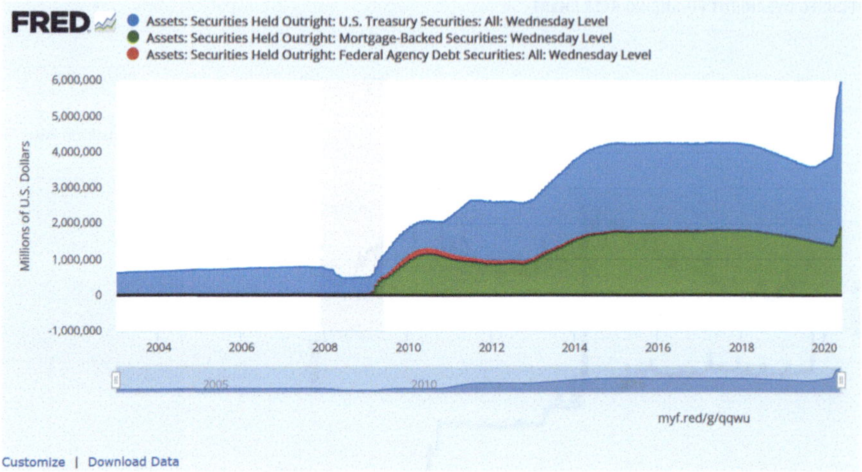

Fig. 4.3 Size of the balance sheet of the US Federal Reserve. (Source: Board of Governors of the Federal Reserve System (US); https://fredblog.stlouisfed.org/2020/03/fourth-large-scale-asset-purchases-program-a-new-hope/)

The Fed acted again during the market turmoil of February and March 2020 (Smialek 3/9/2020), when the S&P dropped from its record peak on February 19 into near bear market territory on March 9, 2020 (Ramkumar 3/9/2020; Otani 3/9/2020). Strains in the repo market were again one of the reasons for prompt action to reassure the markets (Verlaine 3/9/2020), but no action was taken to reform repo markets or to reduce leverage and interconnections. Even after an oval office address by President Trump and further Fed injections of liquidity and interest rate cuts, the stock market had its worst day on March 12, 2020, since Black Monday, October 19, 1987 (Ostroff et al. 2020) (Fig. 4.3).

Massive interventions by the Fed have helped to offset the impact of the pandemic on the stock market and in financial markets (see Appendix below). As of June 16, 2020, at the beginning of 2 days of testimony to Congress by the Fed chair Jerome Powell, the Fed's balance sheet had expanded to almost $7.2 trillion, nearly doubling in 1 year. These actions by the Fed are justified as technical, just to keep the markets operating smoothly, rather than "government intervention." This role of the Fed as acting on behalf of the markets enables it to be exempt from the accusations of "big government," even as it assumes an increasing role in stabilizing financial markets.

7.4 Vulnerabilities

In summary, "capital" in the modern banking system is defined as bankers' equity, meeting certain criteria for safety, regulated to offset leverage (Adrian et al. 2018). Legal coding can create safe assets in the private sector, but the effectiveness of these actions depends on the endorsement of participants in the financial markets, and support from institutions close to the state, such as the Federal Reserve. The extension of shadow banking and the growing size of the repo markets then change the dynamics of the system, potentially creating more risk and slower growth. That is, repos can be treated as money (Gorton and Metrick 2010, 207; Sissoko 2019), but the potential exists for a dramatic loss of confidence, should the institutional backing by the state be too weak or the aggregate returns unable to redeem the existing financial liabilities.

The capitalist state itself can be considered a financial institution (Davis 2017b), collecting taxes (assets) and issuing bonds and currency (liabilities). The state is the backstop for apparently infinite financial markets, an institution whose own future depends on the operation of those financial markets. That is, the state backs financial institutions which helps assure its own perpetuity. The resolution of any debt is then a combination of increased tax collections and extension of the time horizon for debt repayment. The global key currencies are the liabilities issued by the countries in the Western liberal model, Japan, Europe, the United Kingdom, and the United States. The dominance of these states and this model is primarily the result of World War II settlements, even though this model is presumed infinite and optimal, extant since the 1648 Westphalian treaty if not the Glorious Revolution in England of 1688, and all the while challenged by Communist models in the USSR from 1917 to 1989 and China since 1949. The state itself is considered safe and secure and drops from the consideration in the "hierarchy of money" (Mehrling 2013), even though the state is necessary to define, interpret, and enforce laws of property and financial contracts.

This hierarchical pyramid of money with the state at the apex is an inversion of the actual origin of surplus, according to Marx. As he mentions in Vol. I, Chapter 6, the worker gives credit to the firm, by working before receiving payment, and "this credit is no mere fiction" (Marx 1967, Vol. I, Chap. 6, 174–175). This labor is the origin of surplus, realized by the sale of the commodity for money to the household. The corporation can then pay out this extra revenue as dividends to stockholders, repay loans to lenders, and pay taxes to the government. In turn, with these tax collections, the Treasury can issue bonds and the central bank can issue currency, while also monitoring the credit allocated by banks and other financial institutions to firms, to repeat the cycle of production of commodities and realization of surplus value. While taxes are compulsory, the other financial circuits are managed by double-entry bookkeeping, and the requirement of balancing assets and liabilities, as well as the repayment of debt incurred. Rather than treat moneylending and money expansion as an "automaton," this tracing of the origin of the surplus from labor reveals the interlinked, contingent, and complex nature of the source of growth of the entire system. While money is considered valuable in itself, the worker is grateful for a job and for a wage, rather than understanding the entire system as based on her own labor, whose share is declining in the contemporary global economy.

> In the money-market...capital [is] *essentially the common capital of a class*...[which] assumes the nature of a concentrated organized mass, which, quite different from actual production, is subject to the control of bankers, i.e., the representatives of social capital. (Marx 1967, Vol. III, Chap. 22, 368; italics in original)

In contemporary financial markets, the only clue about the social nature of production is the significance of public debt and corporate stock, which are traded on the markets as commodities.

Ironies abound. The ostensible function of the financial system is to intermediate long-term assets with short-term liabilities and to channel savings into profitable real investments. The repo market takes longer-term "safe" assets like Treasury bonds and uses them as collateral for unregulated, highly leveraged, very short-term trades, for the provision of liquidity for wealth holders, and for the extension of credit for consumption (Mian 2019).

The belief in the capacity of private markets to produce safe assets underlies the growth of the shadow banking system. The reliance on increasingly short-term highly leveraged assets requires increasing support by the central bank when market trades become frozen, which then increases the central bank balance sheet and the specialized interventions that facilitate its further expansion. The operation of the private financial system has the capacity to hijack the entire economy to produce "safe" assets for the protection of idle wealth.

> Talk about centralization! The credit system, which has its focus in the so-called national banks and the big money-lenders and usurers surrounding them, constitutions enormous centralization, and gives to this class of parasites the fabulous power, not only to periodically despoil industrial capitalists, but also to interfere in actual production in a most dangerous manner. (Marx 1967, Vol. III, Chap. 33, 544–545)

Even before the pandemic of COVID-19, there were pre-existing conditions that reflected weakness in the credit system. The financial markets, prized for giving market signals, were already flashing red (IMF GFSR 2020, Chap. 2). For example, in the context of low interest rates to stimulate recovery since 2001, there has been a record buildup of corporate debt, often used for stock buybacks instead of new real investment. A number of economies have resorted to negative interest rates, which may cause further instability in financial markets, such as hoarding cash and lowering bank profits. There was already a threat of deflation due to inequality and low global effective demand (see Fig. 4.4). The effect of the pandemic is to reduce growth in emerging countries, previously the arena for investment. The simultaneous impact on the global economy threatens financial crisis, along with the health crisis. Given the recent turn to populism in some countries, a coordinated global strategy has been difficult to formulate and to implement.

When the COVID-19 pandemic hit the financial markets in March 2020, there was an immediate response by the Federal Reserve and other central banks. The central banks of the G7 acquired assets of $7 trillion in 8 months, compared with only $3 trillion in the full year after the collapse of Lehman Brothers in 2008, along with a full panel of special lending facilities (FSB HR, 2020b, 33–34) (see Fig. 4.5 below).

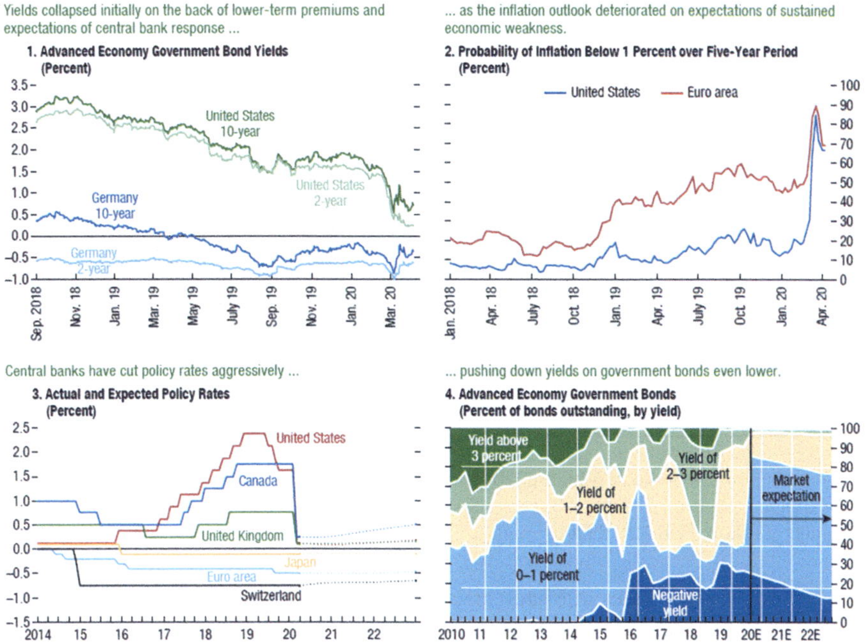

Fig. 4.4 Negative interest rates. (Source: IMF GFSR 2020, 3; Bloomberg Finance LP.; and IMF staff calculations)

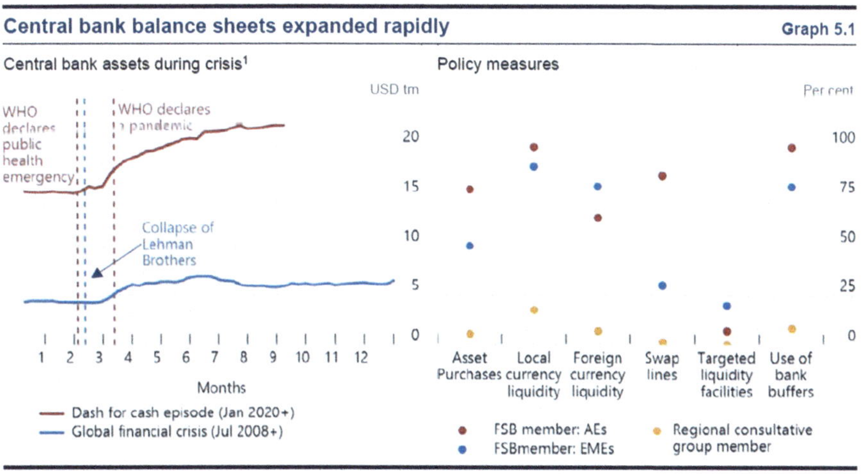

Fig. 4.5 Increase in central bank assets. [1]Includes central bank assets in Canada, the euro area, Japan, United Kingdom and United States. (Source: Datastream; national data; FSB calculations; FSB HR 2020b)

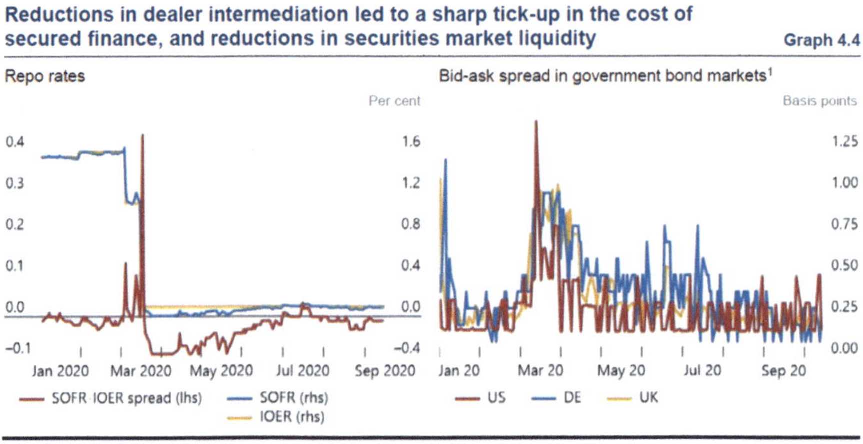

Fig. 4.6 Repo rates spike in March 2020. [1]10-year. SOFR: Secured Overnight Financing Rate; IOER Interest Rate on Excess Reserves. (Source: Federal Reserve Bank of St Louis, FRED; Bloomberg; Eikon; FSB HR, 2020b)

The spike in repo rates in March 2020 provided the signal, once again, for massive central bank intervention (see Fig. 4.6 above).

At the end of the year 2020, there were increases in mortgage originations by non-bank lenders (Eisen 2020), further increases in cash pools (Economist 12/12/2020, 63–64), and signs of another tech bubble on Wall Street (Platt et al. 2020). With stock indices reaching record highs, stockholders were able to benefit from new vaccine development as well as the Fed's expansionary monetary policy, while inequality surged with layoffs and foreclosures among low-wage service workers.

After reaching record stock market peaks, with speculative bubbles in cryptocurrencies and meme stocks, and increases in inflation, the Federal Reserve announced in January 2022 a plan to increase interest rates to beginning in February 2022. These efforts were widely interpreted as an attempt to return to "normal" monetary policy, after the COVID-19 pandemic. Yet stock markets swooned (Zuckerman et al. 2022) and the yield on 10-year Treasury bonds rose immediately (Timiraos 2022), even before the Fed's policy could take effect. The Fed's resolve will be tested once again, especially after the Russian invasion of Ukraine on February 24, 2022.

8 Conclusions

Taking the study of "capital" as a whole complex system, characterized by the commodity labor power, the exchange value of which is represented by money, can explain the anomalies of the present. Money can become "capital" only when it is used to create and expand value in production, a process which is increasingly subject to time lags and risks. The turn to trading a variety of assets on financial markets is a distraction from the actual production of value, making those financial markets increasingly vulnerable. The backing by the Federal Reserve at present only extends and enlarges the distortion, serving to increase even further the ratio of financial assets to GDP.

In the case study of the repo market, legal coding has created a new financial instrument, which became a "safe asset." The trading of this asset in unregulated financial institutions resulted in financial instability, nonetheless, requiring the intervention of the central bank. That is, it is important to consider the individual asset within the context of the entire set of institutions. Even after the series of increasing frequency and scope of financial crises since 1980, the interconnectedness and "systemic risk" are still not fully considered. Financial markets are still considered rational and stable, once the crisis has been resolved. This policy framework has permitted unregulated financial institutions to grow relative to the whole, requiring increasing interventions. In Marx's terms, the attempt to produce "safe assets" has expanded the financial sector, M-M', relative to the industrial sector, which constitutes a series of expanded claims to the surplus while the actual production of surplus stagnates.

The definition of "capital" as an institutional complex is important, including key terms like money and value, and authoritative expertise like law, economics, and finance. Otherwise, there is a tendency to treat "capital" as merely a factor of production or a sum of money and oversimplify understanding of the entire system. This institutional complex shifts over time, such as the separation of industrial and financial capital discussed by Marx, aided by the view of money as a commodity itself and capital as "productive," or "money that begets money." In other words, because money is assumed to expand automatically, markets can be considered "self-regulating." This set of views and values has reinforced the tendency for the financial system to become more market driven since the 1980s, with increasing risks, more frequent financial crises, and stagnation. This private market financial system ultimately relies on the integrity of public finance as a backstop, which the increasing privatization of financial markets actually undermines.

Marx understood the capacity of the credit system to centralize surplus and to allocate it according to the rules of financial markets. The legal claim to a return from moneylending enables a few individuals to reap the returns to social production. As a result, lobbying, deregulation, and legal coding of complex securities is more lucrative than industrial production. The system as a whole becomes more fragile as a result.

A more complete understanding of the capitalist system as a whole is necessary to provide reform and meaningful alternatives.

Appendix

Central Bank Facilities in the Pandemic 2020 (Table 4.1)

Table 4.1 Selected central bank facilities to support funding markets

	Money markets and government securities	Corporate bonds	Other markets
Bank of Canada	**Bankers' Acceptance Purchase Facility** Purchases of eligible bankers' acceptances to maintain credit to small- and medium-sized businesses		
	Provincial Money Market Purchase Program Purchases of provincial money market securities in the primary market		
	Commercial Paper Purchase Program Purchases of eligible commercial paper in the primary and secondary markets to maintain the smooth flow of credit to corporations		
Bank of England	**Asset Purchase Facility** A £200 billion increase in the central bank's holdings of UK government bonds and sterling nonfinancial investment-grade corporate bonds to a total of £645 billion		
	COVID-19 Corporate Financing Facility For 12 months, the central bank and Treasury will purchase commercial paper of maturities up to 1 year issued by companies making a material contribution to the UK economy		
Bank of Japan	**Outright purchases of commercial paper and corporate bonds** A temporary (until the end of September 2020) increase in holdings of corporate bonds and commercial paper, moving from reinvesting proceeds of maturing assets into making net purchases **Policy actions to enhance the liquidity and functioning of short-term funding markets** The Bank of Japan announced funds-supplying operations against pooled collateral and purchases of Japanese government securities with repurchase agreements. In addition, it conducted unscheduled outright purchases of Japanese government bonds and expanded its Securities Lending Facility		**Purchase of exchange-traded funds and real estate investment trusts** A doubling in the pace of exchange-traded fund (ETF) purchases
European Central Bank	**Pandemic Emergency Purchase Program** Purchases of private and public sector securities, until the end of 2020, up to a total amount of EUR 750 billion. Expanded European Central Bank Asset Purchase Program, with additional EUR 120 billion in asset purchases focusing on the corporate sector. The collateral eligibility was amended to promote inclusion of corporate sector securities		

(continued)

Table 4.1 (continued)

	Money markets and government securities	Corporate bonds	Other markets
US Federal Reserve	**Primary Dealer Credit Facility** Provision of credit to primary dealers in exchange for a broad range of collateral for term funding with maturities up to 90 days **Commercial Paper Funding Facility** Purchases from eligible issuers, via a special purpose vehicle (SPV), of 3-month US dollar-denominated commercial paper **Money Market Mutual Fund Facility** Provision of liquidity to eligible money market mutual funds	**Primary Market Corporate Credit Facility** Purchases of investment-grade bonds and some bonds recently downgraded from investment grade from eligible issuers, via an SPV, and loans to eligible borrowers **Secondary Market Corporate Credit Facility** Purchases of investment-grade corporate bonds and some bonds recently downgraded from investment grade in the secondary market from eligible issuers. Purchases of investment-grade exchange-traded funds (ETFs) along with the remaining funds allocated to high-yield ETF purchases	**Term Asset-Backed Securities Loan Facility** Loans to holders of certain AAA-rated asset-backed securities, including collateralized loan obligations and commercial mortgage-backed securities, based on newly and recently originated consumer and small business loans **Municipal Liquidity Facility** Purchases of short-term notes issued by US states, counties, and cities

Sources: National central banks (see URLs in the reference list for more details); IMF GFSR April 2020, p. 23

Bibliography

Adkins, Lisa, Melinda Cooper, and Martijn Konings. *The Asset Economy: Property Ownership and the New Logic of Inequality*. Cambridge, UK: Polity Pres, 2020.

Adrian, Tobias and Hyun Song Shin. "The Changing Nature of Financial Intermediation and the Financial Crisis of 2007-2009." *Annual Review of Economics*, Vol. 2 (2010), 603-608, C1–C14, 609-618.

Adrian, Tobias, John Kiff, and Hyun Song Shin. "Liquidity, Leverage, and Regulation Ten Years After the Global Financial Crisis," *Annual Review of Financial Economics*, 2018, 1–24.

Akerlof, George A. and Robert J. Shiller. *Phishing for Phools: The Economics of Manipulation and Deception*. Princeton, NJ: Princeton University Press, 2015.

Alpert, Daniel. *The Age of Oversupply: Overcoming the Greatest Challenge to the Global Economy*. New York: Penguin, 2013.

Anbil, Sriya, Alyssa Anderson, and Zeynep Senyuz. "What Happened in Money Markets in September, 2019?" *FEDS Notes*. Washington: Board of Governors of the Federal Reserve System, February, 27, 2020.

Avalos, Fernando, Torsten Ehlers, and Egemen Eren. "September Stress in Repo Market: Passing or Structural?" in *BIS Quarterly Review*, fourth quarter, 2019, 12–14.

Baklanova, Viktoria, Adam Copeland and Rebecca McCaughrin. "Reference Guide to U.S. Repo and Securities Lending Markets," Federal Reserve Bank of New York Staff Report No. 740, December, 2015.
Banner, Stuart. *Speculation: A History of the Fine Line Between Gambling and Investing*. New York: Oxford University Press, 2017.
Bass, Alan. Fetishism, Psychoanalysis, and Philosophy: The Iridescent Thing. New York: Routledge, 2018.
Beckert, Jens. *Imagined Futures: Fictional Expectations and Capitalist Dynamics*. Cambridge, MA: Harvard University Press, 2016.
Beckert, Jens. "Markets from Meaning: Quality, Uncertainty and the Intersubjective Construction of Value." *Cambridge Journal of Economics*. Vol. 44, 2020, 285-301.
Beckert, Jens and Richard Bronk (eds.). *Uncertain Futures: Imaginaries, Narratives, and Calculations in the Economy*. New York: Oxford University Press, 2018.
Bellofiore, Ricardo. "Forever Young? Marx's Critique of Political Economy After 200 Years." *PSL Quarterly Review*, December, 2018, Vol. 71, No. 287, 353-388.
Berlin, Isaiah. *Four Essays on Liberty*. New York: Oxford University Press, 1969.
Bhagwati, Jagdish. *In Defense of Globalization*. New York: Oxford University Press, 2004.
Block, Fred L. and Margaret R. Somers. *The Power of Market Fundamentalism: Karl Polanyi's Critique*. Cambridge, MA: Harvard University Press, 2014.
Brine, Kevin R. and Mary Poovey. *Finance in America: An Unfinished Story*. Chicago: University of Chicago Press, 2017.
Cannan, Edwin. "Early History of the Term Capital." *Quarterly Journal of Economics*, Vol. 35, No. 3, may, 1921, 469-481.
Cook, Eli. *The Pricing of Progress: Economic Indicators and the Capitalization of American Life*. Cambridge, MA: Harvard University Press, 2017.
D'Arista, Jane. *All Fall Down: Debt, Deregulation, and Financial Crisis*. Cheltenham, UK: Edward Elgar, 2018.
Daston, Lorraine. *Against Nature*. Cambridge, MA: MIT Press, 2019.
Davis, Ann E. *The Evolution of the Property Relation: Paradigms, Debates, Prospects*. New York: Palgrave MacMillan, 2015.
Davis, Ann E. "Fetishism and Financialization." *Review of Radical Political Economics*. Vol. 49, No. 4, 2017a, 551-558.
Davis, Ann E. *Money as a Social Institution: The Institutional Development of Capitalism*. New York: Routledge, 2017b.
Davis, Ann E. *The End of Individualism and the Economy: Emerging Paradigms of Connection and Community*. New York: Routledge, 2020.
Davis, Ann E. "Postone's Legacy: Capitalism and Time." *Critical Historical Studies*, Spring, 2022, Vol. 9, No. 1, 1-34.
Economist, "A Year of Raising Furiously," December 12, 2020, 63-64.
Eichengreen, Barry J. *Exorbitant Privilege: The Rise and Fall of the Dollar and the Future of the International Monetary System*. New York: Oxford University Press, 2011.
Eichengreen, Barry J.. "Financial History, Historical Analysis, and the New History of Finance Capital." *Capitalism: A Journal of History and Economics*, Vol. 1, No. 1, Fall, 2019, 20-58.
Eisen, Ben. "Mortgage Originations Are on Pace for Top Year as Refinancings Soar," *Wall Street Journal*, December 11, 2020, B1.
Epstein, Gerald A. *What's Wrong with Modern Money Theory? A Policy Critique*. New York: Palgrave MacMillan, 2019.
Fama, Eugene F. "Efficient Capital Markets: A Review of Theory and Empirical Work." *Journal of Finance*, May, 1970, Vol. 25, No. 2, 383-417.
Financial Stability Board. "Global Monitoring Report on Non-Bank Financial Intermediation 2019." January 19, 2020a.
Financial Stability Board. "Holistic Review of the March Market Turmoil." November 7, 2020b.

Garegnani, Pierangelo. "On the Present State of the Capital Controversy." *Cambridge Journal of Economics*. Vol. 36, 2012, 1417-1432.

Gorton, Gary B. *Slapped by the Invisible Hand: The Panic of 2007*. New York: Oxford University Press, 2010.

Gorton, Gary, Stefan Lewellen, and Andrew Metrick. "The Safe-Asset Share." *American Economic Review*, 102:3, May, 2012, 101-106.

Gorton, Gary and Andrew Metrick. "Haircuts." *Federal Reserve Bank of St. Louis Review*, November/December, 2010, 507-519.

Gorton, Gary and Andrew Metrick. "The Federal Reserve and Panic Prevention: The Roles of Financial Regulation and the Lender of Last Resort." *Journal of Economic Perspectives*, Vol. 27, No. 4, Fall, 2013, 45-64.

Gourinchas, Pierre-Olivier, Helene Rey, and Nicolas Govillot. "Exorbitant Privilege and Exorbitant Duty." NBER, 2017.

Graeber, David. *Toward an Anthropological Theory of Value: The False Coin of Our Own Dreams*. New York: Palgrave, 2001.

Graeber, David. *Debt: The First 5,000 Years*. Brooklyn, New York: Melville House, 2011.

Greeley, Brendan and Colby Smith. "Investors Seek Clarity from Fed on Balance Sheet Expansion." *Financial Times*, 1/28/20.

Gutierrez, German and Thomas Philippon. "Investmentless Growth: An Empirical Investigation." Washington, D.C.: Brookings Papers on Economic Activity, 9/7-8/2017.

Haldane, Andrew, Simon Brennan and Vasileios Madouros. "What is the Contribution of the Financial Sector: Miracle or Mirage?" London School of Economics: *The Future of Finance*, London, 2010, 87-120.

Harvey, David. *A Brief History of Neoliberalism*. New York: Oxford University Press, 2005.

Harvey, David. *The Enigma of Capital and the Crises of Capitalism*. New York: Oxford University Press, 2010.

Harvey, David. *Seventeen Contradictions and the End of Capitalism*. New York: Oxford University Press, 2014.

Hawken, Paul, Amory Lovins, and L. Hunter Lovins. *Natural Capitalism: Creating the Next Industrial Revolution*. Boston: Little, Brown and Company, 1999.

Hodgson, Geoff. "What is Capital? Economists and Sociologists Have Changed Its Meaning: Should It be Changed Back? *Cambridge Journal of Economics*. Vol. 38, 2014, 1063-1086.

Hodgson, Geoff. *Conceptualizing Capitalism: Institutions, Evolution, Future*. Chicago: University of Chicago Press, 2015.

Infante, Sebastian, Charles Press, and Zack Saravay. "Understanding Collateral Re-Use in the United States Financial System," paper presented at the ASSA, sponsored by the AEA, in San Diego, January, 2020.

International Monetary Fund. "Global Financial Stability Report: Markets in the Time of COVID-19." Washington, D.C., April 2020.

Ivanova, Maria N. "Inequality, Financialization, and the US Current Account Deficit," *Industrial and Corporate Change*, Vol. 28, No. 4, 2019, 707-724.

Ivanova, Maria N. "Marx's Theory of Money: A Reappraisal in the Light of Unconventional Monetary Policy," *Review of Radical Political Economy*. Vol. 52, No. 1, 2020, 137-151.

Karak, Anirban. "Economy Theory Without Historicity: The Relevance of Marxian Social Theory for a Critique of Capitalism." *Critical Historical Studies*, Spring, 2021, Vol. 8, No. 1, 115-136.

Keynes, John Maynard. *The General Theory of Employment, Interest, and Money*. New York: Harcourt, race & World, 1964.

Kotz, David M. *The Rise and Fall of Neoliberal Capitalism*. Cambridge, MA: Harvard University Press, 2015.

Kotz, David M. "The Rate of Profit, Aggregate Demand, and the Long Economic Expansion in the United States since 2009," *Review of Radical Political Economics*. Vol. 51, No. 4, 2019, 525-535.

Kotz, David M. and Deepankar Basu. "Stagnation and Institutional Structures." *Review of Radical Political Economics*. Vol. 51:1, 2019, 5–30.

Krippner, Greta R. *Capitalizing on Crisis: The Political Origins of the Rise of Finance*. Cambridge, MA: Harvard University Press, 2011.

Lapavitsas, Costas. *Profiting Without Producing: How Finance Exploit Us All*. London: Verso, 2013.

Latour, Bruno. *An Inquiry into Modes of Existence: An Anthropology of the Moderns*. Cambridge, MA: Harvard University Press, 2013.

Levy, Jonathan. "Capital as Process and the History of Capitalism." *Business History Review*, Vol. 91, Autumn 2017, 483-510.

Macaulay, Catherine R. "Financializing Capitalism: 400 Years of Equity Market Development," *Competition and Change*, Vol. 23, No. 5, 2019, 502-523.

Marx, Karl. *Capital*. Volume I, II, III. New York: International Publishers, 1967.

Marx, Karl and Friedrich Engels. *The German Ideology*. New York: International Publishers, 1947.

Mehrling, Perry. "Three Principles for Market-Based Credit Regulation." *American Economic Review*. 2012, 102(3): 107-112.

Mehrling, Perry. "The Inherent Hierarchy of Money." Lance Taylor, Armon Rezai, and Thomas Michl (eds.). *Social Fairness and Economics*. New York: Routledge, 2013, 394-404.

Mehrling, Perry, Zoltan Pozsar, James Sweeney, Daniel H. Neilson. "Bagehot was a Shadow Banker." Institute for New Economic Thinking, 2013.

Mian, Atif. "How to Think About Finance?" Research Brief. Economists for Inclusive Prosperity. Research Brief, January, 2019.

Mirowski, Philip. *More Heat than Light: Economics as Social Physics, Physics as Nature's Economics*. New York: Cambridge University Press, 1989.

Moseley, Fred. "Capital." In David M. Brennan, David Kristjanson-Gural, Catherine P. Mulder and Erik K. Olsen (eds.). *Routledge Handbook of Marxian Economics*. New York: Routledge, 2017, 90-97.

Neal, Larry and Jeffrey G. Williamson (eds.). *The Cambridge History of Capitalism*. Volume I. The Rise of Capitalism: From Ancient Origins to 1848. Cambridge, UK: Cambridge University Press, 2015.

O'Kane, Chris. "Reification and the Critical Theory of Contemporary Society." *Critical Historical Studies*. Spring, 2021, 57-86.

Ostroff, Caitlin, Joanne Chiu, and Caitlin McCabe. "Stocks Plunge 10% in Dow's Worst Day Since 1987," *Wall Street Journal*, March 12, 2020.

Otani, Akane. "Stock Market Enters a New Endurance Test," *Wall Street Journal*, March 9, 2020, B1.

Panitch, Leo and Sam Gindin. *The Making of global Capitalism: The Political Economy of the American Empire*. London: Verso, 2012.

Philippon, Thomas. *The Great Reversal: How America Gave Up on Free Markets*. Cambridge, MA: Harvard University Press, 2019.

Piketty, Thomas. *Capital in the Twenty-First Century*. Cambridge, MA: Harvard University Press, 2014.

Piketty, Thomas. *Capital and Ideology*. Cambridge, MA: Harvard University Press, 2020.

Pistor, Katharina. *The Code of Capital: How the Law Creates Wealth and Inequality*. Princeton, NJ: Princeton University Press, 2019.

Platt, Eric, David Carnevali, and Michael Mackenzie. "IPO Bonanza Stirs Uneasy Memories of Dotcom Mania," *Financial Times*, December 12, 2020, 13.

Polanyi, Karl. *The Great Transformation*. Boston: Beacon Press, 1944.

Poovey, Mary. *A History of the Modern Fact: Problems of Knowledge in the Sciences of Wealth and Society*. Chicago: University of Chicago Press, 1998.

Poovey, Mary. "The Liberal Civil Subject and the Social in Eighteenth-Century British Moral Philosophy," *Public Culture*, Vol. 14, No. 1, 125-145, 2002.

Poovey, Mary. *Genres of the Credit Economy: Mediating Value in Eighteenth-and Nineteenth-Century Britain*. Chicago: University of Chicago Press, 2008.

Postone, Moishe. *Time, Labor and Social Domination: A Reinterpretation of Marx's Critical Theory*. New York: Cambridge University Press, 1996.

Pozsar, Zoltan. "A Macro View of Shadow Banking." Institute for New Economic Thinking, 2015.

Ramkumar, Amrith. "Mixed Technical Signals Feed Stock Volatility," *Wall Street Journal*, March 9, 2020, p. B9.

Riles, Annelise. *Collateral Knowledge: Legal Reasoning in the Global Financial Markets*. Chicago: University of Chicago Press, 2011.

Sartori, Andrew.

Searle, John R. *Making the Social World; the Structure of Human Civilization*. New York: Oxford University Press, 2010.

Shaikh, Anwar. *Capitalism: Conflict, Competition, Crises*. New York: Oxford University Press, 2016.

Shapin, Steven and Simon Schaffer. *Leviathan and the Air-Pump: Hobbes, Boyle, and the Experimental Life*. Princeton, NJ: Princeton University Pres, 1985.

Singh, Manmohan. "Collateral Reuse and Balance Sheet Space." IMF Working Paper WP/17/113. May, 2017.

Sissoko, Carolyn. "Repurchase Agreements and the (De)Construction of Financial Markets." *Economy and Society*. Vol. 48, No. 3, 2019, 315-341.

Skidelsky, Robert. *What's Wrong with Economics? A Primer for the Perplexed*. New Haven: Yale University Press, 2020.

Smialek, Jeanna. "New York Fed Moves to Keep Money Markets Calm Amid Turmoil," New York Times, March 9, 2020.

Smith, Adam. *An Inquiry into the Nature and Causes of the Wealth of Nations*. New York: Modern Library, 1994.

Timiraos, Nick. "With Rates on Hold, Fed Faces Decisions on Its Balance Sheet: Debate on Whether the Central Bank's Intervention Led to a Market Rally Complicates Choices on How, When to Wind it Down." *Wall Street Journal*, January 28, 2020.

Timiraos, Nick. "Fed Tees Up March Interest Rate Increase," *Wall Street Journal*, January 26, 2022.

Tooze, J. Adam. *Crashed: How a Decade of Financial Crises Changed the World*. New York: Penguin Books, 2018.

Verlaine, Julia-Ambra. "Short-Term Loan Sector Worries Banks," *Wall Street Journal*, March 9, 2020, B8.

Vogl, Joseph. *The Ascendancy of Finance*. Cambridge, UK: Polity, 2017.

Wansleben, Leon. "Formal Institution Building in Financialized Capitalism: The Case of Repo Markets." *Theory and Society*, Vol. 49, 2020, 187-213.

Weber, Max. *Protestant Ethic and the Spirit of Capitalism*. New York: Scribner, 1958.

Zuckerman, Gregory, Gunjan Banerji, and Michael Wursthorn. "Turmoil: A High-Speed Investor U-Turn," *Wall Street Journal*, January 27, 2022.

Zuijderduijn, C.J. *Medieval Capital Markets: Markets for Renten, State Formation, and Private Investment in Holland (1300-1550)*. Boston: Brill, 2009.

Chapter 5
The Public Private Divide

1 Introduction

The structure of the modern nation-state is apparently divided into separate spheres. There is consideration on the nature of these divisions, and whether the modern state operates as a whole entity, or "totality," as well as the nature of the unifying forces, if any. This chapter reviews approaches to this question in diverse literature and discusses the potential for disruption and contradiction. The concern in this chapter is the use of this distinction, the public/private divide, to resolve the contradictions which result from the view of "capital" as an impersonal automatic agent, which is typical of capitalism (as discussed in Chap. 4 above). On the other hand, the public/private divide is subject to its own contradictions.

2 Public/Private Divide

In the early modern period, property in land was considered the base of the social structure (Howell 2010, 42–46; Gordon 1996). Most modern industrial economies have a constitutional "separation of powers," with representation of citizens by franchise, and constitutional protections of a private economy based on property. Historically, the franchise was restricted to property owners, with gradual extension to "universal" suffrage. That is, both citizens and owners were "represented" in government, with competing sets of rights, human rights and property rights. According to Polanyi, this separation of powers was a form of restriction of citizens with respect to owners.

> The separation of powers, which Montesquieu (1748) had meanwhile invented, was now used to separate the people from power over their own economic life. The American Constitution, shaped in a farmer-craftsman's environment by a leadership forewarned by the English industrial scene, isolated the economic sphere entirely from the jurisdiction of

A. E. Davis, *Whole Earth*, https://doi.org/10.1007/978-3-031-01934-0_5

> the Constitution, put private property thereby under the highest conceivable protection, and created the only legally grounded market society in the world. In spite of universal suffrage, American voters were powerless against owners. (Polanyi 1944, 225–226)

The economy is considered a separate realm, often self-regulating and automatic, according to the "liberal creed" (Polanyi 1944). "The economy" is one of the "reifying abstractions" characteristic of "modernity" (Poovey 2002; 1995; Bonefeld 2020), studied by professional economists in universities. Idealized versions of the economy are the foundation for various political positions and economic policies.

Formal economic categories are based on universal and abstract axioms, presumably natural, such as property and the individual. In these categories, there are no distinctions made between human and other living things or materials, such as "inputs" into production functions. These abstract institutions like the market have agency, but not the individuals, who are included in the categories. For example, individuals are employed by private firms, whose productivity constitutes socially necessary labor time as an average. What counts as "value" is the average, not the individual worker's output. The metric of macroeconomics of labor productivity is similarly the expression of an average across firms, industries, and countries. While "the individual" is presumably "free," only abstract institutions have agency, such as "the economy" or "the market."

The economy is tracked and monitored based on double-entry bookkeeping (real and financial), for both the firm and the macroeconomy. There are separate flows related to obligations, debts and credits. The commodity is recorded in both concrete and abstract forms (money value).

Money provides a means of differentiating institutions and also reintegrating them. In Habermas's term, money is a "steering medium," which intermediates subsystems, and can differentiate types of social relationships and communication (Habermas 1985). That is, certain types of norms are appropriate for the private sphere of the family, such as altruism and mutual understanding, which are contrary to those permitted in the market, such as competition and self-interest. The boundary between market and society is fraught, nonetheless, as are these normative distinctions, and can shift over time, or by political regime (Davis 2017).

There is also ambiguity of the definition of the public/private divide (PPD), even when considered synonymous with the distinction of state/market. For example, the market is "public" compared with the household, but it is "private" with respect to the state. A single person can be "public" as a citizen and "private" as a property owner, even at the same time. Gal (2004) considers the PPD as "fractal," with further divisions always possible. For Pateman (1988), there are two private spheres. In the public sphere, the citizen is the subject, while in the private sphere, the worker or wife is the object. The objectification of the worker is legitimated as temporary, offset by the agency of the citizen with representation in the state, and with the reward of increasing productivity for the system as a whole. The goals of the system are wealth and growth, justified by the consumer preference for "more," presumably based on "human nature." It is not clear whether "growth" is constituted by material wealth or value (Postone 1993) or human satisfaction.

3 Property and Governance

Property has been linked to governance historically. In the medieval period, land was the foundation for governance, with rights to landlords and serfs based on shared settlement of a particular parcel (Howell 2010). There were trifunctional forms of governance for the country as a whole, with individuals identified by class, with nobles, clergy, and commoners each with distinct roles and responsibilities (Piketty 2020) (see Fig. 5.1).

The notion of individual private property was protected in Roman law, but not recognized in the medieval period in England. This changed with the Enclosure Movement, when ownership of discrete parcels was legally recognized and enforced by the courts (Pistor 2019, 29–39), with rights to exclusion. With this historical view, rather than property viewed as eternal "natural law," according to Locke, property was made by legal codes in particular historical circumstances (Pistor 2019, 45–46). What Piketty calls the "sacralization" of property was part of the "proprietarian" ideology (Piketty 2020, 120–125).

The French Revolution provides another example of the ways in which governance is altered by changing definitions of property. During the French Revolution of 1789, there was a "Great Demarcation" (Piketty 2020), a term which describes a presumably new independence for the newly declared private property. Rather than three functional estates with certain privileges, all property was shifted to private ownership, and "regalian powers" (security, justice) were assigned to the state (Piketty 2020, 99–116). The ownership of this independent private property was no longer tied to obligations to the lord, in terms of service, or rent, but was owned outright (allodial property) (Fig. 5.2).

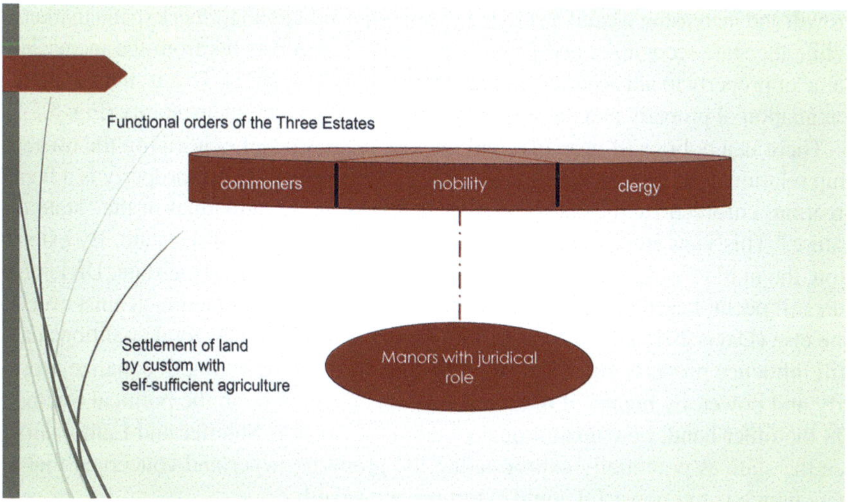

Fig. 5.1 Ancien regime – tripartite orders

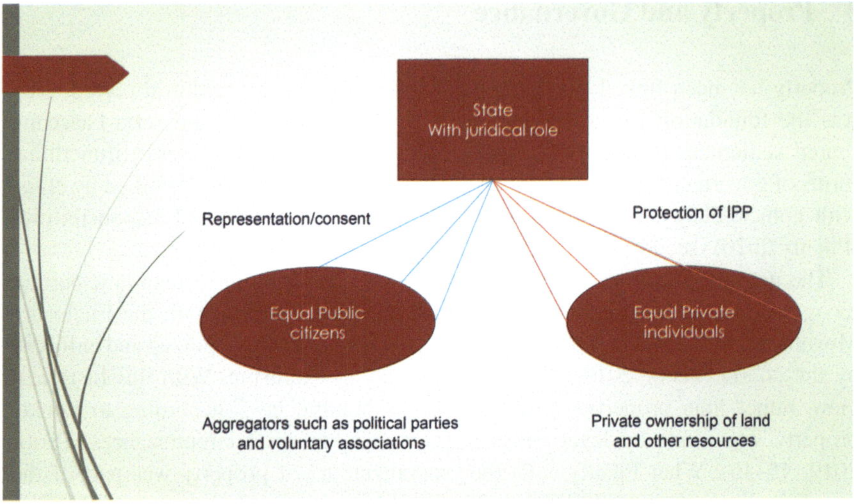

Fig. 5.2 Logic of "great demarcation" in France, 1789

The contention here is that "property" is not as independent as it seems, but is embedded in legal institutions and financial relations managed by the state. Instead of the tripartite corporate relationships of the *ancien regime*, the new mode of organization is the individual and the state. Yet this "free" individual participates in several abstract institutions which manage interconnections by norms and roles, overseen by expert authorities. These abstract institutions which bind the separate individual owners include the law, the market, and finance. To increase the value of one's own property, one must interact with the market and with finance, which exercises influence beyond the individual. Further, the state manages the market and finance, for the purpose of growth and increasing wealth, in order to finance the military to further expand markets. While the state recognizes and protects property, it also benefits from the increasing value of property to aid accumulation and power (Shovlin 2021). That is, there is a differentiation of property and the state, while there is also a complementarity (Fig. 5.3).

There is a politics of property, and two opposite ways of conceiving the ownership relationship for the society as a whole. The view here is that property is a legal creation, enforced by the state, rather than based in the individual in the "state of nature." This view implies that property is social, a creature of the state. By extension, the market which relies upon property is also a creature of the state. Divisions can still occur, based upon income, with wealthy owners as a faction against everyone else (Davis 2015), by a hierarchy of wealth and power. Electoral coalitions can still influence property rules and can influence the state by acting to equalize property and power, by means of universal suffrage, depending on the political regime. On the other hand, new institutional economists, such as Shleifer and Lamoreaux, see the state as potentially expropriating the property owner and concerned that a state which is too powerful could extort private wealth.

To the extent that there is a private property, it is protected by private law, which is a function of the state (Habermas 1989, 53–55, 73–79, 148–151, 177–180). The

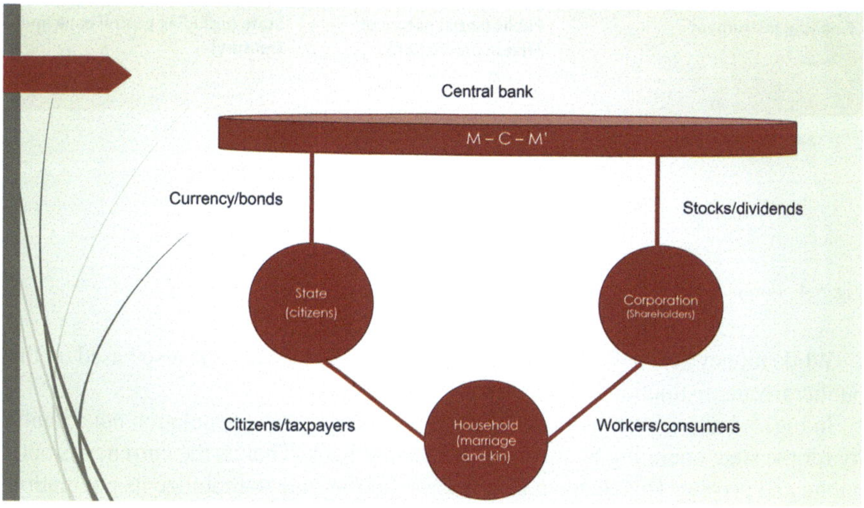

Fig. 5.3 Financial circuit managed by the state

difficulty of differentiating these divergent approaches is based on the paradoxical claim that "individuals" are "autonomous" and independent (Davis 2020), and property is "natural."

4 Divergent Institutions, Unified System

Money can be the "steering medium" of the capitalist system because it expresses the overarching goal of the system, the accumulation of money. In order to achieve this goal, the associated worldview is "commodification," to see every object or person in terms of potential revenue and profit. This "instrumental" worldview is assumed to be only for market participants and only during market interaction. But the goal of the system is pervasive and can influence social orientation, values, and attitudes in all other spheres, in my view.

The operation of the capitalist system is built upon a set of legal or administrative institutions which establish and manage conceptual/categorical dichotomies. There is a history of each one which reveals the ambiguity and complexity involved.

4.1 Public Finance

Money is issued and managed by the state, established in constitutions in modern industrial countries. The state treasury is managed according to standard accounting rules, and the state budget information is public, to provide accountability and to secure the consent of the governed.

Financial instrument	Public (social nature of private production)	State (including central bank and treasury)
Tax capacity (bonds)	Liability	Asset
Fiat currency	Asset	Liability

Fig. 5.4 Public finance

While money sets the boundaries of the public and private, it is also based on the public/private distinction in double-entry bookkeeping.

In Fig. 5.4 above, the national currency is an asset for the population but a liability for the state operating by means of the central bank. That is, the currency is both public and private. This dualism is necessary for the state to mobilize its population as a whole, collective entity to back the currency, which then is the medium of exchange and means of payment for private transactions. The role of money as a store of value is also related to the scale of the "public," with its greater probability of successful production and realization, despite the risk of private credit to individual firms.

The operation of modern credit is based on the scale of the nation as a whole, and on its presumed infinite lifetime, which is nonetheless based on the success in the near term of its public finance. That is, public credibility is the ultimate source of private credit, which then serves to repay public debt.

The modern state itself is formed from this dichotomy of public and private (Davis 2015). The hereditary monarchy was based on the "king's two bodies" (Kantorowicz 1957); first, the royal domain, his own land vs. the boundary of the national territory, and second, his own anatomy vs. the public body as the entire population. The modern state is now based on an ability to tax as managed by a representative body of the "public," which can provide the "consent" of the governed, or "parlement," to finance a standing army and domestic police. This tax authority backs the national currency, which is then expended to increase the wealth and power of the state, both public and private. The modern state is a fiscal/military state, building upon financial flows, and competing on the global market (Polanyi 1944).

The form of the state can vary historically (Davis 2015). For example, Habermas has identified four forms of the modern state (Habermas 1985, 358–373), from the "bourgeois state," the "bourgeois constitutional state," the "democratic constitutional state," and the "welfare state," with different accommodations to property, representation, and adjustment to the divisions associated with property. The "welfare" state allows for the greatest interpenetration of public and private, with politics representing special interest groups and factions, rather than the purely wealth-maximizing rationality of the property owner (Habermas 1989, 196–210).

There is a long-term history of finance in relation to state formation (Davis 2017), as well as histories of financial bubbles and crises. The ambiguity of the public/private divide can help account for the phenomena of financial crises. The state delegates profit-making activities to private corporations and banks, allowing them to make use of public credit. Then the state must regulate them and bail them out when they reap losses instead. The authority and the timing of these public rescues tend to generate conflict and controversy. There is a still-growing literature on the Great Financial Crisis of 2008, for example (see Chap. 4 above; Tooze 2018).

4.2 Property

There are paradoxes with respect to property. Like money, property represents the boundary of the public/private divide and also its contradiction. Property itself is a social relationship (Davis 2019), expressed in language. One could argue that Habermas's "public sphere" is the necessary expression of the public dimension of private property, which is the ostensible foundation of the bourgeois state. That is, the constitutional nature of property belies its "private" dimension and makes explicit the role of the state in its definition and enforcement. Liberal ideology views property as separate and independent of the state, even while the state is essential to authorize changing definitions and norms (Habermas 1989, 89–102).

There is a large literature regarding debates, such as whether property represents theft and coercion (Davis 2015; Malm 2016, 279–326) or freedom and the right to self-preservation and accumulation. There is a long-term history of property and its variable forms.

Even if the property is privately owned, its value depends on the market, which is comprised of a larger public of "rational" individuals. Rather than being "free," property is based on the right to exclusion. It is continually being exchanged and evaluated, influenced by current economic forces and fluctuations. The owners' individual efforts to expand the value of his property is constantly subject to these external or "public" influences.

The notion of property has a connotation of permanence and solidity. Yet the definition itself has been in continual flux. In recent times, the position of an individual parcel with respect to global climate represents a new source of uncertainty, as discussed below.

4.3 From Commons to Factory and Household

The peasant mode of production had the household and the juridical authority in the same location, within the feudal form (Piketty 2020). In this period, there was no separation of state from market, or public from private. With the rise of long-distance trade and production for the market, there was a separate organization of merchants called the "putting out system," to avoid guild restrictions, and then the separation of the factory under the ownership of the entrepreneur, distinct from the household. The private business corporation was differentiated from the guild and from the merchant monopoly corporation by the contingent relation to labor. Rather than members, workers became employees with limited rights and were forced to compete in labor markets with separate laws. Separated from the land and the guild, the private household became more mobile, with less secure access to means of subsistence. These two "private spheres" (Pateman 1988) both involve direct control of labor and secrecy regarding methods of production and relation, or "privacy" (McKeon 2005). The firm and the household are both under the direct control of the individual "owner" or *bourgeois* (Habermas 1989, 28, 43–44, 46–47), producing the "private" commodity for the market and the potential private commodity labor power. The quantity and quality of both of these private "commodities" affect the pace and profit of production, which is a public matter (Commons 1995). Children have been considered a "public good" (Folbre 2008), and the personality and orientation of each generation, or "consciousness," affects the operation of the system overall (O'Kane 2021). Personality has been considered the product of cultural forms like property, such as in Hegel's writings.

In capitalism, there is a cash nexus association with regard to the household (Folbre, 1994). Population is a resource for production, the source of surplus, and also a burden on the wage earner and the state. In contrast to slavery, the institution of the wage labor force rescues the firm from most responsibility for reproduction of the labor force (Weber 1968, 161–164), while creating burdens for the state, and the "unpaid labor" of the household organized by gender.

Notions of the factory and the household are apparently unchanging. There is, nonetheless, a long-term history of the factory and the household which varies by period and by geography. The multiplication of "private spaces," like homes and cars, then covers the landscape, but connects each unit by means of mass and social media and financial circuits. Suburban homes have "picture windows" to increase visibility and image, to meet status expectations (Veblen 1934).

4.4 Self/Social

The security and independence of independent private property is necessary for the personal development of the bourgeoisie, according to Habermas (Habermas 1989, 43–51). The realm of freedom was distinguished from the realm in necessity in ancient Greek philosophy (Habermas 1989, 2–5).

The modern self is often understood to be the foundation of the polity, an original unique human being formed in the image of God. Alternatively, the self is viewed as a type of subjectivity formed by discipline (O'Kane 2021), or whose personality is formed by the ownership relation.

Whether the individual is self-sufficient and "separative", without relying on social relationships, is another debate, vs. reliant on social relations for psychic well-being and personality development (Davis 2020).

The juridical individual is a "legal person" (Habermas 1985, 358), which can include private business corporations.

4.5 Public Opinion/Private Interests

The formation of the modern state depends on the informed involved public sphere, according to Habermas, even when expressing "private" interests related to property. This rational public debate makes the operation of the public sphere more reliable and more representative of the public good.

The open access of the public sphere and its representation depends on the equality of *bourgeois* and *homme* and the opportunity for all persons to become property owners (Habermas 1989, 55–56, 87–88, 124–126, 160–162).

In modern industrial economies, there is an important role of political parties in "will formation" by means of public debate (Habermas 1985, 344–346). In earlier periods, political parties expressed factions, like the Alberghi in Genoa and the Guelfs and Ghibellines in Florence, more based on families and clans and the appropriate role of the church, than rational deliberation. The role of political parties, the Whigs and the Tories, was significant in the ideas of money and credit, as well as the formation of the Bank of England (Wennerlind 2014; Wennerlind 2011, 172–189). There was a similar partisan dispute between the Federalists, led by Hamilton, and the Republicans, led by Jefferson, in the formation of the Bank of the United States. In the postwar period in the United States and Europe, the model was liberal democracy combined with a capitalist economy. The political parties formed during that period were based on the degree to which the market was "free" or regulated, with some movement around the center. After the Great Financial Crisis of 2008 (see chapter 4 above), there was a tendency for anti-system politics, challenging this general consensus by all parties (Hopkin 2020, 50–58). Politics became more characterized by polarization and more extreme views.

The role of media in political formation, and party alliances, is mentioned by Habermas, although he primarily focuses on "information" rather than means of persuasion. Is information more important, for the formulation of positions and recommendations, for the formation of alliances and political parties? Can information be objective, according the standard of journalists, or always particular and performative? Can speech be "free" or necessarily censored and circumscribed to maintain legitimating narratives? Is information and communication both prescriptive and descriptive and so constitutes the subject (Brewer 1995, 17–18)? (Fig. 5.5)

Was the public sphere rational, informed, and independent, or always already suffused with property and financial interests? The coffee shops to which Habermas

Private	Public sphere	State
Firm (bourgeois)	Critical free press	Public officials
Household (homme)	Informed electorate (citoyen)	Bureaucracy

Fig. 5.5 Adopted from Habermas (1989), 30

refers were populated by investors in state and corporate debt, providing liquidity for financial markets (Habermas 1989, 32–33). Their information was related to commercial trends, and the state's efforts to expand the wealth and power of the nation, as well as partisan propaganda (Wennerlind 2011, 169–172). This "bourgeois" component to the public sphere may not have been the ideal foundation for rational public "deliberation" and "communicative action" so celebrated by Habermas.

Does Habermas accept "individualization" (Habermas 1985, 362) and system differentiation (Habermas 1985, 339) as benefits of capitalist modernity, without critique? By contrast, Polanyi (1944) sees individuation as a form of power and discipline.

Habermas analyzes the "real abstractions," building on the Marxian literature, due to the monetization of labor as a commodity (Habermas 1985, 336, 374–375, 378, 402). That is, after the Enclosure Movement, the displaced serfs must work for a wage, becoming part of the mobile labor force. Without a permanent access to land for subsistence, there is a forced mobility and search for access to land for rent or for purchase. Without a regular wage, there is need for credit. That is, with the formation of the labor market and the "steering medium" of the money wage, the major institutions were reorganized.

Habermas may have not realized the similar foundations of such abstractions in the land and credit markets, as well as labor markets. In each case, abstract entities are a key feature of the modern institutions, with authority enforced by the state and interpreted by experts (Davis 2015). These abstract entities represent material objects and concrete outcomes, influenced by norms and rules which affect behavior:

1. Labor market (Polanyi 1944)
2. Land market (Pistor 2019)
3. Credit markets (Wennerlind 2011; Wennerlind 2014; Neal and Williamson 2015)

In each case, the concrete, "real" entity, human labor, a parcel of land, or a promise to repay in the future, is part of a meaning/symbol system. The "lifeworld," in Habermas's term, is restructured in a new language which is socially recognized, with implicit norms and values. These meanings are "intersubjective" and enforced by institutions which channel and reward behavior. As a result, there are new institutions, as well as laws and administrative regulations.

In the labor market, Habermas sees workers as acting in an "objectivating attitude to each other and to themselves," rather than coordinated in terms of norms and values, or to reach mutual understanding. In such a context, "communal and individual life become reified" (Habermas 1985, 336). In such a context, social scientists shift perspective from participant to observer (Habermas 1985, 153, 185, 374). In this context, human actions are oriented to "steering media," like money and bureaucracy, which can be analyzed by system theorists. This shift in orientation of social scientists matches that of the workers, who objectify themselves as commodities, to "make a living," by means of wage labor.

These three abstractions match Polanyi's three "fictional commodities," land, labor, and money. In each case, the production of each of these so-called commodities was not for the purpose for sale for profit, which is typical of market commodities. Rather, these three fictional commodities are constructed by social meanings, temporary in the case of labor, but with real effects. Polanyi sees the abstract entities as enforced by the state and understood as "laissez faire" or the "liberal creed" by theorists (Polanyi 1944).

5 New Institutions

With the formation of new "steering media" of the money and markets, and the state, there is a new set of interlocking institutions founded. Habermas stresses the rationality of the "independent" property owner, without due consideration for the coercion for the worker and the insecure mobile household. With the differentiation of the roles of capital and labor, there is a new potential for factions, and an important role for unifying ideologies, such as the pursuit of the "wealth of nations."

5.1 Public Goods

The definition of "public goods" has always been contested in a state dedicated to wealth and power. According to Adam Smith, investments in infrastructure and education aided commerce, and defense aided territorial integrity and expansion. Forms of the state which included mass democracy and the welfare provided relief and legitimacy (Habermas 1985, 356–373), but were subject to reduction and retrenchment in periods of political or economic crises. Law as a form of power requires legitimation itself (Habermas 1985, 365–367). The definition of public goods is influenced by the type of governance (Tanimoto and Wong 2019) and has provided the basis for a literature on "varieties of capitalism."

Adam Smith emphasized the importance of public education for workers, as a means of increasing productivity and quality of life. Philanthropists have notably donated to public parks, libraries, museums, and conservation areas, to help edify the public. Public health has been one of the more significant improvements in quality of life, with sanitation and innovations in health care (Gordon 2017). The various efforts, and political positions, on vaccines and mask mandates have complicated efforts with respect to the global COVID-19 pandemic of 2020–2022 (Tooze 2021).

5.2 Private Parcel of Land/Global Ecology

In the modern state, the right to own land as individual private property (Pistor 2019) is considered a basic right and privilege, compared with the relationship to the global ecology. The modern liberal state, based upon freedom of property, has difficulty regulating property and its relation to ecology, even with evidence of increasingly extreme impacts of climate change.

5.3 Energy

Energy is defined abstractly as the "ability to do work" per unit of time (Prentiss 2015, 27–28). It is not clear from this term, as defined, that the perspective involved is human, the ultimate judge of useful work, and without regard to environmental limits or implications. Rather, the mobilization of energy is considered the outcome of technological "progress," from an abstract standpoint. There is no location on earth, no relation to earth's energy balance, or any distinction between chemical, atomic, kinetic, electrical, cellular, animal, or human energy, in this definition.

In the context of capitalist production, "energy" can be the means of replacing and disciplining labor. The notion of "power" is not as carefully specified as energy, although common to physics and to sociology, with little notice by its practitioners and little connections across divergent contexts (Malm 2016, 18–19). The "fetish" of steam power enabled the factory owner to gain increasing control over the pace and organization of production (Malm 2016, 194–222), even while destabilizing the climate of the earth.

5.4 Public Media

Commercialized mass media tend to undermine the rationality and legitimacy of the public sphere (Habermas 1989). The "transformation" noted by Habermas has proceeded in intensity, with new means of persuasion, and larger, more integrated social media platforms, as well as print and broadcast (Zuboff 2019). Information provided to markets can be intended to influence expectations, a form of reflexivity, rather than simply sharing data (Davis 2015, 148–149).

5.5 Time

Rather than seasonal time as a guide to agricultural work organization, there is a notion of universal homogeneous time, which is represented in capital markets (Postone 1993). This uniform standard time serves to discipline both labor and capital markets and to provide the foundation for a universal competition among nations and peoples.

5.6 Science

After the formation of the Royal Society in England, the community of science was differentiated from the lay public, with special entry requirements, norms, and privileges. In the contemporary period, science organizations are usually public and nonprofit, such as based in a university or research institute, or private as part of corporate research and development. In either case, basic research is often supported by the state to achieve economic competitiveness and commercialization.

5.7 Church

With the separation of church and state, religion has become a separate institution, rather than a unifying force for a whole society (Habermas 1985). There are norms of pluralism and tolerance in modern secular societies. The formation of clerical organizations as nonprofits must meet certain criteria.

5.8 *Family*

Like the labor relation, the family is represented by a legal contract, in this case the marriage contract (Pateman 1988). This is the method of integrating pair-bonding and kinship into the modern institutions based on property, with historically varying marriage and inheritance rules (Howell 2010).

5.9 *Corporations*

The notion of a unified body of individual persons acting as a unit has a long history (Davis 2019). The chartered merchant monopoly corporations were essential in the formation of global trade and colonies (Harris 2020). The modern private business corporations can operate as both public and private, with rights to representation as a legal individual, as well as protection of private property. This duality represents one of the contradictions of the public/private divide.

6 Ambiguities, Reversals, and Contradictions of Public/Private Divide

According to Smith, there is an internalized "impartial spectator," which can judge each person with respect to potential market values, such as "human capital". This awareness of the viewer creates an image of oneself internal to each person and can be a source of norms or prescriptive behavior. In this way, norms presented in mass media can influence one's self-image and behavior. While each person may seek to view herself "objectively," the capitalist worldview tends to focus on potential market power of each personal characteristic.

Personal expression tends to suffer when there is a shift from the reading/debating public to the consumer public, influenced by advertising and commercial media (Habermas 1989, 159–175, 181–195).

Brewer (1995) points out that the private self often behaves with the view in mind of the observer, which can be represented in media of various types, such as epistolary, print, radio, and video. The reputation and status of each person is also affected by the possession and display of luxury goods (Veblen 1994). The proliferation of images of the person in print, mass media, and social media belies the distinction of public and private, since these images, while presumably private, can affect market behavior and political expression (Zuboff 2019).

What are often considered separate institutions are nonetheless related to the reproduction of the whole. The institutional and conceptual separations prevent an awareness of the interconnections of the whole. Capital is a set of relationships, but appears to be a thing, an object, which makes awareness and critique more difficult. Because of the normative behavior expected in each separate institution, "people within the capital relation are dominated by abstractions they collectively produce" (O'Kane 2020, 268) by their own behavior.

Because of the division of labor by skill and by class, the social whole is divided against itself, a form of "autophagy" (Davis 2020, 85–106). The instrumental use of humans, as either producers or consumers, distorts awareness of the whole and the development of integrated capacities. Political divisions result, which compromise the potential for self-governance, the ultimate promise of classical democracy.

Ultimately, there is a contest between human rights or property rights, or *homme* or *bourgeois*, in Habermas's terms, in the definitions of suffrage and political voice. Habermas tends not to analyze the respective positions of *femme* or *proletarian* and the relevant inequalities in the two private spheres.

The public sphere, the formal representation of the population, and free expression of public opinion are important as legitimation devices (Habermas 1975). The public/private divide can still authorize two legitimate but contrasting political positions: a "protection of property" dimension, in contrast with a promotion of "equal access" dimension, leading to political gridlock.

Would the demands of ecological preservation and the ethical implications of the Anthropocene conflict with a form of governance based on individual private property?

The commitment to democracy seems to be wavering in the face of a global resurgence of populism in the wake of the financial crisis of 2008, the COVID-19 pandemic, and the accelerating impact of climate change (Muller 2016; Levitsky and Ziblatt 2018; Hopkin 2020).

Capitalism and democracy are inconsistent, creating tensions (Bowles and Gintis 1986; Habermas 1985, 345–346). If capitalism truly divides the population and restricts the personal development of certain categories, then the promise of democracy can never be met. The compromise between property rights and human rights tends to unravel when there are serious threats to economic growth.

Bibliography

Bonefeld, Werner. "On Capital as Real Abstraction," in Antonio Oliva, Angel Oliva, and Ivan Novara (eds.). *Marx and Contemporary Critical Theory: The Philosophy of Real Abstraction*. New York: Palgrave MacMillan, 2020, 153-170.

Bowles, Samuel and Herbert Gintis. *Democracy and Capitalism: Property, Community and the Contradictions of Modern Society Thought*. New York: Basic Books, 1986.

Brewer, John D. "This, That and the Other: Public, Social and Private in the Seventeenth and Eighteenth Centuries." Dario Castiglione and Lesley Sharpe (eds.). *Shifting the Boundaries: Transformation of the Languages of Public and Private in the Eighteenth Century*. Exeter: University of Exeter Press, 1995, 1-21.

Commons, John R. *Legal Foundations of Capitalism*. New Brunswick, NJ: Transaction Publishers, 1995.

Connolly, William E. *Climate Machines Fascist Drives and Truth*. Durham: Duke University Press, 2019.

Davis, Ann E. "Is there a History of Property? Periodization of Property Regimes and Paradigms," in Staci M. Zavattaro, Gregory R. Peterson, and Ann E. Davis (eds.). Property Rights in Contemporary Governance. Albany: SUNY Press, 2019, 5–24.

Davis, Ann E. *The End of Individualism and the Economy: Emerging Paradigms of Connection and Community*. New York: Routledge, 2020.

Davis, Ann E. Davis. *The Evolution of the Property Relation: Understanding Paradigms, Debates, Prospects*. New York: Palgrave MacMillan, 2015.

Davis, Ann E. *Money as a Social Institution: The Institutional Development of Capitalism*. New York: Routledge, 2017.

Folbre, Nancy. *Who Pays for the Kids? Gender and the Structures of Constraint*. New York: Routledge, 1994.

Folbre, Nancy. *Valuing Children: Rethinking the Economics of the Family*. Cambridge, MA: Harvard University Press, 2008.

Gal, Susan. "A Semiotics of the Public/Private Division." In Joan W. Scott and Debra Keates (eds.) *Going Public: Feminism and the Shifting Boundaries of the Private Sphere*." Urbana: University of Illinois Press, 2004, 261-277.

Gordon, Robert J. *The Rise and Fall of American Growth: The US Standard of Living Since the Civil War*. Princeton, NJ: Princeton University Press, 2017.

Gordon, Robert W. "Paradoxical Property" in John Brewer and Susan Staves (eds.). Early Modern conceptions of Property. New York: Routledge, 1996, 95-110.

Habermas, Jurgen. *Legitimation Crisis*. Boston: Beacon Press, 1975.

Habermas, Jurgen. *The Theory of Communicative Action: Lifeworld and System: A Critique of Functionalist Reason*. Volume 2. Boston: Beacon Press, 1985.

Habermas, Jurgen. *The Structural Transformation of the Public Sphere: An Inquiry into a Category of Bourgeois Society*. Cambridge, MA: MIT Press, 1989.

Harris, Ron. *Going the Distance: Eurasian Trade and the Rise of the Business Corporation, 1400-1700*. Princeton, NJ: Princeton University Press, 2020.

Hopkin, Jonathan. *Anti-System Politics: The Crisis of Market Liberalism in Rich Democracies*. New York: Oxford University Press, 2020.

Howell, Martha C. *Commerce Before Capitalism in Europe, 1300-1600*. New York: Cambridge University Press, 2010.

Kantorowicz, Ernst H. *The King's Two Bodies: A Study in Medieval Political Theology*. Princeton, NJ: Princeton University Press, 1957.

Levitsky, Steven and Daniel Ziblatt. *How Democracies Die*. New York: Crown, 2018.

Malm, Andreas. *Fossil Capital: The Rise of Steam Power and the Roots of Global Warming*. New York: Verso, 2016.

McKeon, Michael. *The Secret History of Domesticity: Public, Private, and the Division of Knowledge*. Baltimore: Johns Hopkins University Press, 2005.

Muller, Jan-Werner. *What is Populism?* Philadelphia: University of Pennsylvania Press, 2016.

Neal, Larry and Jeffrey G. Williamson (eds.). *The Cambridge History of Capitalism*. Volume I: The Rise of Capitalism: From Ancient Origins to 1848. Volume II: The Spread of Capitalism: From 1848 to the Present. Cambridge, UK: Cambridge University Press, 2015.

O'Kane, Chris. "The Critique of Real Abstraction: From the Critical Theory of Society to the Critique of Political Economy and Back Again," in Antonio Oliva, Angel Oliva, and Ivan Novara (eds.). *Marx and Contemporary Critical Theory: The Philosophy of Real Abstraction*. New York: Palgrave MacMillan, 2020, 265-287.

O'Kane, Chris. "Reification and the Critical Theory of Contemporary Society," *Critical Historical Studies*, Vol. 8, No. 1, Spring, 2021, 57-86.

Pateman, Carole. *The Sexual Contract*. Stanford, CA: Stanford University Press, 1988.

Piketty, Thomas. *Capital and Ideology*. Cambridge, MA: Harvard University Press, 2020.

Pistor, Katharina. *The Code of Capital: How the Law Creates Wealth and Inequality*. Princeton, NJ: Princeton University Press, 2019.

Polanyi, Karl. *The Great Transformation*. Boston: Beacon Press, 1944.

Postone, Moishe. *Time, Labor, and Social Domination: A Reinterpretation of Marx's Critical Theory*. Cambridge, UK: Cambridge University Press, 1993.

Poovey, Mary. *Making a Social Body: British Cultural Formation, 1830-1864*. Chicago: University of Chicago Press, 1995.

Poovey, Mary. "The Liberal Civil Subject and the Social in Eighteenth-Century British moral Philosophy," *Public Culture*, Vol. 14, No. 1, 125-145, 2002.

Prentiss, Mara. *The Energy Revolution: The Physics and the Promise of Efficient Technology*. Cambridge, MA: Harvard University Press, 2015.

Scott, Joan W. "Feminist Family Politics." In Joan W. Scott and Debra Keates (eds.) *Going Public: Feminism and the Shifting Boundaries of the Private Sphere*. Urbana: University of Illinois Press, 2004, 225-237.

Shovlin, John. *Trading with the Enemy*. New Haven: Yale University Press, 2021.

Tanimoto, Masayuki and R. Bin Wong (eds.). *Public Goods Provision in the Early Modern Economy*. Oakland: University of California Press, 2019.

Tooze, J. Adam. *Crashed: How a Decade of Financial Crises Changed the World*. New York: Penguin, 2018.

Tooze, J. Adam. *Shutdown: How Covid Shook the World's Economy*. New York: Viking, 2021.

Veblen, Thorstein. *The Theory of the Leisure Class: An Economic Study of Institutions*. New York: Modern Library, 1934.

Weber, Max. *Economy and Society: An Outline of Interpretive Sociology*. Volume I. Berkeley, CA: University of California Press, 1968.

Wennerlind, Carl. *Casualties of Credit: The English Financial Revolution, 1620-1720*. Cambridge, MA: Harvard University Press, 2011.

Wennerlind, Carl. "Money: Hartlibian Political Economy and the New Culture of Credit" in Philip J. Stern and Carl Wennerlind (eds.). *Mercantilism Reimagined: Political Economy in Early Modern Britain and Its Empire*. New York: Oxford University Press, 2014, 74-93.

Zuboff, Shoshana. *Surveillance Capitalism: The Fight for a Human Future at the New Frontier of Power*. New York: Public Affairs, 2019.

Chapter 6
Abstraction and Reification

1 Historical Institutional Methodology

There have been many accounts of the tendency for abstraction in capitalism (Sohn-Rethel 1978; Poovey 1995, 1998, 2002, 2008; Davis 2017; Patel and Moore 2017, 47–63).

Whether "abstractions" can have "real effects" is an issue of intense debate. Words seem to be ephemeral, to provide only fodder for the imagination, or "fiction." Recent contributions to linguistic theories provide mechanisms for words to matter concretely in coordinating human behavior, nonetheless. Key statements from authoritative persons can create institutions which perform functions (Searle 2010). These "illocutionary" statements both describe and create a real effect. Listeners perform a function by their coordinated actions. This process can account for the evolution of institutions in the modern era (Davis 2015, 28–30).

Earlier institutions were based on symbols which helped form cohesive societies involving ritual practice. The role of holy scriptures performed a similar function in early monotheistic religions like Islam and Judaism, with collective reading and chanting. The role of the church in authorizing the monarch was central in the early modern period. With the rise of secular knowledge, the role of consent and political process, including speaking and debate, performed an essential role in the formation of modern institutions, like the fiscal/military state (Brewer 1990). These institutions performed the function of legitimation, in the process of active participation and deliberation, and the subsequent formalization of authorized action in decrees and laws. The evolution of law and the role of the legal profession is the subject of ongoing debate, regarding its natural origins, rationality, progressive direction, or legitimation of power (Banner 2021; Gordon 2017; Tomlins 2016).

The description of the market may be another example of an abstraction, where a certain term describes behavior that becomes habitual and normative. The writing of Adam Smith described the operation of a market economy before it was fully

A. E. Davis, *Whole Earth*, https://doi.org/10.1007/978-3-031-01934-0_6

operational. The presentation of the market as a system helped structure relationships that were only emerging at the time. This development of the concept, and the enumeration of its effects, helped to propagate the notion of the market as a self-regulating mechanism useful in governance (Poovey 1998, 15, 236–248; Poovey 2008, 139–144). Adam Smith's abstractions, like the "invisible hand," were capable of agency, without apparent human volition, like other modern abstractions (Poovey 2002; Vogl 2015, 23–33; Bonefeld 2020, 160–164). In this way, the economy can operate as an automatic system (Polanyi 1944), which can "steer" the human behavior, even while celebrating personal freedom.

Based on these elements, I am proposing here a theory of historical institutional evolution, which overcomes the dichotomies of self/other, individual/social, ideal/material, and structure/process, as developed in earlier work. Language forms the "social synthesis" (Sohn-Rethel 1978) by means of abstract categories which have meaning in capitalism, like property, money, and commodity. These terms are the foundation of laws and practices, as well as formal expertise and authoritative interpretation in the context of disputes. As a result of such review and ongoing experience, the terms and institutional practice may change, resulting in a modification of the meaning. The process of "collective intentionality" (Searle 2010) describes such an iterative process of social and institutional change. The concepts of "commodification" and "proletarianization" drawing from Marx can provide a comprehensive worldview which can accommodate and incorporate these long-term changes in institutions, while providing some coherence and stability in the evolution of capitalism.

Capitalism forms a "totality" (Postone 1993) in a particular period and geography, a global system integrated by world finance. The "standpoint" is that of a "capitalist," a person who uses capital and labor to increase the monetary value of one's own property (Levy 2021). Every person in the system understands this set of incentives, like a form of cultural literacy, and positions oneself to "make a living" and to gain advantage. This view of the whole then shapes the "subjectivity" of every participant, in order to survive and to thrive in such a system. Smith's "impartial spectator" is always looking over her shoulder, imagining what each customer and competitor might be doing, and trying to develop strategies for self-advancement and security in that context.

Marxist theories of abstraction were based on the role of the labor process (Postone 1993; Davis 2017) and the experience of trade. Sohn-Rethel emphasizes the contradiction between exchange value and use value as contributing to an abstraction of the commodity. As Marx emphasized, exchange value is based on the quantity of socially necessary labor time in production, while the use value is the imagined utility derived from the commodity by the owner when it can be consumed in the private sphere after the purchase. Exchange value abstracts from the specific skills of labor and use value abstracts from the concrete traits of the commodity. A trading society like ancient Greece would encounter these strict divisions, which would contribute to the abstract form of reasoning, according to Sohn-Rethel. The "social synthesis" in such a society would come from the abstraction of the commodity form, with both aspects evident in different locations in different times. The tendency towards abstraction would enable Greek philosophers to develop concepts which provide "universal" knowledge which is not reliant upon workers, who were slaves in that period. The division between intellectual and manual labor would result, along with mathematics and geometry, which arose in the same period, along with coinage (Sohn-Rethel 1978, 58–67).

The relations of exchange are among humans, for whom language and symbols have meaning. "Money, then, acts as the concrete material bearer of the form of exchangeability of commodities" (Sohn-Rethel 1978, 44). In the context of trade, "time and space assume thereby that character of absolute historical timelessness and universality which must mark the exchange abstraction as a whole and each of its features" (Sohn-Rethel 1978, 49). A conceptual division between humans and nature also results from this abstraction (Sohn-Rethel 1978, 55–57, 70–74), since humans are viewing the entirety of the earth as potential commodities for exchange and for human use.

> The notion of nature as a physical object-world independent of man emerges from commodity production when it reaches its full growth of monetary economy…This conception of nature is rooted in history; it arises when social relations assume the impersonal and reified character of commodity exchange. (Sohn-Rethel 1978, 72)

There is a process of formation of a "second nature," strictly among humans, as if there were no essential interchange with nature in the processes of human life.

> The formal structure of commodity exchange constitutes the core of the second nature: the purely social, abstract, functional reality which I earlier contrasted with primary nature where man exists on the same level as animals. Second nature finds its external expression in money….This occurs through the necessity for a social synthesis which is in total separation from any of the operations of man's material interchange with nature. (Sohn-Rethel 1978, 60)

With this separation of types of abstract cognition, the division of intellectual and manual labor became the basis for a class division, according to Sohn-Rethel. The developments in natural science were based on methods from experimentation and observation, which are not dependent on direct involvement in the work process. The independent intellectual labor can then design a labor process to reduce the reliance on direct manual labor and so increase labor productivity. The knowledge of the worker can then be extracted and become the basis for innovation, as well as education in formal institutions, unrelated to guilds or unions. The innovations of "scientific management" initiated by Frederick Winslow Taylor paved the way for a new discipline of management (Sohn-Rethel 1978, 147–163), which developed in universities to train executives, reinforcing the hierarchy of mental over manual labor.

The emphasis on mechanization, production of machines by machines (Marx 1967), information technology and automation, culminating in artificial intelligence, can be viewed as a continuing trend of substitution of capital for labor and deskilling. What Poster (1984) calls the "mode of information" is made possible by this extension of the replacement of direct labor in production, complete with information technology firms which pervade social relations, such as "social media" giants Facebook, Amazon, and Google (Zuboff 2019). Natural science has been applied to the development of new methods of production, new types of products, along with innovations in psychology aimed at managing human relations at the workplace, and marketing.

Habermas's notion of "steering media" can be explained by the role of money in capitalist economics (Milios 2020). The abstraction which results in the designation of a specific commodity as representing the exchange value of all commodities occurred over time, a form of institutional evolution discussed in Vol. I of *Capital* (Marx 1967). The priority of this specific money commodity was related to its role in accumulation of wealth and power for competing European nations and the emerging class of merchants who were skilled in the requirements of accounting, credit, and the expansion of wealth. The role of bureaucracy emerged in the development of the state after feudalism, with the replacement of tax collections by formal bureaucracy instead of the sale of offices (Brewer 1990), and the organization of the standing army instead of merchant monopoly corporations authorized to use force. That is, the "steering media" identified by Habermas, money and bureaucracy, were the result of long-term institutional evolution, which then further shaped the subsequent development of those institutions. That is, the abstract notion of "steering media" can be specifically located in the history of the human institutions of the market and the state, rather than reified abstractions which seem to have agency.

2 Long-Term Evolution of Institutions

The approach of historical institutionalism would study the development of abstractions like property and money, and the associated evolution of institutions, in order to retain the awareness that these institutions are human, in spite of their appearance otherwise. That is, "reifying abstractions" are assumed to have agency themselves.

One role of key terms like money and property is that the system appears to have stable foundations, even as the meanings of the pillars change. For example, money and property are the foundation of institutions that have themselves changed historically (Banner 2011). Institutions can evolve significantly, even while supporting actions which have normative support.

The role of law may provide a useful example. The statements of authoritative laws, resulting from consultation and interpretation, then have a type of standing and respect. Law may have a special relationship to society, a "systemization of social relations" (Gordon 2017, 18). Law can be defended as the ultimate expression of rationality of a self-governing state, with informed deliberation on collective rules. There is the question, nonetheless, of the origin of law. Does the role of law result from conjectural history or from Enlightenment reason? Was the "ancient constitution" of English history an invention by lawyers, claiming special status for the "liberty" of the English (Gordon 2017, 6–7; Pocock 1975)? The test of history is one method of claiming a "transcendent standpoint" necessary for claims to authority (Gordon 2017, 308).

Historians of ancient law, such as Henry Sumner Maine, have discussed stages of development, from code to custom, and from status to contract (Maine 1917, 179–215). He makes note of the concept of "legal fiction," where the operation of the law has been changed even while the letter has not been altered, in the example of adoption. That is, the relationship of kinship is adjusted by law, to make a person a relative in the same way as biological kinship, although with complete knowledge that this is a social arrangement agreed to among the parties involved (Maine 1917, 15–18).

Another example of a "legal fiction" is the notion of the corporation, a group of individuals who can act as a single person (Maitland 2003; Searle 2010; Harris 2020, 251–274), with perpetual life, irrespective of the changing membership of the group. That is, the concept of the corporation enables a group of human persons to have a single "legal personality," recognized by law with privileges and powers. In this way, a legal concept can enable certain types of coordinated behavior which would not otherwise be possible. The long-term evolution of the corporate form and its advantages may account for the "rise of the West" and the "organizational revolution" after 1600 (Harris 2020, 252–255).

Karl Polanyi (1944) notes that there are three "fictional commodities" in market economies, land, labor, and money. That is, these three resources for market were not produced as commodities for profit for sale; yet they are treated and behave as though they were commodities. With the rise of the market economy, Poovey notes the rise of new genres of writing. The fact/fiction continuum did not exist until there was a need to differentiate "true" money from imaginative fiction. She argues that money is a type of writing which seems to have unusual powers, but is maintained as "true" with respect to purchasing power and payment of debt enforced by the state. The new genre of political economy can seem like pure fiction, as well, creating imaginative beings with unusual behavior, like self-regulating markets and "invisible hands." Yet political economy became a formal discipline and the subject of study in universities. The "problematic of representation" remains an issue, nonetheless, when money loses confidence of the populace and needs to be enforced by the state (Poovey 2008).

3 Property

Property is another example of a "real abstraction," a specific term with varying meanings historically, which is a fundamental pillar of governance and a guide to specific types of behavior (Davis 2015). Blackstone's image of property as "individual absolute dominion" has been a "central trope" of public discourse (Gordon 1996, 95). In spite of challenges by legal realists at the turn of the twentieth century, this notion remains popular, which serves "to suppress and to deny the collective and collaborative elements" of law and the economy (Gordon 1996, 108). Lawyers understand that property is an abstraction, not a thing, but rights or relationships among people with respect to things (Banner 2011, 45). There is a "bundle of rights" that are involved in the conception of property, which historically began to include expectations of financial return, which could be guaranteed by the courts (Banner 2011, 69).

There is debate within the Marxist literature with respect to whether property is involved with the material "base" of the economy, or with the ideological "superstructure." According to Gordon, "it is just about impossible to describe any set of 'basic' social practices without describing the legal relations among the people involved" (Gordon 2017, 262). For example, whether a person is a slave or a stockholder or a worker can have dramatic impacts on the person's rights and access to legal recourse. The importance of key categories of gender, race, place of birth, citizenship status, ethnicity, and even religion is increasingly relevant because of this implicit legal institutional infrastructure, in my view. There is a long and variable history of labor law, for example, with changing rights to organization and minimum wages and standards (Stone 2009). These changes and the associated debates have had a significant effect on the varieties of capitalism and the various trajectories of economic growth, as well as the normative consensus in the economics profession and the legal profession. In spite of its claim to neutrality and objectivity, the legal profession itself has undergone significant variations based on certain regimes, or "paradigms" (Gordon 2017, 110–134). While Gordon provides a critique of the view of law as "evolutionary-functionalist," Tomlins (2016) argues for an integral relationship between capitalism and law.

> To think of law structurally is to imagine a language of consequence that produces effects. In a capitalist society the effects it produces are manifestations of a system of action called capitalism that exists independently of law but is knowable only though the operations of law. (Tomlins 2016)

Recent work has recalled the analysis of Marxist literature that law is an ideological apparatus (Glass 2021, 333, 340).

4 Gender

Gender is another category of describing and prescribing the position of persons who have a set of certain biological criteria relative to human reproduction. There are a variety of methods for analyzing gender (Scott 1986). The salience of gender as a social category has varied historically. The roles of women have changed along with the structure of the household, which has been affected by the organization of work and varieties of land tenure. In a peasant subsistence economy, the household is defined by rights to the land, as in medieval serfdom. In a guild economy, the household could include apprentices as well as biological kin (Surkis 2021, 351). With the Enclosure Movement and the development of the market for land, the role of women in agriculture was restricted (Valenze 1995). The household became more mobile with the extension of the labor market, and the size was restricted to biological relatives in the "nuclear" family. The norm of the "family wage" was intended to support the factory worker and his dependent spouse and children, who need not be employed in the wage labor force themselves (Fraser 2013; Cooper 2017), even though that norm did not routinely apply to working class households. As standard of living improved in advanced capitalist countries, the consumer market developed as a status marker. After the Great Depression, private, single-family housing was used as an economic stimulus, and the house itself was a marker of status. To expand the size of the house and the lot, suburbanization increased the relevant status differential and tended to stratify neighborhoods by race and class, which would also affect schooling, social networks, and employment opportunities. The separation of home from work with the rise of factory production tended to increase the salience of gender, along with certain ideals such as the Victorian "angel of the house" (Poovey 1995). Although women were part of the wage labor force from its earliest emergence, the normative gender division of labor facilitated the characterization of the factory workforce as male.

As women were increasingly understood as part of the "private sphere," the notion of spheres can be further explored. In fact, the entire distinction of public and private law can be understood in contrast to the "private" household and family and the associated binaries (Surkis 2021, 348). There is an abstraction of space which accompanies the development of capitalism (Poovey 1995, 9, 15, 27–31). For example, the factory is a space separate from the household, owned and controlled by the owner. This space of the factory is physical, with boundaries, walls, and gates, and is also represented in law as the rights of the owner to his property. Similarly, the household is a physical space, with the size and architectural features varying historically, but it is also represented as the "private sphere" of the household, separated from government. It is here that different norms can be manifested, whether special treatment of children or maintenance of patriarchal authority. The independence of women in the household has varied with marriage law, and the rights to married women's property, as well as women's opportunities for education and wage labor. There is also a racial dimension to the household, from slave plantations (Cheney 2017), to the legal relation of marriage (Surkis 2021, 352–353), to "white flight" in the suburbs (Keil 2018). To the extent that the separation of home and work has been naturalized, as private space for families and intimate personal relations, suburbs have transformed the landscape, and other "private" spaces have proliferated, such as cars, trucks, and sports utility vehicles. In this way, the separate spheres have actual geographical manifestations, as well as abstract norms which shape the house by period, its style, size, and other features. The "Malthusian family" exerts a discipline on family size (Foucault 1978, 100, 105), to have only the number of children which can be supported by the wage earners, without resort to social welfare, a form of moralization of sexuality (Cooper 2017; Surkis 2021, 358–359). The family is considered "dependent" on the wage earner or public welfare (Fraser 2013), instead of capitalism dependent on the reproduction of the population. For Foucault, sexuality is a form of power, managing the individual body and the population, to adjust both to the requirements of capitalism (Foucault 1978, 25, 140–141, 145–147). The true identity of each individual is related to sex (Foucault

1978, 69–70, 155–156), but there is no discussion of families and communities, what might be considered other forms of cohesive "social" relations.

Women's activism has included pressure for equal rights, feminism and socialism, as well as abolition of slavery, women's suffrage, and reproductive freedom (Valenze 2004). Women have also formed an important constituency for conservative values and protection of property (McGirr 2001).

The study of population has continued the legacy of Malthus, considering the limits of the earth, while only periodically studying the connection between household formation, sexuality, women's fertility, and access to contraception. While Reverend Malthus and Garrett Hardin presumed a continual increase in the human population, the "second demographic transition" may have been influenced by changing values related to modernity and to gender roles (Zaidi and Morgan 2017). Whether sexuality is the sign of "original sin" or the source of liberation continues to be debated (Bashford 2014; Bashford and Chaplin 2016). The notion of the limits of the earth has persisted in different periods, such as between the World Wars, and in the 1970s. Awareness of the "Anthropocene" has recently renewed attention to world population growth, while there is no consistent global policy towards women's empowerment and education, compared with religious imperatives prohibiting contraception and family planning.

5 The Power of Money: Credit and Finance

Money as a "real abstraction" may become more important as a result of institutional differentiation into separate "domains" (Poovey 1998, 5), like the public/private divide. Money then can serve as the "social synthesis," which links all of the separate domains together, like systems theory. Money can be portrayed as a neutral tool, a matter of convenience, even while it is the essential link among the component parts.

Money becomes more powerful for each component domain: (a) as corporations are subject to capital markets, instead of royal charter; (b) as households are reliant on money wages to survive, after enclosure and limits on social benefits; (c) as states must raise funds through taxes and bond issue to finance military to expand markets and territory, in competition with other states; and (d) as all three institutions, corporations, household, and states, rely on financial markets to manage perpetuation, rather than explicit human descendants and progeny. That is, institutional division and spatial separation makes the integration of money more essential, especially for a system with the goal of expansion of money.

Even while life is separated into fragments by time, space, and age, these divisions are naturalized. The corporation is the site of professional management and division of labor, instead of the guild with its mysteries. The household is the sphere of intimacy and freedom, rather than exclusion and isolation. States are the manifestations of rationality and debate, the highest achievements of humans, expression of rationality, and the Enlightenment.

6 Money and Credit

Money is an integrating device, or "social synthesis" (Sohn-Rethel 1978). I propose that "credit" is another term which is a "real abstraction." That is, credit is understood by participants as referring to the future, as relying on promises, based on current plans which may become unrealistic with changing circumstances. Given uncertainty regarding the borrower and the future conditions, decisions regarding credit are often based on analysis of probability and insured to protect against loss. The term credit is widely understood, supported by institutions such as banking and finance, and interpreted and enforced by law and government. That is, the term "credit" has meaning, not only by a common definition, but a set of behaviors which are expected and enforced. While the acceptance of the loan is voluntary, the repayment of the debt can be coercive (Wennerlind 2011).

There is a history of credit, as an evolving set of interlinked institutions. For example, the capital market evolved from early long-distance trade and the "commercial revolution" (Lopez 1971). City-states with active regular market participation, such as Florence, began to use the expected future outcome as a means to offer credit in the present. One example is the dowry fund (Molho 1971) which enabled the city to acquire funds in the present with a promise to pay a dowry in the future. This resource was useful for families who may otherwise lack the means of assuring proper marriage for their daughters. This is an early example of the way in which finance is intertwined with the normal life cycle.

Like the normal life cycle, a regular repeatable commodity circuit became the foundation of the early public debt. The global reach of financial circuits began with the exploration and long-distance trade of European powers. Genoese bankers helped to finance the global explorations and military conquests by Spain in the fifteenth and sixteenth centuries (Patel and Moore 2017, 74–81). Founded in the early seventeenth century, the chartered monopoly trading companies, the Dutch East India Company and the English East India Company, provided the model for colonies, long-distance trade of commodities, and trading of corporate stock (Moore 2015, 208; Marx 1967, Vol. I, Chap. 31, 751–752). The competition for markets and colonies among European powers provided a premium on public credit, to support shipping and defense.

The Bank of England was founded in 1694 to help manage the public debt (Davis 2017, 2020; Murphy 2019). The plan for the BOE was based on Whig notions of the potential for infinite wealth based on labor, as opposed to land (Pincus 2012; Acemoglu and Robinson 2012). The South Sea Company was chartered in 1711, so that government debt could be consolidated and traded for its shares. To make the South Sea stock attractive, the UK government awarded the South Sea Company the international monopoly on the slave trade, the Asiento de Negros, which had been acquired by the Treaty of Utrecht in 1714 (Moore 2020, 2; Price and Whatley 2020; Marx 1967, Vol. I, Chap. 31, 759; Wennerlind 2011, 197–234). Lord Treasurer Robert Harley established the South Sea Company to restore public credit, hiring the most able writers to promote the profitability of the slave trade, such as Daniel

Defoe (Habermas 1989, 59; Shovlin 2021, 99, 129). The genre of "fiction" emerged to enhance the real fiction of paper money (Poovey 2008).

> By tying the public debt to the profits from the Atlantic slave trade a closer mental association was forged between the urban milieu of London, the slave forts on the African coast, and the colonial towns of New Spain. This sophisticated time-space compression transferred value from the future to the present, from the sphere of commerce to public finance, and from the Atlantic world to the city of London….at the very center of English political and economic life. (Wennerlind 2011, 198–199)

The emergence of chartered monopoly corporations, like the English East India and the Dutch East India Companies in the early seventeenth century, had made stock markets attractive for safe investments in Amsterdam and in London (Vogl 2017, 67–92). With the formation of the South Sea Company and the John Law's Mississippi Company (Shovlin 2016) in the eighteenth century, the increasingly liquid financial markets enabled the trading of public debt and corporate stock among investors. The BOE was able to use the government gold stock, as well as public debt and corporate shares as backing for the issue of paper currency. The associated bubbles were managed by increased government regulation and backup (Levenson 2020), such as the Bubble Act in the United Kingdom. The association of the BOE with these secondary markets for public debt and corporate shares facilitated the financing of the UK debt, and the subsequent victory over France, and the consolidation of UK hegemony as a global empire.

The emergence of these sister corporations helped to support the "financial revolution" in England. Holders of the stocks need only be concerned with the movements of share prices, rather than the human cargo that was the subject of global slave trade, purchased with cowries from India (Hunt 2013, 37). This institutional and spatial separation enabled investors to focus only on safety and rate of return of the corporate stock, a form of blissful ignorance, while the first "factories" were on the coast of Africa to assemble slaves for the Middle Passage (Baucom 2020, 1). The term "credit fetishism" has been used by Wennerlind to suggest the abstraction from concern with the lack of agency of the slaves themselves, or "credit's general capacity to obfuscate its underlying social reality" (Wennerlind 2011, 199, 229–230).

> "The social imaginary of credit…is a form of unwilled or built-in blindness grounded in a particular understanding of the world" (Wennerlind 2011, 230).

The slave trade facilitated the expansion of the sugar plantation economy, from Madeira and Brazil and ultimately to the Caribbean and Louisiana (Follett 2016), enabling the expansion of the English shipping and development of export markets for its manufacturing (Mintz 1985). The expansion of scale facilitated the formation of plantations and the importation of slave labor, with the impact on the colonies with deforestation, soil erosion, and climate change as the result of intensive agricultural production (Moore 2000). Sugar plantations were perhaps another form of "modern factory" because of the necessary discipline, the reordering of the landscape, the use of expensive equipment, and the large-scale relocation of labor (Pomeranz and Topik 1999, 95).

> Slave ships landed more than 1.5 million African captives on British Caribbean islands...by the late 1700s and had brought more than 2 million to Brazil....while New England slave traders were responsible for 130,000 of the human beings shipped in the Middle Passage before 1800. (Baptist 2014, 4)

New England involvement in the triangular trade facilitated its surplus with the West Indies to finance its trade deficits with England. In the colonial period, New England exports of whale oil, lumber, and fish were exchanged for slaves and molasses, the latter for re-export as rum (Kimball 2016).

The fact that these slaves were also human beings led to forms of resistance historically and continuing in the present (Robinson 1983). Even after abolition and end of colonial regimes, the bars to migration and property ownership for the non-white populations left in place unequal or "dual" economies (Mintz 1985, 69–73), along with underdevelopment in former colonies (Pomeranz and Topik 1999, 95–96). Even after independence, colonies were forced to repay the costs of their independence through debt to the former imperial countries (Piketty 2020, 276–283).

Access to global finance enabled the early monopoly merchant corporations to reorganize the landscape, relocate populations, and produce global commodities for profit, returning increments of money to the original lenders and stockholders. This reorganization of land use, in particular, made land a factor of production, subject to the profit calculus, instead of species habitat, human abode, and access to means of subsistence, with sugar plantations an early model (Moore 2015, 59). What followed was a long series of such transformations across the globe (Moore 2015, 182–189), facilitating Europe's imperial expansion.

According to Moore, the definition of "modernity" relies on the concept of "human exceptionalism...[such that] humans are regarded as ontologically prior to the relations of nature" upon which they can act (Moore 2015, 77). According to Gilroy, the role of slavery in this emergence of world trade made blacks the world's first "truly modern people," connected to the revolution of modern finance (cited in Baucom 2020, 2). The colonial triangular trade was like the modern supply chain, producing commodities for consumption, the origin and impact of which are distant and obscure.

That is, credit is a "real abstraction," with a key term, along with associated institutional regularities, and authoritative expertise and enforcement. Credit involves imagination of the future, but relies on real commodity circuits (Menard 2006; Ghosh 2021). The Bank of England became a model for the United States, by means of Hamilton's erudite explorations. Mercantilism was articulated as a system and supported by policies such as the Navigation Acts (Wennerlind 2011; Zahedieh 2010). The fiscal/military nation-state (Brewer 1990) was established on this foundation of public credit. The possibility of credit changed the awareness of the public and willingness to speculate (Banner 2017) and was manifested in real trade routes, ships, colonies, plantations, and slavery.

7 Information and Media Technology

"Information" is another key term with associated institutions and expertise. In my view, "information" is also a "real abstraction," which omits the human dimensions of its meaning and associated behavior and actions. It is an abstraction with agency, like property and money, while typically disregarding the human users.

In the development of information theory, Claude Shannon abstracted from meaning, unlike Habermas's theory of communication. For Shannon, the key elements of information theory were the following (Gleick 2011, 217–231, 372, 416):

- The information source
- The transmitter
- The channel
- The receiver
- The destination

As a result of this definition, information theory could be applied to communication among humans, but also among machines, like computers and telephones.

Information is related to probability, since the information value describes content that was not already expected, like the statistical likelihood of certain letter combinations in a given language. Information is also related to entropy and the second law of thermodynamics, because information is a form of order and requires energy (Gleick 2011, 246–247, 272–281). "The body itself is an information processor" (Gleick 2011, 8) and information is physical (Gleick 2011, 279, 361–367).

> The universe, by existing, registers information [according to Seth Lloyd]. By evolving in time, it processes information. (Gleick 2011, 397)

In Gleick's discussion, he moves from tangible forms of communication and information like distant drumbeats to quantum computers, increasingly abstract. It is not clear whether he believes that this process of abstraction is "natural," a feature of the universe, or related to the structure of the human brain, or a function of the technological innovations of capitalism. For example, the invention and development of information theory and the computer were in the context of World War II and the massive effort to crack the German military code (Duguid 2021; Fara 2009, 332–338). The increasing speed and capacity of information technology also aids in the management of labor in the corporation, as well as global supply chains (Baldwin 2016) and financial trades. Information technology is capital saving as well as labor saving, with network externalities. That is, platform companies with massive investments in computer servers can serve millions of customers at zero marginal cost. These virtual platforms can replace the costs of physical "bricks and mortar" retail spaces, as well as cumulate information specific to each customer, providing a "big data" resource that is proprietary. Platform companies can also store and process sufficient quantities of information that approximates human intelligence, known as "artificial intelligence," and can observe and influence behavior (Zuboff 2019).

It is important to study a concept like "information" and to specify its uses in specific institutional contexts. For example, information can be synonymous with knowledge, referring to the historic accumulation of science and humanities (Burke 2021). Information can also mean "code" and computer software as well as DNA and genetic code. Information can also be protected as intellectual property (Banner 2011) or can be "free" to support any community of users, like Richard Stallman and the Free Software Foundation (Levy 1984, 415–436; Lessig 1999, 100–108). Information can be used to make economic decisions and can also be the product of the market system. Information can support speculation, placing bets on the future value of a financial asset and the rate of change of its prices (Banner 2017).

Was "information" always already present, or the result of progressive technological innovation and scientific innovation? Were the laws of physics "governing the world" before they were theorized by human scientists like Newton and Einstein? While historians (Blair et al. 2021) have compiled a broad, long-term history of information, it is clear that its meanings and uses have varied by periods. The "objective" perspective of modern science can be explained by the extraction and use of information for commerce, the military, and control, like cybernetics (Gleick 2011, 235–243), as one segment of the population managing another, instrumentally (Merchant 2020; Wennerlind 2014), without acknowledging these segmentations and divisions. The Internet also evolved from military applications and favored automation and less reliance on human intervention (Greenstein 2015, 26).

Consider the range of information technologies, including manuscript, print, mass media, social media, mobile personalized media, search, social networks, virtual reality, augmented reality, and avatars in the "metaverse." Does technology have its own dynamic, becoming increasingly abstract to facilitate machine processing and to reduce time? Automaticity is an ideal, from the "automaton" in the factory and the expansion of financial circuits (Marx 1967) to the "Internet of Things" (Boyes et al. 2018).

The privatization of the Internet may have led inadvertently to the further "transformation of the public sphere," as support for newspapers declined and financial support migrated to search sponsored by advertising on the Internet. The role of social media in potentially fostering extremism and political polarization is widely discussed.

8 Real Abstractions

The "real abstractions" of capitalism, such as money and property, take the form of knowledge, expertise, and institutions which manage life processes of the earth and the human population. Yet these real abstractions do not appear lifelike, but rather obscure the connection to living things. The "fiction" at the foundation of capitalism, that money is "real," maintains the notion that money is generative, creative, and can "grow." In fact, the "growth" that takes place in capitalism is entirely attributable to humans and living beings on the earth. This foundational fiction of capitalism, that money can grow, undergirds the requirement that knowledge take the form of abstractions, which appear to be real, and can be measured by quantities and empirical observation. These abstractions are maintained by forms of knowledge characteristic of capitalism, which provide the foundation of its continuity.

The tendency for abstraction in capitalism has been noted by Sohn-Rethel and Postone, related to the labor process and the process of exchange. This abstraction leads to new design in the workplace, to replace labor and to speed production, aiding throughput and increasing profit. The corporation was then subject to abstraction by means of the financial markets, and capital markets subsequently developed algorithms and models to perform in the context of financial abstractions. Human behavior can be modified and predicted, leading to more targeted advertising and sales efforts (Zuboff 2019). Political campaigns then make use of the same techniques of persuasion, rendering "democracy" subject to the whims of campaign finance and commercial media.

There is an inherent logic of capitalism which influences the direction of technology (Zuboff 2019, 15–16, 221–225), which changes behavior and social norms. As noted by Adam Smith in *The Wealth of Nations*, any owner of capital will use his stock to improve the productivity of labor (Smith 1994; Book II Introduction, 299–301; 309–312). The capitalist system has a systematic bias towards labor-saving technology, according to Postone's "treadmill." This tendency can be traced with institutional evolution of capitalism.

The "real abstractions" of capitalism are ideas, key terms, that have real effects on organizing, coordinating, and motivating human behavior. These particular abstractions, like property, gender, money, and information, provide functions to assist capitalism, by organizing human behavior in ways that appear as "natural." That is, ideas are integral to action, and difficult to separate, forming a complex interactive whole, like the software which operates the hardware in the computer which performs machine learning, which is tested over time based on its predictions of actual events, and then revised.

Bibliography

Acemoglu, Daron and James A. Robinson. *Why Nations Fail: The Origins of Power, Prosperity, and Poverty*. New York: Crown Publishers, 2012.

Baldwin, Richard. *The Great Convergence: Information Technology and the New Globalization*. Cambridge, MA: Harvard University Press, 2016.

Banner, Stuart. *American Property: A History of How, Why, and What We Own*. Cambridge, MA: Harvard University Press, 2011.

Banner, Stuart. *Speculation: A History of the Fine Line Between Gambling and Investing*. New York: Oxford University Press, 2017.

Banner, Stuart. *The Decline of Natural Law: How American Lawyers Once Used Natural Law and Why They Stopped*. New York: Oxford University Press, 2021.

Baptist, Edward E. *The Half Has Never Been Told: Slavery and the Making of American Capitalism*. New York: Basic Books, 2014.

Basch, Norma. *In the Eyes of the Law: Women, Marriage and Property in Nineteenth Century New York*. Ithaca: Cornell University Press, 1982.

Bashford, Alison. *Global Population: History, Geopolitics, and Life on Earth*. New York: Columbia University Press, 2014.

Bashford, Alison and Joyce E. Chaplin. *The New Worlds of Thomas Robert Malthus: Rereading the Principle of Population*. Princeton, NJ: Princeton University Press, 2016.

Baucom, Ian. *History 4 degrees Celsius: Search for a Method in the Ageof the Anthropocene*. Durham, North Carolina, Duke University Press, 2020.

Blair, Ann, Paul Duguid, Anja-Silvia Goeing, and Anthony Grafton (eds.) *Information: A Historical Companion* edited by. Princeton, NJ: Princeton University Press, 2021.

Bonefeld, Werner. "On Capital as Real Abstraction," in Antonio Oliva, Angel Oliva, and Ivan Novara (eds.). *Marx and Contemporary Critical Theory: The Philosophy of Real Abstraction*. New York: Palgrave MacMillan, 2020, 153-170.

Boyes, Hugh, Bil Hallaq, Joe Cunningham, Tim Watson, "The Industrial Internet of Things (IIoT): An Analysis Framework." *Computers in Industry*. Vol. 101 (2018), 1-12.

Brewer, John. *Sinews of Power: War, Money, and the English State, 1688-1783*. Cambridge, MA: Harvard University Press, 1990.

Burke, Peter. "Knowledge," in *Information: A Historical Companion* edited by Ann Blair, Paul Duguid, Anja-Silvia Goeing, and Anthony Grafton (eds.). Princeton, NJ: Princeton University Press, 2021, 538-544.

Cheney, Paul. *Cul De Sac: Patrimony, Capitalism, and Slavery in French Saint-Domingue*. Chicago: University of Chicago Press, 2017.

Cooper, Melinda. *Family Values: Between Neoliberalism and the New Social Conservatism*. Brooklyn, New York: Zone Books, 2017.

Davis, Ann E. *The Evolution of the Property Relation: Understanding Paradigms, Debates, Prospects*. New York: Palgrave MacMillan, 2015.

Davis, Ann E. *Money as a Social Institution: The Institutional Development of Capitalism*. New York: Routledge, 2017.

Davis, Ann E. *The End of Individualism and The Economy: Emerging Paradigms of Connection and Community*. New York: Routledge, 2020.

Duguid, Paul. "Communication, Computation, and Information" in *Information: A Historical Companion* edited by Ann Blair, Paul Duguid, Anja-Silvia Goeing, and Anthony Grafton (eds.). Princeton, NJ: Princeton University Press, 2021, 238-258.

Fara, Patricia. *Science: A Four Thousand Year History*. New York: Oxford University Press, 2009.

Follett, Richard. "The Rise and Fall of American Sugar" in Richard Follett, Sven Beckert, Peter Coclanis, and Barbara Hahn (eds.). *Plantation Kingdom: The American South and its Global Commodities*. Baltimore: Johns Hopkins University Press, 2016, 61-90.

Foucault, Michel. *The History of Sexuality*. Volume I: An Introduction. New York: Pantheon Books, 1978.

Fraser, Nancy. Fortunes of Feminism: From State-Managed Capitalism to Neoliberal Crisis. London: Verso, 2013.

Ghosh, Amitav. *The Nutmeg's Curse: Parables for a Planet in Crisis*. Chicago: University of Chicago Press, 2021.

Gleick, James. *The Information: A History, a Theory, a Flood*. New York: Pantheon, 2011.

Glass, Maeve. "Theorizing Constitutional History," *History and Theory*. Vol. 60, No. 2, June, 2021, 331-346.

Gordon, Robert W. "Paradoxical Property" in John Brewer and Susan Staves (eds.). *Early Modern Conceptions of Property*. New York: Routledge, 1996, 95-110.

Gordon, Robert W. *Taming the Past: Essays on Law in History and History in Law*. New York: Cambridge University Press, 2017.

Greenstein, Shane. *How the Internet Became Commercial: Innovation, Privatization, and the Birth of a New Network*. Princeton, NJ: Princeton University Press, 2015.

Habermas, Jurgen. *The Structural Transformation of the Public Sphere: An Inquiry into a Category of Bourgeois Society*. Cambridge, MA: MIT Press, 1989.
Harris, Ron. *Going the Distance: Eurasian Trade and the Rise of the Business Corporation, 1400-1700*. Princeton, NJ: Princeton University Press, 2020.
Hunt, Lynn, "The Global Financial Origins of 1789," in Suzanne Desan, Lynn Hunt, and William Max Nelson. *The French Revolution in Global Perspective*. Ithaca: Cornell University Press, 2013, 32-43.
Keil, Roger. *Suburban Planet: Making the World Urban from the Outside In*. Cambridge, UK: Polity, 2018.
Kimball, Eric. "'What Have We to Do with Slavery?' New Englanders and the Slave Economies of the West Indies" in Sven Beckert and Seth Rockman (eds). *Slavery's Capitalism: A New History of American Economic Development*. Philadelphia: University of Pennsylvania Press, 2016, 181-194.
Lessig, Lawrence. *Code and Other Laws of Cyberspace*. New York: Basic, 1999.
Levenson, Thomas. *Money for Nothing: The Scientists, Fraudsters, and Corrupt Politicians Who Reinvented Money, Panicked a Nation, and Made the World Rich*. New York: Random House, 2020.
Levy, Jonathan. *The Ages of American Capitalism: A History of the United States*. New York: Random House, 2021.
Levy, Steven. *Hackers: Heroes of the Computer Revolution*. New York: Penguin, 1984.
Lopez, Robert S. *The Commercial Revolution of the Middle Ages, 950-1350*. Englewood Cliffs, NJ: Prentice-Hall, 1971.
Maitland, F. W. *State, Trust and Corporation*. Edited by David Runciman and Magnus Ryan. New York: Cambridge University Press, 2003.
Maine, Henry Sumner. *Ancient Law*. New York: Everyman's Library, 1917.
Marx, Karl. *Capital*. Volumes I - III. New York: International Publishers, 1967.
McGirr, Lisa. *Suburban Warriors: The Origins of the New American Rights*. Princeton, NJ: Princeton University Press, 2001.
Merchant, Carolyn. *The Anthropocene and the Humanities: From Climate Change to a New Age of Sustainability*. New Haven: Yale University Press, 2020.
Menard, Russell R. *Sweet Negotiations: Sugar, Slavery, and Plantation Agriculture in Early Barbados*. Charlottesville: University of Virginia Press, 2006.
Milios, John. "Value Form and Abstract Labor in Marx: A Critical Review of Alfred Sohn-Rethel's Notion of 'Real Abstraction,'" in Antonio Oliva, Angel Oliva, and Ivan Novara (eds.). Marx and Contemporary Critical Theory: The Philosophy of Real Abstraction. New York: Palgrave MacMillan, 2020, 25-39.
Mintz, Sidney W. *Sweetness and Power: The Place of Sugar in Modern History*. New York: Penguin Books, 1985.
Molho, Anthony. *Florentine Public Finances in the Early Renaissance, 1400-1433*. Cambridge, MA: Harvard University Press, 1971.
Moore, Jason W. "Sugar and the Expansion of the Early Modern World-Economy: Commodity Frontiers, Ecological Transformation, and Industrialization," Review (Fernand Braudel Center) 2000, Vol. 23, No. 3, 409-433.
Moore, Jason W. *Capitalism in the Web of Life: Ecology and the Accumulation of Captial*. London: Verso, 2015.
Moore, Sean. "Exorcising the Ghosts of Racial Capitalism from the South Sea Bubble: Pent-Up Racist Liquidity and the Recent Four-Year Stock Surge." *Eighteenth-Century Studies*, Volume 54, No. 1, Fall, 2020, 1–11.
Murphy, Anne L. "Performing Public Credit at the Eighteenth-Century Bank of England." *Journal of British Studies*, Vol. 58, No. 1, 2019, 58-78.
Patel, Raj and Jason W. Moore. *A History of the World in Seven Cheap Things: A Guide to Capitalism, Nature, and the Future of the Planet*. Oakland: University of California Press, 2017.
Piketty, Thomas. *Capital and Ideology*. Cambridge, MA: Harvard University Press, 2020.

Pincus, Steve. "Rethinking Mercantilism: Political Economy, the British Empire, and the Atlantic World in the Seventeenth and Eighteenth Centuries." *William and Mary Quarterly*, Vol. 69, No. 1, January, 2012, 3–34.

Pistor, Katharina. *The Code of Capital: How the Law Creates Wealth and Inequality*. Princeton, NJ: Princeton University Press, 2019.

Pocock, J.G.A. *The Machiavellian Moment: Florentine Political Thought and the Atlantic Republican Tradition*. Princeton, NJ: Princeton University Press, 1975.

Polanyi, Karl. *The Great Transformation*. Boston: Beacon Press, 1944.

Pomeranz, Kenneth and Steven Topik. *The World that Trade Created: Society, Culture, and the World Economy, 1400-the Present*. Armonk, NY: M.E. Sharpe, 1999.

Poovey, Mary. *Making a Social Body: British Cultural Formation 1830-1864*. Chicago: University of Chicago Press, 1995

Poovey, Mary. *A History of the Modern Fact: Problems of Knowledge in the Sciences of Wealth and Society*. Chicago: University of Chicago Press, 1998.

Poovey, Mary. "The Liberal Civil Subject and the Social in Eighteenth-Century British Moral Philosophy." *Public Culture*, Vol. 14, No. 1, 2002, 125-145.

Poovey, Mary. *Genres of the Credit Economy: Mediating Value in Eighteenth-and Nineteenth-Century Britain*. Chicago: University of Chicago Press, 2008.

Poster, Mark. *Foucault, Marxism and History: Mode of Production versus Mode of Information*. Cambridge, UK: Polity Press, 1984.

Postone, Moishe. *Time, Labor, and Social Domination: A Reinterpretation of Marx's Critical Theory*. Cambridge, UK: Cambridge University Press, 1993.

Price, Gregory and Warren Whatley. "Did Profitable Slave Trading Enable the Expansion of Empire: The Asiento de Negros, the South Sea Company, and the Financial Revolution in Great Britain." *Cliometrica*, November, 2020.

Robinson, Cedric J. *Black Marxism: The Making of the Black Radical Tradition*. London: Zed Press, 1983.

Scott, Joan W. "Gender: A Useful Category of Historical Analysis." *American Historical Review*, December, 1986, Vol. 91, No. 5, 1053-1075.

Searle, John R. *Making the Social World: The Structure of Human Civilization*. New York: Oxford University Press, 2010.

Shovlin, John. "Jealousy of Credit: John Law's 'System' and the Geopolitics of Financial Revolution," in *Journal of Modern History*, Vol. 88, June, 2016, 275-305.

Shovlin, John. *Trading with the Enemy: Britain, France, and the 18th-Century Quest for a Peaceful World*. New Haven: Yale University Press, 2021.

Smith, Adam. *An Inquiry into the Nature and Causes of the Wealth of Nations*. New York: The Modern Library, 1994.

Surkis, Judith. "Family Law Matters," in *History and Theory*. Vol. 60, No. 2, June, 2021, 37-362.

Sohn-Rethel, Alfred. *Intellectual and Manual Labour: A Critique of Epistemology*. Atlantic Highlands, New Jersey: Humanities Press, 1978.

Stone, Katherine V.W. "John R. Commons and the Origins of Legal Realism; Or, The *Other* Tragedy of the Commons." In Daniel W. Hamilton and Alfred L. Brophy. *Transformations in American Legal History: Law, Ideology, and Method*, Vol. 2, Cambridge MA: Harvard University Press, 2009.

Tomlins, Christopher. "Organic Poise? Capitalism as Law" in *Buffalo Law Review*, Vol. 64, No. 1, 2016.

Trivellato, Francesca. *The Promise and Peril of Credit: What a Forgotten Legend About Jews and Finance Tells Us About the Making of European Commercial Society*. Princeton, NJ: Princeton University Press, 2019.

Valenze, Deborah M. *The First Industrial Woman*. New York: Oxford University Press, 1995.

Valenze, Deborah M. "Gender in the Formation of European Power, 1750-1914" in Teresa A. Meade and Merry E. Wiesner-Hanks (eds.). A Companion to Gender History. Oxford, UK: 2004, 459-476.

Vogl, Joseph. *The Specter of Capital*. Stanford, CA: Stanford University Press, 2015.

Vogl, Joseph. *The Ascendancy of Finance*. Cambridge, UK: Polity, 2017.
Wennerlind, Carl. *Casualties of Credit: The English Financial Revolution, 1620- 1720.* Cambridge, MA: Harvard University Press, 2011.
Wennerlind, Carl. "Money: Hartlibian Political Economy and the New Culture of Credit" in Philip J. Stern and Carl Wennerlind (eds.). *Mercantilism Reimagined: Political Economy in early Modern Britain and its Empire*. New York: Oxford University Press, 2014.
Zahedieh, Nuala. *The Capital and the Colonies: London and the Atlantic Economy 1660-1700.* New York: Cambridge University Press, 2010.
Zaidi, Batool and S. Philip Morgan. "The Second Demographic Transition Theory: A Review and Appraisal." Annual Review of Sociology. Vol. 43. 2017, 473-492.
Zuboff, Shoshana. *The Age of Surveillance Capitalism: The Fight for a Human Future at the New Frontier of Power*. New York: Public Affairs, 2019.

Part III
Alternatives

Chapter 7
Proletarianization and Commodification

1 Introduction

Building on concepts developed in earlier chapters, we now examine the history of the United States more specifically, to analyze the long-term impact of the "real abstractions" of property and money on economic and human development. We will find an arc of global rise and fall for both the United States as global hegemon and for capitalism, with the remaining power based on a key currency and strong military, with degraded human skills and environment, insecure employment, economic instability, and intense political polarization.

The primary form of documentation of these abstractions over the entire period of the growth of the market is the accounting method of double-entry bookkeeping (Poovey 1998). First in the mercantile era, but later with global trade and international balance of payments, there is a potentially contradictory relation between the two sides: money and real (Brine and Poovey 2017; Marx 1967), while both are necessary to complete the circuit. A second issue is the coercive power behind the need to balance commodity trade with financial payments, which is exerted by the creditors in alliance with the state (Wennerlind 2011). These are important considerations in the maintenance of credit in the modern era, on which capitalism depends.

Neoclassical theory of money does not address these two issues by having no consistent theory of money. In these neoclassical theories, money is "neutral" or simply a "veil" which is driven by real decisions. This approach fits with the mainstream assumptions that markets are voluntary exchanges of equal value, which reach equilibrium costlessly, a result of natural law and human nature. A historical institutional view, by contrast, uses these two issues to trace the long-term development of markets and institutions (Vogl 2017; Ferguson 2008).

A. E. Davis, *Whole Earth*, https://doi.org/10.1007/978-3-031-01934-0_7

2 The Long Duréé: Human Relation to Land

Over the long history of human evolution and migration, there has been a changing relation to the land. Before language and agriculture, the land was a direct source of subsistence for hunter-gatherers. With permanent settlements, there were improvements in agriculture, writing, and technological development. Empires in Sumer, Greece, and Rome extended their territory for the acquisition of surplus. With urbanization, there was a division of labor between agriculture and crafts, with trade expanding as skills improved. With the decline of the Roman Empire, Western Europe was left in the "dark ages," while there were advanced civilizations in China and India and the Middle East. Attracted by luxury goods and spices, Europe was able to regain hegemonic power with the use of general-purpose money, along with the fiscal/military state, to acquire trade routes and territories (Hoffman 2015).

From a source of direct subsistence, land became a territory to conquer, to form bounded states for the production and management of surplus. Aristocracy was derived from landownership and the associated skills of jurisprudence and stewardship (Pocock 1975). Land represented "nature," and the source of knowledge and improvement as well as romantic landscapes and parks to provide escape from modernity (Wulf 2016). From feudal relations, the development of markets in land provided the template for "property," for exclusive use, entitlement, and exchange (Levy 2021, 44–54; Starr 2019, 32–55). Once land was considered "property," there were laws for its management, protection, and use and the expanded role of money and credit for the exchange of property (Priest 2021). Property managed for the motive of financial "gain" then reduced its use for subsistence and the concern with the quality of the soil and the habitat. Trade and globalization organized by Britain and later the United States was managed to acquire surplus and backing for state money, which shaped the view of the earth towards the purpose of economic gain. Land became "property" which was used as collateral to back "money," which mediated access to the means of subsistence by means of market participation of the population as producers and consumers. By this process, the "abstractions" of property and money became "real" in their effects on life, earth, and livelihood. Money and property became the "real abstractions" which are "steering mechanisms" for the society, affecting values and priorities, the quality of life, and distribution of income and life opportunities.

3 Emergence of Capitalism

Once capitalism emerged, there is an imperative to make use of one's property to increase its market value (Levy 2021, xiii–xxi), by means of regular circuits managed by proletarianization and commodification. These processes of abstraction can be illustrated with the example of the British colonies in North America and then the United States.

3.1 From Land to Property and Finance

In the seventeenth and eighteenth centuries, financial circuits were backed by commodity circuits from long-distance trade and colonies (Hoppit 2000, 262–277). Colonial sugar plantations in the West Indies were driven by the need to make capital investments, to judge the state of the market, and then seek revenue from sales to repay the debt. In order to minimize the capital outlay, slaves and soil were driven to exhaustion, due to the need to serve the market efficiently (Cheney 2017, 42–60). Other examples of cash crops and "commodity frontiers" (Moore 2015) are from cotton and coal.

Given the strategic importance of trade, the major ports were particularly important in the development of the colonies. Colonial corporations, such as New York and Philadelphia, were self-governing entities which owned their own land, according to charters granted by the crown. These municipal corporations were able to charter, in turn, corporations for specific public functions, such as harbor development and water. After the American Revolution, the model of the liberal state was to distribute this land as individual private property. New York City identified standard lot sizes along perpendicular street grid patterns to facilitate the land sales. The new Western states followed the same policy of land distribution, with land auctions and land grants. There was no limit to the ownership of an individual person, which allowed land speculators to acquire large tracts to distribute to tenants at higher prices. Reliance on credit to buy land, acquire implements, or for mortgages could result in foreclosures, especially with unregulated state banks. As a result, by 1860, agriculture accounted for only 40% of total employment (Gates 1960, 420). Later, the US government sold public lands acquired by conquest or war, by the Homestead Acts of 1862, 1909, and 1916. This intentional land distribution to private ownership was designed to stimulate the economy and to attract population.

The model of independent private property ownership of land was part of the Jeffersonian myth of the yeoman farmer and his independence and helped justify the expansion across the continent (Grandin 2019). There were processes in place, such as speculation and mortgage debt, which facilitated the consolidation of landownership, nonetheless, and the formation of a wage labor force (Levy 2012; Bauerly 2018). With new technologies of production for farm implements, as well as transportation and communication infrastructure, production of commodities for the market spread across the country (Larson 2010). The decades of "internal improvement" in the early nineteenth century were brought to an end by the Panic of 1837 (Bauerly 2018, 36–39), nonetheless, and the passage of state constitutional amendments which prohibited budget deficits (Wallis 2000). Small farmers remained an important political force, demanding easier credit, especially in the Midwest, with the rise of populism (Bauerly 2018, 111–134; Levy 2021, 297–314). Although farmers were able to make use of futures markets, with the rise of commodity exchanges (Cronon 1991), there remained residual distrust of financial centers in the Northeast.

A system of national banks was formed to aid in finance of the Civil War. Industrialization led to larger-scale corporations and the turn of the century merger wave (Lamoreaux 1985). The mobilization of farmers, the formation of large corporations, as well as economic instability helped consolidate the alliance that passed the Federal Reserve Act in 1913. The Progressive Movement represented a compromise of allowing the scale economies in return for regulation by experts and professionals (Levy 2021, 320–324). Stock markets were essentially unregulated until the New Deal and led to the bubble of the 1920s and then to large losses during the Great Depression (Ott 2011).

Early cities were based on pedestrian mode of transportation, skilled manual crafts and guilds, with dense development and narrow, winding streets. With the development of mobile energy technology, based on steam and electricity instead of hydropower, manufacturing became "footloose," capable of relocating to be near markets and natural resources, balancing investment in fixed costs and transportation costs (Krugman 1991, 1998). With the development of urban transportation technology, from horse-drawn carriages to electric rail, residential settlement became more land intensive and dispersed, allowing the differentiation by class and race into suburbs (Warner 1962; Warner and Whittemore 2012; Glaeser 2013). The infrastructure was often provided by states competing for development, to smooth out the topography, to provide water and waste disposal, and to lower transaction costs (Larson 2001).

After World War II and the New Deal, private housing was a strategy for economic recovery, with finance guaranteed by the federal government (Kruse and Sugrue 2006; Levy 2021, 430). The single-family home was the norm, with appliances and goods provided by large-scale branded consumer corporations. Interstate highways provided the means to transportation, enabling the spread to the suburbs, along with the growth of the auto industry. Cities were redesigned to accommodate cars (Norton 2008; Feagin and Parker 1990) and turned the streets from public to private spaces. The financial patterns of the suburbs tended to reinforce class and race stratification, which provided a substantial challenge to racial integration in schools, and contributed to urban fiscal crises (Phillips-Fein 2017). New York City provided a model for the restriction of public services, to achieve a balanced budget, advised and enforced by the financial sector.

Large corporations focused on producing standardized consumer goods, with large fixed costs and Fordist methods of managing the labor force (Kotz 2015, 50–62; Sargent 2015). To lower costs, firms first moved from cities to the suburbs, then to the South of the United States (Norton 2001), and to Mexico, to make use of lower taxes and rates of unionization and less regulation. The computer and improved information technology allowed for the extraction of skills from the workers and subsequently the management of distributed methods of production and fragmentation of production with global supply chains. Jobs became less skilled and more unstable, and unionization declined.

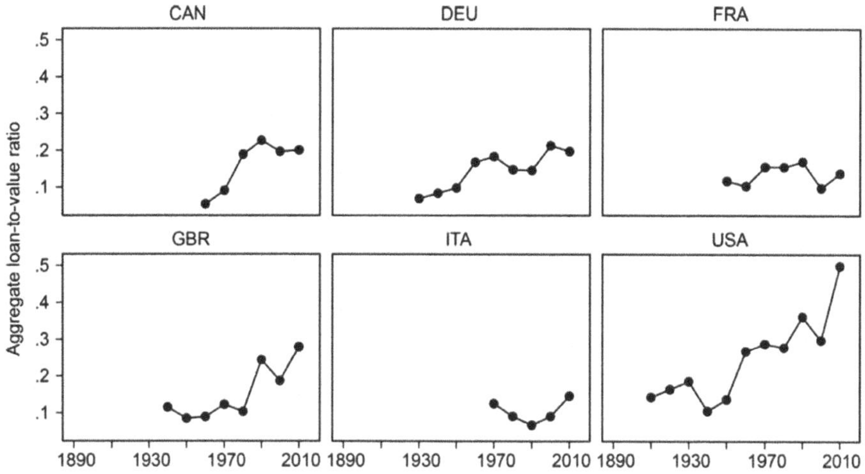

Fig. 7.1 Ratio of household mortgage lending to the value of the housing stock

Housing has remained a significant form of credit across advanced industrial countries, especially since 1980 (Jorda, Schularick, and Taylor 2016). There is what they term a "financial hockey stick," a graph which shows a dramatic increase in lending relative to GDP, particularly in mortgages. At the same time, the size and number of loans have increased, along with leverage. For example, in the United States, mortgage debt increased from 28% of home value in 1980 to 40% in 2013. See chart above for comparison across countries, from Jorda, Schularick, and Taylor 2016, 224 (Fig. 7.1).

The role of housing finance was important as a countercyclical policy, also undergirding the secular expansion of the financial sector.

3.2 *Corporations and the Management of Financial Circuits*

Because the early settlement of the North American colonies was managed by corporations chartered by the crown, the role of corporations in the early decades of the United States was unpopular and the subject of partisan political debate. There was a backlash against Hamilton and the Federalists who wanted to centralize the government of the United States, in the Constitution of 1787 (Holton 2007), and to allow for a Bank of the United States in a corporate form. By the early nineteenth century, nonetheless, with general incorporation laws, the corporate form became very widespread and provided the vehicle for the consolidation of small businesses to achieve scale economies, gain market share, and attract investment (Wright 2012, 2014). The issue of corporate stock along with government bonds stimulated the formation and liquidity of US financial markets.

The corporate form is long-standing, as an enduring "legal fiction" (Pistor 2019, 47–67), a "legal person" (Bloch and Lamoreaux 2017; Winkler 2017; Brine and Poovey 2017, 29–36) with widespread legitimacy, even as the formal definition of corporations has changed historically (Harris 2020). As merchant monopoly corporations chartered by the crown, the initial corporations, such as the English East India Corporation, were agents empowered by the government to conquer territories and to secure trade routes. Once secure financing was able to support a standing army, the English government managed the colony of India as a state bureaucracy and conducted military policy by means of a standing army. The wave of incorporation served a similar function in the nineteenth-century United States, mobilizing resources to produce commodities for sale for profit, which provided tax revenue for the state and central governments. Arguably, the corporation became the preferred method for balancing the "real" side of production, with the "financial" side of money and credit (Brine and Poovey 2017, 15–16). That is, the corporation obtained raw materials and labor, often in increasing size firms, like the vertically integrated form of the Ford auto plant at River Rouge. The corporation also obtained revenue from the sale of its products, while also tapping into capital markets, by issuing stocks and bonds, and later commercial paper.

The importance of stockholders increased as professional managers replaced the founders, such as Andrew Carnegie and Thomas Edison. With the separation of ownership from control, the interests of shareholders may not match the needs of the corporations, as shareholders prefer liquidity compared with locked-in capital for the security of the corporation (Brine and Poovey 2017, 141–147). The Progressive Movement chose to allow large firms to persist after the merger wave in the late nineteenth century, while managing them with regulation by experts instead of nationalization (Levy 2021, 320–324). Later in the twentieth century, the maximization of shareholder value was viewed as a method to bring these divergent interests in line, along with incentive pay for chief executive officers based on stock options (Levy 2021, 611–622). The American system was characterized by an interest in short-term returns instead of long-term investments, compared with other advanced industrial countries, and stock buybacks. The financial model of the corporation has resulted in mergers and layoffs, LBOs, and recently SPACs, to launch initial public offerings while skirting listing requirements of the SEC.

With the rise of corporations and regulation of stock markets, especially after the New Deal, financial markets gained legitimacy. In pursuit of liquidity and information regarding "price discovery," markets developed for an increasing array of assets. From the interests of farmers to hedge the future value of their crops after the growing season, the "bucket shop" which exchanged commodity futures for the purpose of gain became regulated to separate speculation from gambling. The requirement of "contemplating delivery" of the commodity was one means of enforcing such a distinction, even while allowing the settlement of the futures contracts by cash. With increasing financial deregulation in the 1980s and continuing into the present, futures contracts based on stock indices and derivatives did not require ownership at all, and positions were possible with increasing leverage and scale. With computerized trading and computer-driven algorithms, trading became driven by speed, in order to place an order early in the queue, to achieve the greatest financial gains from access to information (Banner 2017, 88–104; Staheli 2013, 75–92; MacKenzie 2021, 32–38).

When the type of property is no longer land used for subsistence, there is a more fundamental uncertainty with respect to valuation. With the rise of new forms of financial assets, changing accounting methods (Levy 2014), and changing legal property forms, the issue of valuation may have loomed large. Increasing scale and frequency of trading may have been one strategy, to continually reinforce liquidity by the observable phenomena of trading. On the other hand, the taboo against alternative economic models may be another. As Polanyi notes, the threat of socialism is the potential threat to the rights of property.

> For the mere possibility that [socialist parties] might decide to [undermine the motive of gain] undermines that type of confidence which in liberal economy is vital, namely, absolute confidence in the continuity of titles to property. While the actual content of property rights might undergo redefinition at the lands of legislation, assurance of formal continuity is essential to the functioning of the market system. (Polanyi 1944, 234)

Do corporations serve their own interests or their country of domicile, or incorporation? The long-standing debate has posed the interests of the corporation to make profit, compared with recent statements by the Business Roundtable regarding concern for stakeholders (Friedman vs. Business Roundtable 2020).

The international dominance of the United States was manifested in a balance of payments (BOP) surplus, based on superior manufacturing capacity after World War II. The erosion of this trade surplus due to import competition from Germany and Japan in the United States led to the abrogation of the Bretton Woods agreement to convert dollars to gold in 1973. The "Volcker shock" enabled the United States to manage this balance of payments deficit with the use of US Treasury bonds as reserves for foreign central banks (Levy 2021, 597–608), while the Plaza Accord of 1987 allowed the yen to adjust. This expanded role of capital flows with the "Washington Consensus" and the role of the dollar as a "safe asset" in global financial markets resulted in a flow of capital "uphill," from poor countries to rich (Prasad 2014, 31–46). While the US BOP deficit became the new norm, the United States assumed the role of "consumer of last resort" for export-oriented development strategies, accompanied by the erosion of the domestic manufacturing belt, and cheap credit for consumer debt and suburban home construction.

For emerging market countries (EMCs), balance of payments deficits are subject to "structural adjustment" in which the International Monetary Fund imposes governance changes in order to qualify for international credit. The US capacity to issue a reserve currency enables it to balance its deficits with the export of "safe" highly liquid financial assets, like US Treasury bonds, instead of real commodities. In a situation similar to the US deficit with Germany and Japan, China has allowed its reserves to accumulate, for the purposes of exchange rate stability and export markets in the United States, a situation that has been dubbed as "Chimerica" (Ferguson 2008; Ferguson and Schularick 2009).

4 American Constitution and Protection of Property

There is a long-standing debate regarding the structure of the US Constitution and its protection of private property (Bauerly 2018, 33). Some credit the influence of Alexander Hamilton for the successful passage of the Constitution of 1787.

4.1 Structure

Aware of the innovations of the Bank of England and the fiscal/military state, Alexander Hamilton sought to form a stronger central government with the Constitution of 1787, to protect the currency, to enable tax collection, and to support a strong military. Property is under highest protection in the US Constitution of 1787 (Polanyi 1944, 225–226), plus reinforced by judicial review initiated by the Federalist Party and John Marshall as chief justice.

4.2 Party Formation

As in other liberal economies, the formation of political parties helped to structure debate, such as the Federalists and Anti-Federalists in the early years of the United States (Holton 2007). In the case of Hamilton vs. Jefferson, and the formation of the Republican Party, the debates ranged from tariff policy to protect infant industry, to formation of a central bank, to the distribution of land. In the twentieth century, parties differed regarding the preservation of the "free market" compared with government regulation. The partisan debates regarding the New Deal in the 1930s were with respect to "freedom of contract" (Atiyah 1979).

In order to preserve the myth of property and freedom, and limited government, there is the presumed separation of public and private spheres (Bauerly 2018, 15–20). There are contradictions in this division, nonetheless: first, property is the creature of the state, including definition and enforcement; second, property is increasingly defined as expected future profits (Brine and Poovey 2017, 31–36). Yet future profits are the outcome of the operation of the entire system, which involves both state and market. Third, in financial crises, there is reliance on the state as backstop. Fourth, credit is provided by the state in projection of its own future revenue from taxable "private" economic activity; without the anchoring role of "safe" public debt, financial markets would be unstable. In exploring the "financial revolution" in eighteenth-century England, Wennerlind finds that public opinion is a foundation for imagining the future which could be achieved by credit, as well as notions of scientific progress, and the coherence of the nation as a public body. That is, the "credibility" surrounding credit required new ideas and behaviors, as well as a "credit fetishism" in which the public was willing to abstract from the specifics of particular investments like slavery (Wennerlind 2011, 229–230). With something as abstract as credit projected into the future, personification was also useful, such as the image of "Fortuna" (Pocock 1975, 446–461), "Lady Credit" (Wennerlind 2011, 191–195; Murphy 2019), or "Moneybags" (Wolff 1988), and later "Uncle Sam."

The consideration of the well-being of the economy as a whole requires a comprehensive perspective more likely from the government. In the United States, the only industrial policy has been based on military and spin-offs (Civil War and railroads; WWI and airplanes; WWII and computers). Corporations which have benefitted from public R&D have squandered their advantage by short-term behavior, such as Texas Instruments sharing its intellectual property with Japan as a condition of market entry. Later, US multinational corporations shared intellectual property to gain access to the China market and to its increasingly productive technology clusters.

5 Class Formation

Government policies affected class formation, from landownership to labor force and proletarianization (Bauerly 2018), along with varieties of legal protection for labor, and rise and decline of unionization. Due to speculation, cost of credit, and equipment, the share of the population who owned their own land declined, along with the share of employment in agriculture as shown in Fig. 7.2 below, even though average farm size has continued to increase (Sumner 2014).

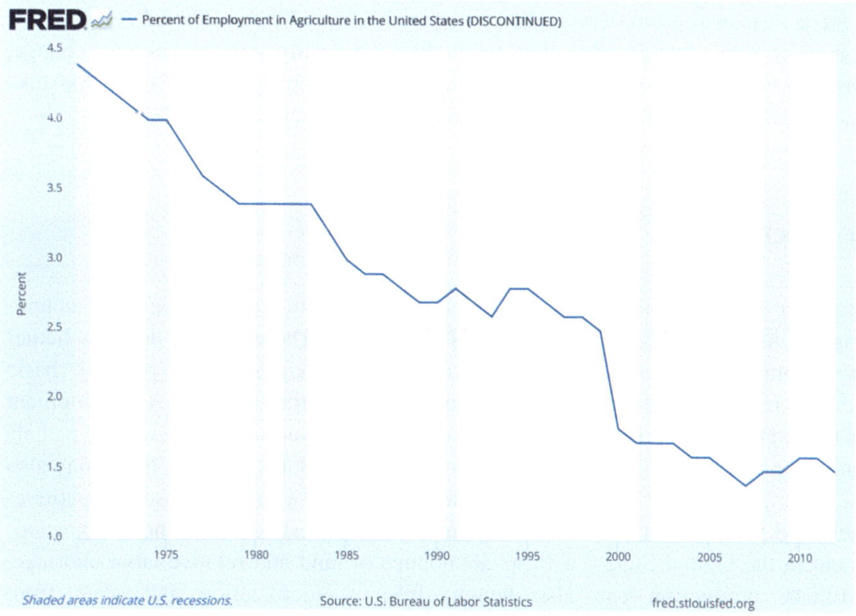

Fig. 7.2 Source: The Federal Reserve Bank of St. Louis

Similar trends took place in manufacturing employment, as productivity increased as well as outsourcing (Baily and Bosworth 2014).

The migration of African Americans after the end of Reconstruction to industrial centers in the Northeast added to the numbers and diversity of the working class in those areas.

The distribution of property in single-family homes provided a means of democratization of property (Lamoreaux 2011). The turn in politics to the right was partly founded on the imperative to protect that property, from taxes, and from neighbors from different class and ethnic groups (Phillips-Fein 2017). The anti-tax movement propelled Ronald Reagan to the presidency and stoked the right turn in American politics (Kruse and Zelizer 2019). The growth in the Sun Belt, and the Southern Strategy of the Republican Party, helped undermine the postwar New Deal alliance of the Democratic Party.

As aggregate concentration has increased, with increasing share of assets and employment with large corporations, compared with small business, inequality has increased (Temin 2017; Averitt 1968). The share of employment in services has increased FRED graph, where salaries and productivity are typically lower, except for health care and finance.

New style Republican Party tactics also changed the norms of governance, beginning with Newt Gingrich (Zelizer 2020), supported by right-wing talk radio hosts like Rush Limbaugh. Mass media, and then social media, further fragmented the information provided to the public, as polarization was an important method to keep the public engaged.

Changes in campaign finance helped prevent the return of progressive taxation and maintained the trend towards increasing inequality.

The turn away from democratic principles has been noted in the US, as the challenges of public health, education, inequality, job quality, a well as climate change, would otherwise create sizable demands on public policy. Dani Rodrik has also noted that globalization places constraints on democracy (Rodrik 2000).

6 Technology

Building on Kondratieff and Schumpeter, there is a notion of long waves of technological innovation (Perez 2009, 2010; Norton 1986). There is some debate whether development of technology has its own trajectory, building upon previous basic science research, instruments, and inventions, or whether technology development is related to financial markets, access to credit, and government policies like patents and support for research and development. In the capitalist system, there may also be an imperative for labor-saving technology, which would increase competitiveness and profit. Such innovation may have been well suited to economic development in the United States, with its abundance of land and relative labor shortage. Military production can also benefit from standardization and scale from interchangeable parts and automation, what became called the "American system" of manufacture, and later "Fordism."

With development in the information technology (IT) industry, a "general-purpose technology" with military, finance, and automation applications, there was some prospect for a "new economy" (Norton 2001). The initial development of semiconductors was conducted by Bell Labs in New Jersey, under the consent decree for AT&T, but subsequently moved to California. As a result of its widespread applications, there is some consensus for an industrial policy to support development of IT (Norton 1986; Borrus, Tyson, and Zysman 1986; Brown and Linden 2011), with its ongoing transformational impact, including capital and labor saving, communication, information processing, and control. In the 1980s, there was fierce competition from Japan, which was managed with development aid from the government for a consortium organized by the Semiconductor Industry Association and leading firms like IBM and Intel, called Sematech. The application of information technology to finance, in the development of pricing models for new financial assets, as well as technical capacity to perform high-speed trades (MacKenzie 2021), was also a powerful incentive for continuing improvement in information technology.

The information technology industry provided the first product to be traded in components, the semiconductor, with high value and low transportation costs. The resulting advances enabled management of the widely distributed global supply chains, which are recorded in the US Balance of Payments as imports from China. The consequent reduction of manufacturing employment, with less market adjustment to new jobs or outmigration, has had a political impact in the United States (Autor, Dorn, and Hanson 2021; Hochschild 2016). The information technology advances provided the foundation of the new "big tech" firms, such as Facebook (now Meta), Apple, Amazon, and Google, now the largest and most profitable. There is also a new generation of business leaders, with immense wealth and political power, some supporting a new Libertarian Right, such as Peter Thiel, and now supporting space tourism (Jeff Bezos) as well as the typical left-leaning persuasion of Silicon Valley and its global philanthropy (Bill Gates). There is a new potential for digital currency (Prasad 2021) which could have global financial and political implications.

7 Globalization Under Pax Americana

The potential divergence of finance and real provided the financial sector with its challenge and also with its opportunity. The development of financial models which project into the future based on probability (Brine and Poovey 2017; Weatherall 2013) and the design of new financial assets has allowed the financial sector to grow relative to the "real" sector measured by GDP (Krippner 2011), to help manage the risk of fluctuating exchange rates.

With military and industrial power, the US hegemony after World War II was notable. During the Bretton Woods system, 1944–1973, the US dollar was as a key currency with a managed exchange rate and convertible to gold. These were the circumstances in which the reification of the US dollar could occur, in which it represented value itself, rather than the entire global economic system. The turn to financialization occurred after 1980 (Levy 2021, 597–622; Krippner 2011; Vogl 2015, 62–67) with the end of the Bretton Woods system in the 1970s and the rise of the market-oriented "Washington Consensus." The International Monetary Fund, dominated by the United States, was tasked with managing global balance of payments adjustment and opening emerging market economies to foreign direct investment. This was a period of growth and consolidation of investment banks, which then in turn lobbied for deregulation (Tooze 2018, 51–56). The growth of finance, and the shadow banking system, provided a means to escape regulation, along with competition from European banks, and contributed to the Great Financial Crisis of 2008 (GFC). This crisis, in turn, reduced confidence in government and further supported the polarization of politics (Packer 2013; Kruse and Zelizer 2019).

Banks themselves became corporations which were "too big to fail" (Brine and Poovey 2017, 370–371), with the merger of investment banks and commercial banks after the Great Financial Crisis. Protection of TBTF banks from off-balance sheet SIVs drains liquidity towards rescuing those firms, imposing austerity on the public (Vogl 2017).

The ramifications of the GFC affected Europe and reduced the appeal of free market capitalism (Hopkin 2020). The refugee crisis in Europe from the Civil War in Syria, and slowing economic growth, had the same polarizing impact in Europe.

The IT industry is sophisticated enough in the twenty-first century, ironically, to challenge the global hegemonic currency of the US dollar, by means of cryptocurrencies and its libertarian acolytes.

The rise of China as a site for global production, and the oppositional politics of Putin, made Russia and China into formidable opponents for the liberal democracies. Now China is turning to foreign direct investment with its own currency by Belt and Road Initiative (BRI) and Asian Infrastructure Investment Bank (AIIB), rather than continue to tie its economy to the United States.

The global level playing field of the "free trade" regime (GATT and then WTO) had already begun to resort to regional alliances, and bilateral agreements favored by multinational corporations, with private conflict resolution devices (Rodrik 2018a).

8 Financialization and Abstraction

Capital mobility and liquidity is sought by financial markets, but there is no such thing as liquidity for the earth as a whole (paraphrasing Keynes). That is, the built environment persists, even if it is devalued in financial terms. The corporate form has allowed investors to attain liquidity in the secondary markets for corporate assets, even while the corporation attains capital lock-in for its own stability. For example, investors in corporations were allowed limited liability (Pistor 2019), to stimulate its ability to raise capital. After World War II during the Bretton Woods system, capital flows were restricted, until the adoption of the "Washington Consensus" to allow international capital flows after 1980. Even in a period of fluctuating exchange rates, there was effectively a "Bretton Woods II" informally maintained by China, called "Chimerica" (Ferguson 2008). That is, China performed manufacturing at low cost for US-based multinational corporations like Apple, but then held US Treasury bonds as reserves, to allow the United States to run a continuing balance of payments deficit on current account. As a result of the World War II settlement, the United States still dominates international financial institutions like the IMF and the WTO, to maintain policies and standards of international credit. As its economy has grown, China has increased its participation in these institutions, as well as initiated its own (Belt and Road Initiative and Asian Infrastructure Investment Bank). After following the Japanese model of "flying geese" in Asia, China may now be "decoupling" from its export-oriented strategy and more towards developing its own alliances independently of the United States.

The United States has sought to develop financial markets to improve liquidity of its Treasury bonds and to help manage and to finance the debt (Panitch and Konings 2008). The resulting market-based financial system is then more difficult to regulate (Brine and Poovey 2017, 342–347), especially buttressed by theories of efficient capital markets (Banner 2017, 313–320), and the country is subject to the whims of the global bond markets (Vogl 2017; Ferguson 2008). On the other hand, financing the public debt is easier with the "US Treasury/Wall Street/IMF complex," to support its military commitments abroad and to enforce global capital rules (Harvey 2005). Global financial markets have expanded far beyond the capacity of any central bank to provide effective backstop, nonetheless, in a period of increasing public debt due to the COVID-19 pandemic.

Knowledge about capital markets may influence their operation, a form of "performativity" (Vogl 2015, 36). Capital markets may be efficient or subject to information cascades and bubbles (Vogl 2015, 67–70).

The ideological insistence on the distinction of states vs. markets or the public/private divide obscures the way in which the market is a governance device (Mazower 2012; Vogl 2017), with implications for national sovereignty and democracy (Rodrik 2000).

Competing corporations and nations for profits and investment may actually undermine human and ecological resilience. Rising inequality may lead to a resurgence of class conflict and political polarization (Rodrik 2018b).

9 Contemporary Global Politics

With "real abstractions" like money and property, and "legal fictions" like corporation, the "bottom line" is the cash payment. The "real effects" of these abstractions occur when debts must be settled, and remaining assets distributed to secured creditors, which is a function of courts of law and the state. Ironically, in times of crisis, the US dollar has remained the "safe haven," in spite of the reduced appeal of its model of political economy. In a disturbance in financial circuits, if the valuation and realization of commodities in money is uncertain, there is a sudden insistence on "hard cash." The US dollar retains its role as a reified global symbol of value.

> On the eve of the crisis, the bourgeois, with the self-sufficiency that springs from intoxicating prosperity, declares money to be a vain imagination. Commodities alone are money. But now the cry is everywhere: money alone is a commodity! As the hart pants after fresh water, so pants his soul after money, the only wealth. In a crisis, the antithesis between commodities and their value-form, money, becomes heightened into an absolute contradiction. Hence, in such events, the form under which money appears is of no importance. The money famine continues, whether payments have to be made in gold or in credit money such as bank-notes. (Marx 1967, Vol. I, Chap. 3, Sect. 3.b, 138)

In the aftermath of GFC and COVID-19, the "original sin" of emerging countries is still apparent (Carstens and Shin 2019), which may further intensify domestic political conflicts as the US Federal Reserve raises interest rates and capital flows "uphill" again in 2022. The US reliance on exporting resources like LNG and agricutural commodities can worsen ecological disruption, as drought complicates vegetable and fruit production in California and the depletion of the Ogallala aquifer in the Mid-West potentially disrupts the "bread basket" (Opie 2000). Export of tourist services is potentially disrupted by the declaration of emergency for the Colorado River and its effect on Las Vegas casinos, while fracking, and the export of liquid natural gas, has the effect of polluting ground water. As the global governance of "free trade" and "free markets" gains less support, the use of military power may be increasing (Cooley and Nexon 2020), with the threats of war, Russia in Ukraine and China in Taiwan.

While politics has become more polarized, with the backlash against race, gender, and environmental politics in the 1970s (Kruse and Zelizer 2019), the effects of climate change are increasingly evident. At the beginning of 2022, reports from several science agencies indicated that 2021 was the hottest year on record, with records beginning in 1880. Gavin Schmidt, Director of the Goddard Institute for Space Studies at the National Aeronautics and Space Administration, said that "the last eight years have been the eight warmest" (Subbaraman 2022). At the same time, differences among Democrats in the Senate appear to jeopardize movement on President Biden's "Build Back Better" initiative, which includes provisions for climate change adaptation and mitigation, along with unified opposition from the Republican Party still dominated by former President Trump.

Bibliography

Atiyah, P. S. *The Rise and Fall of Freedom of Contract*. New York: Oxford University Press, 1979.

Autor, David, David Dorn, and Gordon H. Hanson. "On the Persistence of the China Shock." Cambridge, MA: NBER Working paper #29401, October 2021.

Averitt, Robert T. *The Dual Economy: The Dynamics of American Industry Structure*. New York: W. W. Norton, 1968.

Baily, Martin Neil and Barry P. Bosworth. "U.S. Manufacturing: Understanding Its Past and Potential Future." *Journal of Economic Perspectives*, Vol. 28, No. 1, 2014, 3–26.

Bauerly, Brad. *The Agrarian Seeds of Empire: The Political economy of Agriculture in US State Building*. Chicago: Haymarket Books, 2018.

Banner, Stuart. *Speculation: A History of the Fine Line Between Gambling and Investing*. New York: Oxford University Press, 2017.

Bloch, Ruth H. and Naomi R. Lamoreaux. "Corporations and the Fourteenth Amendment" in Naomi R. Lamoreaux and William J. Novak (eds.) *Corporations and American Democracy*. Cambridge, MA: Harvard University Press, 2017, 286-328.

Borrus, Michael, Laura D'Andrea Tyson, and John Zysman. "Creating Advantage: How Government Policies Shape International Trade in the Semiconductor Industry," in Paul R. Krugman (ed.). *Strategic Trade Policy and the New International Economics*. Cambridge, MA: MIT Press, 1986.

Brine, Kevin R. and Mary Poovey. *Finance in America: An Unfinished Story*. Chicago: University of Chicago Press, 2017.

Brown, Clair and Greg Linden. *Chips and Change: How Crisis Reshapes the Semiconductor Industry*. Cambridge, MA: MIT Press, 2011.

Carstens, Agustin and Hyun Song Shin. "Emerging Markets Aren't out of the Woods Yet," *Foreign Affairs*, March 15, 2019 based on a BIS speech of March 22, 2019.

Cheney, Paul. *Cul De Sac: Patrimony, Capitalism, and Slavery in French Saint-Domingue*. Chicago: University of Chicago Press, 2017.

Cooley, Alexander and Daniel H. Nexon. *Exit from Hegemony: The Unraveling of the American Global Order*. New York: Oxford University Press, 2020.

Cronon, William. *Nature's Metropolis: Chicago and the Great West*. New York: W. W. Norton, 1991.

Feagin, Joe R. and Robert E. Parker. *Building American Cities; The Urban Real Estate Game*. New York: Prentice-Hall, 1990.

Ferguson, Niall. *The Ascent of Money: A Financial History of World*. New York: Penguin, 2008.

Ferguson, Niall and Moritz Schularick, "End of Chimerica." Cambridge, MA: Harvard Business School Working Paper 10-037, 2009.

Gates, Paul W. *The Farmer's Age: Agriculture 1815-1860*. New York: Holt, Rinehart and Winston. Volume III The Economic History of the United States. 1960.

Glaeser, Edward L. "A Nation of Gamblers: Real Estate Speculation and American History." *American Economic Review*, Vol. 103, No. 3, May 2013, 1–42.

Graeber, David. *Toward an Anthropological Theory of Value: The False Coin of Our Own Dreams*. New York: Palgrave, 2001.

Grandin, Greg. *Empire's Workshop: Latin America, the United States, and the Rise of the New Imperialism*. New York: Metropolitan Books, 2006.

Grandin, Greg. *The End of the Myth: The Final Frontier to the Border Wall in the Mind of America*. New York: Metropolitan Books, 2019.

Harris, Ron. *Going the Distance: Eurasian Trade and the Rise of the Business Corporation, 1400-1700*. Princeton, NJ: Princeton University Press, 2020.

Harvey, David. *A Brief History of Neoliberalism*. New York: Oxford University Press, 2005.

Hochschild, Arlie. *Strangers in their Own Land: Anger and Mourning on the American Right*. New York New Press, 2016.

Holton, Woody. *Unruly Americans and the Origins of the Constitution*. New York: Hill and Wang, 2007.

Hopkin, Jonathan. *Anti-System Politics: The Crisis of Market Liberalism in Rich Democracies*. New York: Oxford University Press, 2020.

Hoppit, Julian. *A Land of Liberty? England 1689-1727*. New York: Oxford University Press, 2000.

Hoffman, Philip T. *Why did Europe conquer the World?* Princeton, NJ: Princeton University Press, 2015.

Jorda, Oscar, Moritz Schularick, and Alan Taylor. "Macrofinancial History and the New Business Cycle Facts," NBER Macroeconomics Annual, 2016, 213-263.

Kotz, David M. *The Rise and Fall of Neoliberal Capitalism*. Cambridge, MA: Harvard University Press, 2015.

Krippner, Greta R. *Capitalizing on Crisis: The Political Origins of the Rise of Finance*. Cambridge, MA: Harvard University Press, 2011.

Krugman, Paul. *Geography and Trade*. Cambridge, MA: MIT Press, 1991.

Krugman, Paul. "Space: The Final Frontier." *Journal of Economic Perspectives*. Vol. 12, No. 2, Spring, 1998, 161-174.

Kruse, Kevin M. and Thomas J. Sugrue (eds.). *The New Suburban History*. Chicago: University of Chicago Press, 2006.

Kruse, Kevin M. and Julian E. Zelizer. *Fault Lines: A History of the United States Since 1974*. New York: W. W. Norton & Company, 2019.

Lamoreaux, Naomi R. *The Great Merger Movement in American Business, 1895-1904*. New York: Cambridge University Press, 1985.

Lamoreaux, Naomi R. "The Mystery of Property Rights: A US Perspective," *Journal of Economic History*, Vol. 71, No. 2, 2011, 275-306.

Larson, John Lauritz. *Internal Improvement: National Public Works and the Promise of Popular Government in the Early United States*. Chapel Hill: University of North Caroline Press, 2001.

Larson, John Lauritz. *The Market Revolution in America: Liberty, Ambition, and the Eclipse of the Common Good*. New York Cambridge University Press, 2010.

Levy, Jonathan. "The Mortgage Worked the Hardest: The Fate of Landed Independence in Nineteenth Century America," in Michael Zakim and Gary J. Kornblith (eds). *Capitalism Takes Command: The Social Transformation of Nineteenth-Century America*. Chicago: University of Chicago Press, 2012, 39-68.

Levy, Jonathan. "Accounting for Profit and the History of Capital," in *Critical Historical Studies*. Vol. 1, No. 2, Fall, 2014, 171-214.

Levy, Jonathan. *The Ages of American Capitalism: A History of the United States*. New York: Random House, 2021.

Marx, Karl. *Capital*. New York: International Publishers, 1967.

MacKenzie, Donald. *Trading at the Speed of Light: How Ultrafast Algorithms are Transforming Financial Markets*. Princeton, NJ: Princeton University Press, 2021.

Mazower, Mark. *Governing the World: The History of an Idea*. New York: Penguin Press, 2012.

Moore, Jason W. *Capitalism in the Web of Life: Ecology and the Accumulation of Capital*. London: Verso, 2015.

Murphy, Anne L. "Performing Public Credit at the Eighteenth Century Bank of England." *Journal of British Studies*, Vol. 58, No. 1, January, 2019, 58-78.

Norton, Peter D. *Fighting Traffic: The Dawn of the Motor Age in the American City*. Cambridge, MA: MIT Press, 2008.

Norton, R.D. "Industrial Policy and American Renewal," in *Journal of Economic Literature*, Vol. 24, No. 1, March, 1986, 1–40.

Norton, R.D. *Creating the New Economy: The Entrepreneur and the US Resurgence*. Cheltenham, UK: Edward Elgar, 2001.

Opie, John. *Ogallala: Water for a Dry Land*. Lincoln: University of Nebraska Press. 2nd ed., 2000.

Ott, Julia C. *When Wall Street Met Main Street: The Quest for an Investor's Democracy*. Cambridge, MA: Harvard University Press, 2011.

Packer, George. *The Unwinding: An Inner History of the New America*. New York: Farrar, Straus, and Giroux, 2013.

Panitch, Leo and Martijn Konings (eds.). *American Empire and the Political Economy of Global Finance*. New York: Palgrave MacMillan, 2008.

Phillips-Fein, Kim. *Fear City: New York's Fiscal Crisis and the Rise of Austerity Politics*. New York: Metropolitan Books, Henry Hold and Company, 2017.

Perez, Carlota. Technological Revolutions and Financial Capital: The Dynamics of Bubbles and Golden Ages. Cheltenham, UK: Edward Elgar, 2002.

Perez, Carlota. "The Double Bubble at the Turn of the Century: Technological Roots and Structural Implications." *Cambridge Journal of Economics*, Vol. 33, 2009, 779-805.

Perez, Carlota. "Technological Revolutions and Techno-Economic Paradigms," *Cambridge Journal of Economics*, Vol. 34, 2010, 185-202.

Pistor, Katharina. *The Code of Capital: How the Law Creates Wealth and Inequality*. Princeton, NJ: Princeton University Press, 2019.

Pocock, J.G.A. *The Machiavellian Moment: Florentine Political Thought and the Atlantic Republican Tradition*. Princeton, NJ: Princeton University Press, 1975.

Polanyi, Karl. *The Great Transformation*. Boston: Beacon Press, 1944.

Pollin, Robert. *Contours of Descent: U.S. Economic Fractures and the Landscape of Global Austerity*. London: Verso, 2003.

Pomeranz, Kenneth. *The Great Divergence: Europe, China, and the Making of the Modern World Economy*. Princeton, NJ: Princeton University Press, 2000.

Poovey, Mary. *A History of the Modern Fact: Problems of Knowledge in the Sciences of Wealth and Society*. Chicago: University of Chicago Press, 1998.

Prasad, Eswar. *The Dollar Trap: How the U.S. Dollar Tightened Its Grip on Global Finance*. Princeton, NJ: Princeton University Press, 2014.

Prasad, Eswar S. *The Future of Money: How the Digital Revolution is Transforming Currencies and Finance*. Cambridge, MA: Harvard University Press, 2021.

Priest, Claire. *Credit Nation: Property Laws and Legal Institutions in Early America*. Princeton, NJ: Princeton University Press, 2021.

Rodrik, Dani. "How Far Will Economic Integration Go?" *Journal of Economic Perspectives*. Vol. 14, No. 1, Winter 2000, 177-186.

Rodrik, Dani. "What Do Trade Agreements Really Do?" *Journal of Economic Perspectives*, Vol. 32, No. 2, Spring, 2018a, 73-90.

Rodrik, Dani, "Is Populism Necessarily Bad Economics?" *American Economic Review*, Vol. 108, May Proceedings Issue, 2018b, 196-199

Rosenthal, Jean-Laurent and R. Bin Wong. *Before and Beyond Divergence: The Politics of Economic Change in China and Europe*. Cambridge, MA: Harvard University Press, 2011.

Sargent, Daniel J. *A Superpower Transformed: The Remaking of American Foreign Relations in the 1970s*. New York: Oxford University Press, 2015.

Servan-Schreiber, Jean-Jacques. *American Challenge*. New York: Athenium, 1968.

Staheli, Urs. *Spectacular Speculation: Thrills, The Economy, and Popular Discourse*. Stanford, CA: Stanford University Press, 2013.

Starr, Paul. *Entrenchment: Wealth, Power, and the Constitution of Democratic Societies*. New Haven: Yale University Press, 2019.

Stephen S. Cohen and John Zysman. *Manufacturing Matters: The Myth of the Post-Industrial Economy*. New York: Basic Books, 1987.

Subbaraman, Nidhi. "2021 was Earth's Sixth Hottest Year on Record, Temperature Reports Say," *Wall Street Journal*, January 13, 2022.

Sumner, Daniel A. "American Farms Keep Growing: Size, Productivity, and Policy." *Journal of Economic Perspectives*, Vol. 28, No. 1, Winter, 2014, 147-166.

Taylor, Charles. *The Language Animal: The Full Shape of the Human Linguistic Capacity*. Cambridge, MA: Harvard University Press, 2016.

Temin, Peter. *The Vanishing Middle Class: Prejudice and Power in a Dual Economy*. Cambridge, MA: MIT Press, 2017.

Tooze, J. Adam. *Crashed: How a Decade of Financial Crises Changed the World*. New York: Penguin, 2018.

Vogl, Joseph. *The Specter of Capital*. Stanford: Stanford University Press, 2015.

Vogl, Joseph. *The Ascendancy of Finance*. London: Polity, 2017.

Wallis, John Joseph. "American Government Finance in the Long Run: 1790-1990" in *Journal of Economic Perspectives*, Vol. 14, No. 1, 2000, 61-82.

Warner, Sam Bass, Jr. *Streetcar Suburbs: The Process of Growth in Boston, 1870-1900*. Cambridge, MA: Harvard University Press and MIT Press, 1962.

Warner, Sam Bass and Andrew H. Whittemore. *American Urban Form: A Representative History*. Cambridge, MA: MIT Press, 2012.

Weatherall, James Owen. *The Physics of Wall Street: A Brief History of Predicting the Unpredictable*. New York: Houghton Mifflin Harcourt, 2013.

Wennerlind, Carl. *Casualties of Credit: The English Financial Revolution, 1620-1720*. Cambridge, MA: Harvard University Press, 2011.

Winkler, Adam. "*Citizens United*, Personhood, and the Corporation in Politics," Naomi R. Lamoreaux and William J. Novak (eds.) *Corporations and American Democracy*. Cambridge, MA: Harvard University Press, 2017, 359-387.

Wolff, Robert Paul. *Moneybags Must be so Lucky: On the Literary Structure of Capital*. Amherst, MA: University of Massachusetts Press, 1988.

Wright, Robert E. "Capitalism and the Rise of the Corporation Nation," in Michael Zakim and Gary J. Kornblith (eds). *Capitalism Takes Command: The Social Transformation of Nineteenth-Century America*. Chicago: University of Chicago Press, 2012, 145-168.

Wright, Robert E. *Corporation Nation*. Philadelphia: University of Pennsylvania Press, 2014.

Wulf, Andrea. *The Invention of Nature: Alexander Von Humboldt's New World*. New York: Alfred A. Knopf, 2016.

Zelizer, Julian E. *Burning Down the House: Newt Gingrich, and the Rise of the New Republican Party*. New York: Penguin, 2020.

Chapter 8
Alternatives: Regional Ecological Communities

1 Introduction

According to the social contract theory of Locke and Rousseau, individual property owners form a state to protect their property from each other and from the state (Lamoreaux 2011). The Lockean proviso, nonetheless, provides an opening to examine how much is good enough and left for others.

In the age of the "Anthropocene," the relationship among humans becomes as important as the relationship between humans and nature. The ways in which humans conceptualize nature influence the forms of behavior that are authorized as normative. There are long-standing narratives of the relation of humans to nature, some characterizing nature as female and "mother earth," and some viewing the role of science as the domination of nature and the extraction of her secrets (Merchant 1979; Merchant 2003, 77–84). In the process of developing an "objective" science, nature became viewed as a machine rather than a living organism and as the opposite of human.

For some scientists, there was a process of rediscovery, an integrated view of humans and the earth as an organic unity, a connection of vitalism among all living things. That is, the earth is a "world organism" (Merchant 1980, 99–236; Wulf 2015; Schwagerl 2014, 55–69, 171–173). Terms like Gaia and Medea help to conceptualize the earth as an integrated system, along with other metaphors and spheres, concepts and narratives (Turner 2018, 4–12, 53–76, 249–256).

2 Green Capitalism

As discussed in earlier chapters, the existing financial system of the capitalist world system is based on public credit to support private commerce and military capacity for each nation in a competitive framework. As a result, any diversion from a focus

A. E. Davis, *Whole Earth*, https://doi.org/10.1007/978-3-031-01934-0_8

on "the wealth of nations" risks losing advantage in the tight race for global hegemony. The existing efforts to achieve global agreements on efforts to address climate change are often sacrificed to that implicit primary objective of economic growth and power. The structure of existing global institutions remains divided according to the state/market dichotomy (Turner 2018, 181–192).

2.1 Market-Based Solutions

There have been efforts over the course of decades to put a price on carbon, to make use of the market mechanism to induce innovation towards renewable energy. In the United States, political support for these proposals has been lacking, and the organization of the United Nations Intergovernmental Panel on Climate Change is separated institutionally from the IMF and the World Bank which manage the economy. The notion of an economic emergency from climate change has not altered the typical decision-making methods of leading industrial countries, in spite of persuasive arguments to the contrary (Stern 2009).

To communicate to the public the importance of "nature," there have been estimates of "ecosystems services," the values produced by ecology for "free" (Costanza 1997; Daily 1997). The term "natural capital" also conveyed the importance of earth resources, which were priced by considering the expense for human-made substitutes, or "willingness to pay" for aspects for which there was no existing market (Hawken et al. 1999). Estimates for the value to humans of such earth systems as temperature, for example, are very complex. The substitute of air conditioning is available, but refrigerants such as CFCs deplete the ozone layer and HFCs are greenhouse gases. Further, such a strategy would require extending the built environment, which itself would have an impact on land use. Geoengineering solutions to prevent incoming solar radiation would have global effects, with uncertain impacts on other earth systems. The definition of "sustainability" often includes human-produced as well as "natural capital," but no existing human system is globally integrated in design or implementation, at present. The payments for ecosystems services method has been applied for specific functions, such as water and forests, in various regions and countries around the world (Salzman et al. 2018).

More sophisticated methods were developed to find the "social cost of carbon." Nobel Prize-winning economist William Nordhaus famously has compared climate change to a "Colossus" and the "ultimate challenge for economics" (Nordhaus 2019, 1992–1993). His method was to use an earth system model to estimate the rise in global temperature from CO_2 emissions and then the loss of production due to that increase in temperature. Using standard economic models such as Cobb-Douglas and integrating over time with a discount rate, the loss of consumer utility due to climate damage was estimated. The results were sensitive to assumptions regarding the discount rate, because the default method of "present discounted value" reduces the value today of benefits which are derived in the future. Other efforts to estimate the costs of climate change include a model with greater spatial delineation, and a wide variety of human impacts, including agricultural yields, health, mortality, trade, population growth, and violence (Carleton and Hsiang 2016), which could then have impacts on global population trends (Turner 2018, 167–170).

Other approaches include the notion of a "Green New Deal" (Pollin 2015; Chomsky and Pollin 2020; Barbier 2010; Pettifor 2019). Modeled on the activist role of the government in the 1930s, this strategy would engage the government in an industrial policy to manage the substitution of renewable energy for fossil fuels. In the process of this conversion, new jobs would be created to substitute for the ones eliminated in the coal and oil industry. Such a process of transition, while having widespread impact, does not exceed the capacity of a government with expansive vision and technical expertise.

There have been advances in sciences which could support such a technological redesign. For example, there are a variety of earth systems models (Turner 2018), which examine the major biogeochemical cycles, and their interaction. Findings from the UNIPCC Assessment Reports and other formal global ecological institutions (such as Grantham Research Institute on Climate Change) make use of these models to make climate projections regarding such indicators as temperature and precipitation. Unlike the "integrated assessment models," the earth systems models primarily consider "natural" variables, rather than also including the effects of human settlement on ecology and the ecological impacts on humans. The major exception is the focus on human CO_2 emissions and accumulation and their impact on other cycles. There are considerable challenges to the development of these models, nonetheless, due to interactions and synergies across particular nutrient cycles. For example, temperature, acidification, and oxygen depletion can interact to result in rapid onset extreme events, resulting in habitat compressions for ocean species (Gruber et al. 2021). Rather than quantify these impacts with prices and damage to economic production, the earth systems models often compare findings and projections with a normal distribution of an observed variable, even as it may shift over time. Other studies try to identify major axes of terrestrial ecosystem function, to estimate deviations which would result from changing patterns, using principal component analysis rather than indices or prices (Migliavacca et al. 2021).

There has been progress in the availability and relative costs of renewable energy technologies, with research and development support from the government (ARPA-E), on the model of support for defense spending (DARPA), as well as investments in the private sector (Prentiss 2015). Central banks have increasingly identified risks to the financial system from climate change (Carney 2015) and have organized a network of central banks to accomplish the "greening" of the financial system (https://www.ngfs.net/en). Private investors on the model of "responsible" investment, or concern for stakeholders, have begun to use ESG criteria, for the environmental, social, and governance quality of a particular corporation (Hill 2020). While this movement has gained adherents and recognition, there are as yet no consistent global standards to make these criteria uniform and no global organization to assess environmental priorities.

In the meantime, some corporations, political parties, and think tanks continue to resist climate change science and operate to increase the "doubt" in these scientific findings (Oreskes and Conway 2010; Michaels 2008; Mooney 2005), reducing the capacity for consensus.

Efforts by legal theorists to address climate change have made important advances. One such effort is the concept of "greenwood in the bundle of sticks," a term by Robert J. Goldstein at West Point to assign special responsibilities for property in land. This approach (Goldstein 1998, 2004a, b) would add to the "bundle of sticks" of property rights a special twig which refers to the ecological dimensions of land. Other approaches develop the concept of "Public Trust," a doctrine from Roman law, which is meant to protect essential resources for public access (Blumm and Wood 2013; Wood 2014). There have been important applications in the United States, including protection of Mono Lake in a dispute with Los Angeles Department of Public Water, in a case considered by the California Supreme Court decided in 1983. More recently, Blumm and Wood have filed a public trust lawsuit against the US EPA in 2015 on behalf of Kelsey Juliana and 21 of her peers regarding climate change impacts on future generations (Blumm and Wood 2017; Schiermeier 2021), supported by Our Children's Trust and Earth Guardians. This effort to apply public trust can provide a comprehensive approach to ecological processes, rather than be bound by individual property parcels or state lines. It builds on the concept of sovereignty and the rights of all citizens and seeks to balance public and private property. These approaches would protect the environment on behalf of citizens, instead of the "takings" approach promoted by the school of law and economics in the 1980s (Fischel 1995), to protect property against government environmental regulation.

There is a long history of the conservation movement, consumer, and climate change movements, some of which are anti-capitalist (Klein 2014). There is also a literature promoting redesign, of products and of the entire economic system (Raworth 2017; McDonough and Braungart 2002; D'Alisa et al. 2015), challenging the sole focus on growth.

2.2 *Assessment of Market-Based Solutions*

The adequacy of the market economy and mainstream economics to address ecology is in question, for at least ten reasons.

First, the "target" of capitalist production is realization from sales to the consumer. To increase speed and scale, there is a tendency to provide products that are addictive, like fat, salt, and sugar, and not necessarily edifying, like social media and advertising.

Second, a consumer culture is a likely result of the persistent sales effort. Values such as convenience, speed, and social status are profitable, but do not necessarily improve broader awareness. Such a culture encourages self-interested behavior, even if this is not necessarily "human nature" (Bowles and Gintis 2011).

Third, to add a price to carbon or carbon permits trading relies on elasticity of supply and demand to have much effect. If prices of carbon do rise, there are impacts on low-income consumers. If they do not rise, there is little effectiveness of the policy. Further, elasticity is improved by government-supported research and development and innovation, which may be more important than market-based policies.

Fourth, there is a preference in the economics profession for market-based solutions. Yet such approaches may still emphasize the short term, due to time discounting, and a simplistic approach to the problem. One example is the development of water markets to address the issue of water shortages. This can lead to stress on low-income families and countries who are then forced to pay for a necessity. Second, privatization of water resources may lead to extraction of rents by for-profit commodification. Third, there are alternative policies, such as reforestation to retain more moisture in the soil, and conservation. Since property rights in water differ in various regions of the United States, there is a tendency for "water wars" and negative externalities by exercising first usage rights. Fourth, industrial substitutes like desalination rely on low cost energy; even so, transport of water to distant markets is still costly compared with its market value.

Another example of a market-based solution is the use of guano and then industrial fertilizer to compensate for soil exhaustion. The application of fertilizer may not improve soil fertility and may actually require greater applications to achieve the same effect, due to diminishing returns. Then nutrient runoff can accumulate in "dead zones" in coastal areas, depleting fish and other species. The alternative of soil regeneration may require more labor-intensive techniques, and require more time with soil fallow, but support long-run sustainability. A cost/benefit analysis in the usual market terms would render such an approach unprofitable even if it were more sustainable.

Fifth, market solutions tend to increase inequality and industrial concentration. One example is the food industry, which is highly concentrated, relies heavily on advertising, and operates complex global supply chains and geographically distributed retail grocery chain stores. Information technology firms like Amazon may be entering the food and restaurant industry and may revolutionize its distribution network, like WalMart in retail. For example, Amazon Go is a retail food outlet which requires no clerical staff, but rather utilizes cell phone application. Such a global integration of supply chains could support ecological regeneration, instead of entrenching the market position of for-profit firms.

Sixth, mainstream economics is based on individual private property and the individual rational consumer analyzing marginal costs/marginal benefits. The notion of individual private property does not easily incorporate environmental externalities, and marginal analysis does not apply to the complex system of climate which is path dependent characterized by irreversible tipping points (Dietz et al. 2021).

Seventh, macroeconomics assumes an infinite financial market, with continuous compounding. As a result, the value today of any future benefit must be discounted, which tends to reduce the value of long-term perspectives.

Eighth, with the existing global trade and currency regime, the dominant ideas of "free markets" and global capital flows are likely to worsen climate change.

Emerging market countries are more likely to emphasize cash crops to repay debt, rather than preserve the environment and enhance the education of the population.

Ninth, economics conceptualizes the earth as an abstract homogeneous plane, a platform for the built environment. These assumptions are not suitable for envisioning the complex interaction of land, ocean, and atmosphere that is being discovered by earth system scientists (Turner 2018).

Tenth, economics assumes discreet units like individuals and individual private property, rather than interconnections and complexity, just when modern science reveals the salience of such interconnection and increasing returns (Arthur 2015).

As discussed in Chapter 4 above, the notion of "capital" is broadly generalized, a teleological worldview applied to nature and to humans indiscriminately, implying the motive of gain as the overarching value.

3 Values

The market presumes to solve the problem of "values," by enabling consumers and firms to observe market prices. Yet externalities are rarely taken into account, along with the other issues of inequality and concentration, and assumptions which are not accurate representations of industrialized economies, like exogenous preferences and "rational" economic decision-making.

Even among classical economists, there is debate about "value." For example, the concept of the labor theory of value was based on the writings of Adam Smith even before Karl Marx.

> The property which every man has in his own labour, as it is the original foundation of all other property, so it is the most sacred and inviolable. (Smith 1994, 140).

Marx comments on and extends the discussion by Adam Smith. Marx claims that he was the "first to point out and to examine critically the two-fold nature of the labour contained in commodities" (Marx, Vol. I, Chap. 1, Sect. 2, 41–46), which has both use value and exchange value. Later in Chapter 7, Sect. 2, Marx summarizes:

> We know that the value of each commodity is determined by the quantity of labour expended on and materialized in it, by the working-time necessary, under given social conditions, for its production. (Marx 1967, Vol. I, Chap. 7, Sect. 2, 186).

Still, within capitalism, the social nature of value is a mystery, as discussed in the analysis of "Commodity Fetishism," and is not understood by the classical political economics of Smith and Ricardo (Foley 2006). For Marx, the "mystical veil" of value will be stripped off only when production is managed by an association of free men [sic] who can consciously regulate in accordance with a "settled plan" (Marx 1967, Vol. I, Chap. 1, Sect. 4, 80–81).

The notion that "value" is based on embodied labor time is true for capitalism, where wage labor produces independently the social product, which they must then purchase with their wages. Postone makes clear that these value relations are not universal, but are particular to capitalism, and may not extend beyond the capitalist system (Davis 2022).

Without the "veil" of money, the community may then be capable of directing production and distribution without this method of valuation, as have communities in the past. The distinction between intrinsic value and economic value may have also originated with capitalism (Poovey 1998). So when considering economic systems beyond capitalism, value and price may not be necessary to identify clear priorities and decisions (Graeber 2001). In fact, advances in information technology may make comprehensive democratic planning more feasible. Simple notions like secure provision of necessities and opportunities for education are quite straightforward, such as the work focused on "capabilities" by Amartya Sen and Martha Nussbaum. Methods developed and explored by Elinor Ostrom and the International Association for the Study of the Commons have demonstrated the capacity of many communities to preserve resources (Turner 2018, 233–247), but they are often hampered by the priority attached to cash crops and debt repayments for emerging countries in the current international political economy.

4 Post-capitalism

In the early years of the United States, public lands were distributed to individual ownership, as consistent with the model of the liberal state. In the current era, it may be important to reconsider this move to privatization, and rather to declare the entire earth as a "public good" (Davis 2021). Rather than protect the property of each individual owner, this would allow a consideration of the complex interactions of the earth's global ecology. Studying and stabilizing these biogeochemical cycles may be the most urgent task for human well-being. The role of property was to provide subsistence, security, and permanence. But in the context of rapidly changing global systems, this function of property is no longer reliable, and projections of the future value of property are at risk. The existing system of property is associated with the fiscal/military nation-state and international economic competition, rather than an efficient system of allocation of scarce resources (Heller and Salzman 2021).

In the context of capitalism, the principle function of earth is to serve as the most reliable collateral for finance, and the key function of humans is commodity production, consumption, and realization of profit. It is important to envision other types of relationships and other purposes.

More progress on the ecology may be possible in a "post-capitalist" society, where one can establish the priority of peace and human development. Without capitalism, there is no longer need to separate workers from the means of production and means of subsistence and to finance wars of capitalist competition.

With a revisioning of the meaning of earth, it becomes more feasible to reserve large areas for preservation for species diversity, as leading scientist E.O. Wilson recommended (2016). A fundamental redesign of human settlement patterns would be possible, with collective ownership of regional ecological units, such as watersheds, with guaranteed access to basic necessities and natural amenities. With a direct immediate relation to the land as a source of life and growth, more attention, as well as formal scientific research and development, could be focused on regeneration. More astute observation would be encouraged and rewarded in each region, regarding biogeochemical cycles and biodiversity. Without the requirement of competitive labor markets and product markets, knowledge could be shared among all residents, and all regions, in cooperation to restore ecological resilience at a global scale (Hess and Ostrom 2007). Rather than use property ownership to extract minerals or grow cash crops, one important step would be to take ecology and labor out of global competition, with specific global standards.

Modern production methods are adequate to meet basic minimum needs for the existing global population, if shared. The existing food system has led to inequality, ill-health, and famines (Bittman 2021).

A global peace pact would assure countries of security and reduce the need for military and economic competition, with the associated peace dividend. Instead of protected intellectual property, there would be shared research and development towards the common goal of earth sustainability.

4.1 Changing Human Sciences

Consciousness of collective impact on the earth by the human species is not aided by the current structure of human sciences. Instead of collective awareness and mutual responsibility, there is an objectification of the "real abstractions" with agency, as if humans were not in control of their own institutions (Graeber 2001). There are "steering media" which determine human destiny, in the short and long run. Rather than humans deliberating collaboratively, there is a "view from nowhere" with no clear standpoint (Latour 2018, 68), with the possible exception of global bondholders (Vogl 2017).

The right to property includes the right of owners to dominate other people and the earth, by human "individuals" which could include corporations as "legal persons." The right to property then includes the instrumental use of other humans and living things, and is not moral, according to Kant. This right includes extraction of resources and production for sale for profit for monetary reward, regardless of the impact on the worker or the environment. The dominant economic model assumes that the market is the most efficient governance mechanism, and "laissez faire" of the market will achieve the greatest human happiness. The result is division and degradation of humans and the environment, and the alteration of earth's self-regulation systems, such as climate. Money is considered valuable in itself, rather than the earth's ecosystems and the human capacities.

Common consciousness of the human impact on the environment has been aided by the research in natural science concerning the "Anthropocene." What has been called the "Great Acceleration" of carbon emissions into the atmosphere coincided with the Pax Americana, the global "free trade" regime led by the United States, and the movements of decolonialization (Chakrabarty 2021, 61–65). The nations of the world have been united in pursuing wealth, by means of markets, money, and property.

Rather than "objective" natural and social science, in which the role of the scientist is invisible, there is need for a new form of community. This research community would search in common for new forms of collaboration in human development, ecological restoration, and global governance. There would be acknowledgment of the complexity of the task and the value of different perspectives on the common problem of preservation of living species on earth. In contrast with a property model, in which humans objectify themselves and then exchange tasks or time units, a collaborative community would deliberate with mutual respect and recognition in search of new forms of knowledge and cooperation.

4.2 Changing Human Settlement Patterns

In a new form of global governance, regional ecological communities would be based on watersheds and other specific ecological features. Land would be owned and managed collectively, with basic needs guaranteed, including food, clothing, shelter, health, and education.

With the regeneration of agriculture (Hawken 2021), the tendency for urbanization and centralization would be modified (Keil 2018). There would be decentralized solar energy and global personal digital communication technology for public communication, not for private profit. Technology and means of production would be available to all, to be used for common purposes. Knowledge would be a public good, with shared access and recognition of innovation.

4.3 Changing Culture

The regional ecological communities would share and rotate essential tasks, integrating mental and manual, across the public/private divide, including agricultural and manufacturing labor as well as social and human reproduction. Specialization would be based on interest and capacity, with wide recognition of the diverse types of contributions which are essential to the community.

There would no longer be a consumer culture based on invidious distinctions and conspicuous consumption.

Wealth would be distributed to assure equal opportunity in education and work.

Collaboration would ensure fair rules to support the development of human capacities.

4.4 Changing Politics

There would be a global federation of regional ecological communities, each guided by global and regional biogeochemical cycles with equitable participation (Ostrom 1990; Agarwal 2010). Rather than a focus on cash crops and debt repayments, communities could more effectively design their own priorities and responsibilities and land use.

Rather than a public/private divide distinction between mobile for-profit private business corporations and territorial-based municipal public corporations, collectives would be focused on distinct collaborative missions and purposes, both global and local.

Information technology would be used to monitor the status of human development and ecology and to express priority needs and issues (beyond the Lange/Hayek debate of plan vs. market; Morozov 2019).

The choices of education, work, and consumption would be mediated by public information technology, like a global Internet remade into an electronic public sphere for public deliberation, instead of privatized surveillance capitalism and advertising.

4.5 Priority on Global Biogeochemical Cycles

With advances in climate science, there has been analysis of both short-term and long-term global ecological trends and the continuing development of earth systems models. With a new awareness of ecology and its impact on human health, there is need of a new concept of "infrastructure," like public water systems after cholera, to consist of global monitors regarding climate resilience. Instead of an "Internet of Things" (IoT) with global interconnection for commodity production, logistics, and distribution, there could be a global network to provide real-time information with an "Internet of the earth" (IoE), or "ecological modernization theory" (Turner 2018, 161–166).

4.6 Earth Monitoring System

Instead of general-purpose capitalist money, there would be an earth monitoring system for ecological indicators. Based on climate models, such a list could include air temperature, atmospheric circulation, ocean circulation, sea level rise, cryosphere dynamics, carbon cycle behavior, net primary production, vegetation distribution, biodiversity, agriculture, hydrological impacts, and land use/land cover. There are ongoing monitoring projects in the United States and with global collaboration among scientists (Turner 2018, 106, 130–133, 211–226). With improving technologies, there are possible methods to reconceive the human/planetary interface, with such efforts as the "smart planet" like Gaia 2.0 (Lenten and Latour 2018) from the standpoint of "terrestrials," humans now clearly residing on the earth rather than the abstract universe (Latour 2018).

4.7 Integration of Time and Geographic Scales

History has been used to narrate a cohesive conception of nation-states and can be a form of political power. Rather than the very long-term view of the evolution of the history of the earth, the dominant contemporary perspective is the time of finance, which focuses increasingly on the very short run.

Instead of homogeneous time of the capitalist treadmill (Postone 1993; Tomba 2019), there could be awareness of the life cycles of the biodiversity of living species and earth's long-term evolution (Chakrabarty 2021).

4.8 Ecological Credit

Money and credit systems would be based on investments in education, health, and ecological restoration. Rather than a future based on extraction and exploitation for financial circuits, investments would be in basic needs, social capacity and political voice (Davis 2021). Instead of reified notions of money, the existence and operation of a new social and ecological contract would make specific each person's contribution and obligation to regenerative ecological resilience. Rather than the individualized disciplinary operation of capitalist financial systems, the global ecological monitoring efforts would treat each region as a collective, or "commons."

A global credit system could be established to make credit conditional on environmental protection, the real assurance of future ability to repay based on earth's processes. General-purpose money would be replaced with ecological indicators, such as Rockstrom's planetary boundaries and Smil's biogeochemical metrics. A new composite metric based on ecological resilience and regeneration based on earth systems models would be the guide for prioritizing global investments. This new metric, the *VITAcoin*, would prioritize life processes instead of symbolic wealth creation by extraction and degradation of natural and human resources. It would represent a new form of social contract based on a new form of community, humans residing on the earth for mutual benefit.

The new institutions backing "money" could consist of regional ecological communities (Davis 2017, 2019), whose residents make decisions regarding ecological and economic assets, coordinated at the global level, informed by biogeochemical cycles and ecological resilience. Rather than the focus on digital or paper currencies, the important determinants would be the structure and mission of the basic institutions. Instead of abstract money, the new money and credit would be based on

Consolidated Balance Sheet	Assets (public and private)	Liabilities
	Population and labor force (health and education)	
	Global cooperatives of science and technology	
	Regional ecological communities (managing Land, Air, Water With VITAcoin reserves)	VITAcoin issued by a global ecological bank

Fig. 8.1 Ecological institutions

explicit shared human decision-making at the local, regional, and global levels (Fig. 8.1).

In such a case, the issue of notes could serve to maintain credit within the limits of the ecology (Raworth 2017; Sheng 2021), and strategies of regeneration (Hawken 2021) could turn "finite" resources like soil and water into properly managed renewable global cycles. Credit could be provided to all who invest in the ecology and human development, and potentially providing access to a larger number of players than the for-profit private financial system. Such a system would also overcome the ambiguity of the public/private divide. Rather than competitive for-profit private entities, there would be coordinated global investment in the most "public" of all goods, the ecology of the earth.

On the asset side of the balance sheet, there would be a new range of alternative institutions. Instead of a series of interlocking balance sheets of public and private entities, the regional ecological communities would operate in a public manner (Ostrom 1990). What had been the owner's authority to command the "property in the person" is in fact a method of objectifying persons (Pateman 1988), who are then subject to control by the owner. This authority of ownership, to consume the commodity which has been purchased, is a form of power. These commodities circulate by means of monetary exchange in the market based on the "equality" of owners, while in fact different types of property have widely different implications for autonomy and "freedom." The notion of the "freedom" of the property owner has been the subject of a long debate (Friedman vs. MacPherson; Hirschman 1977).

There has been much work on alternative types of institutions, such as the "commons," and worker cooperatives, as well as regenerative farms (Agarwal 2010; Ostrom 1990; Hawken 2021). Collective organization of work, combined with political deliberation within a residential community, with integrated ties to the land (preservation as well as cultivation) is a new challenge, instead of the template of "rational calculation" of financial returns on property invested in "capital".

One could design an "open" process of formation of corporations, with a mission orientation like the franchise model of Omarova (2021), or public investment banks (Hockett 2019). Conceptually, these institutions are feasible, but would not produce a profit rate as high as those corporations which can externalize costs. The responsiveness to local initiatives could be regulated by ESG criteria, with standardized accounting. Such a model could be truer to the local initiatives and democracy that so impressed de Tocqueville, while maintaining community and ecological preservation.

On the liability side of the balance sheet, the issue of notes called VITAcoin would be based on ecological indicators, instead of projected profitability of private banks and corporations. Instead of enforcing the discipline of competition for profit on these private players, the total set of public assets would be backing public credit, with greater assurance of future ecological resilience. The users of notes would gain the privilege of accessing public resources, on the condition and promise for supporting regeneration of human and ecological resources.

5 Different Narratives and Visions of the Future

According to Larson, there is a "Culture of Exploitation" that developed in the early decades of the United States. To foster sustainability would require a paradigm shift on the order of magnitude of the abolition of slavery (Larson 2020, 3). There is some similarity to the "growth coalition" by which municipalities, states, and regions compete for location of production, even though the incentives offered are often greater than the public benefits (Logan and Molotch 1987). At the global scale, there is use of the term "empire" with respect to the United States (Immerwahr 2019), in contrast to its claim of leading and protecting world democracy.

Narratives are influential in explaining origins, expressing values, and the socialization of behavior (Shiller 2019; Hulme 2009). For example, in spite of their focus on the "ecological rift" and Cartesian dualism, Patel and Moore discuss the manner of seeing the world from the point of view of the colonial conqueror and capitalist developer. They understand Christopher Columbus as viewing the "New World" with an "appraiser's eye" and as an "assessor" (Patel and Moore 2017, 50). That is, there is a totalizing perspective associated with capitalism which can encompass humans, other species, land, and other resources, for the purposes of commodification and "development" for gain. In a culture driven by these imperatives, it is difficult to envision an alternative. For this reason, Moore stresses the analysis of worldviews and "real abstractions," which influence how humans view each other and the world, and have real effects on ecology (Moore 2016, 88). Graeber stresses critique and study of alternative cultures as well (Graeber 2001, 240–251).

There is a story of capitalism which is told in different ways in different eras. A student radical in the 1960s could alert his audience of a wave of new awareness by daring them to name the system (Block 2018, 15–16). Yet by the 1980s, capitalism was named and defended by Milton Friedman and President Ronald Reagan, which galvanized a "free market" Republican Party. In the 2020s, President Trump could claim dire threats by socialists and communists, in spite of the marginal role of the left in the contemporary United States.

There are now history wars, as well as ideological ones. There is a new "history of capitalism" in leading universities, such as Harvard, Princeton, and the University of Chicago. The work of these scholars is also reinvestigating the role of slavery in the expansion of the US economy (Beckert and Rothman 2016; Beckert and Desan 2018) and increasing awareness of its ecological implications.

The viability of capitalism has also been an explicit subject, with competition from former Communist countries like China and Russia, and global market instability. Recent books on saving capitalism (Reich 2015; Rajan and Zingales 2004; Posner 2010, 2011; Zingales 2012; Philippon 2019) express concern about inequality, increasing concentration, and deregulation.

A naming of the system, development of a history and critique, and formulation of alternatives is an important project in the age of the Anthropocene.

In summary, the entitlements of the property owners enable them to acquire the product of humans, other species, and the earth, for the purposes of commodity production for sale for profit. The investments in the reproduction of these living beings are reduced so that lifeless money can "grow." This capacity of property is backed by the ability to inscribe into law these privileges. The nation-state which protects this property benefits from the wealth generated in this way, in competition with other nation-states, for which their citizens are willing to sacrifice their own lives and the lives of other species. The financial system which governs these states and monetizes these commodities is international in scope and enables the ongoing tendency for competition, both economic and military.

Surely a direct focus on supporting living things and promoting the sustainability of earth's processes is a more direct path to well-being; world peace is necessary, but only the beginning.

Compared with the ideas of global governance examined by Mazower (2014), regional ecological communities are another utopian dream providing an alternative vision.

Bibliography

Agarwal, Bina. *Gender and Green Governance: The Political Economy of Women's Presence Within and Beyond Community Forestry*. New York: Oxford University Press, 2010.

Arthur, W. Brian. *Complexity and the Economy*. New York: Oxford University Press, 2015.

Arthur, Rudy and Arwen Nicholson. "Selection Principles for Gaia," *Journal of Theoretical Biology*. Vol. 533, 2022, 1-16.

Barbier, Edward B. *A Global Green New Deal: Rethinking the Economic Recovery*. Cambridge, UK: Cambridge University Press, 2010.

Beckert, Sven and Christine Desan. *American Capitalism: New Histories*. New York: Columbia University Press, 2018.

Beckert, Sven and Seth Rockman. *Slavery's Capitalism: A New History of American Economic Development*. Philadelphia: University of Pennsylvania Press, 2016.

Bittman, Mark. *Animal, Vegetable, Junk: A History of Food, from Sustainable to Suicidal*. New York: Houghton Mifflin Harcourt, 2021.

Block, Fred L. *Capitalism: The Future of an Illusion*. Oakland, CA: University of California Press, 2018.

Blumm, Michael and Mary Christina Wood. *The Public Trust Doctrine in Environmental and Natural Resources Law*. Durham, North Caroline: Caroline Academic Press, 2013.

Blumm, Michael and Mary Christina Wood. "“No Ordinary Lawsuit”: Climate Change, Due Process, and the Public Trust Doctrine." *American University Law Review*, Vol. 67, No. 1, 2017, 1–87.

Bowles, Samuel and Herbert Gintis. *A Cooperative Species: Human Reciprocity and Its Evolution*. Princeton, NJ: Princeton University Press, 2011.

Carleton, Tamma A. and Solomon M. Hsiang. "Social and Economic Impacts of Climate," *Science*, September, 2016, Vol. 353, No. 6304, aad9837-1 to aad9837-15.

Carney, Mark. "Breaking the Tragedy of the Horizon: Climate Change and Financial Stability," Bank of England speech, London, 9/29/2015.

Chakrabarty, Dipesh. *The Climate of History in a Planetary Age*. Chicago: University of Chicago Press, 2021.

Chomsky, Noam and Robert Pollin. *Climate Crisis and the Green New Deal: The Political Economy of Saving the Planet*. London: Verso, 2020.

Clark, Christopher. *Time and Power: Visions of History in German Politics, from the Thirty Years' War to the Third Reich*. Princeton, NJ: Princeton University Press, 2019.

Costanza, Robert, et al. "The Value of the World's Ecosystem Services and Natural Capital." *Nature*, Vol. 387, May 15, 1997, 253-260.

Daily, Gretchen C. *Nature's Services: Societal Dependence on Natural Ecosystems*. Washington, D.C.: Island Press, 1997.

Davis, Ann E. "The Practical Utopia of Ecological Community," in Richard Westra, Robert Albritton and Seongjin Jeong (eds.). *Varieties of Alternative Economic Systems: Practical Utopias for an Age of Global Crisis and Austerity*. New York: Routledge, 2017, 52-68.

Davis, Ann E. "“Salvation or Commodification?” The Role of Money and Markets in Global Ecological Preservation." *Review of Radical Political Economics*. Vol. 51, No. 4, 2019, 536-543.

Davis, Ann E. "“It's Humanity, Stupid”: Values and the Definition of Public Good." *Journal of Economic Issues*, Vol. LV, No. 2, June 2021, 382-387.

Davis, Ann E. "Postone's Legacy: Capitalism and Time." *Critical Historical Studies*, Spring, 2022, Vol. 9, No. 1, 1-34.

D'Alisa, Giacomo, Federico Demaria, Giorgos Kallis (eds.). *Degrowth: A Vocabulary for a New Era*. New York: Routledge, 2015.

Dietz, Simon, James Rising, Thomas Stoerk, and Gernot Wagner. "Economic Impacts of Tipping Points in the Climate System." *PNAS*. Vol. 118, No. 34, 2021, 1–9.

Fischel, William A. *Regulatory Takings: Law, Economics, and Politics*. Cambridge, MA: Harvard University Press, 1995.

Foley, Duncan K. *Adam's Fallacy: A Guide to Economic Theology*. Cambridge, MA: Harvard University Press, 2006.

Goldstein, Robert J. "Green Wood in the Bundle of Sticks: Fitting Environmental Ethics and Ecology into Real Property Law," *Boston College Environmental Affairs Law Review*, Vol. 25, No. 2, 1998, 347-430.

Goldstein, Robert J. *Ecology and Environmental Ethics*, Ashgate, 2004a.

Goldstein, Robert J. (ed.), *Environmental Ethics and Law*, Ashgate, 2004b.

Graeber, David. *Toward an Anthropological Theory of Value: The False Coin of Our Own Dreams*. New York: Palgrave, 2001.

Gruber, Nicolas, Philip W. Boyd, Thomas L. Frolicher, and Meike Vogt. "Biogeochemical Extremes and Compound Events in the Ocean," *Nature*, Vol. 600, December 16, 2021, 395-407.

Hartog, Francois. *Regimes of Historicity: Presentism and Experiences of Time*. New York: Columbia University Press, 2015.

Hawken, Paul, Amory Lovins, and L. Hunter Lovins. *Natural Capitalism: Creating the Next Industrial Revolution*. Boston: Little, Brown and Company, 1999..

Hawken, Paul. *Regeneration: Ending the Climate Crisis in One Generation*. New York: Penguin Books, 2021.

Heller, Michael and James Salzman. *Mine! How the Hidden Rules of Ownership Control our Lives*. New York: Doubleday, 2021.

Hess, Charlotte and Elinor Ostrom. *Understanding Knowledge as a Commons: From Theory to Practice*. Cambridge, MA: MIT Press, 2007.

Hill, John. *Environmental, Social, Governance (ESG) Investing: Analysis of the Theory and Practice of a Sustainable Portfolio*. London: Elsevier, 2020.

Hirschman, Albert O. *The Passions and the Interests: Political Arguments for Capitalism before Its Triumph*. Princeton, NJ: Princeton University Press, 1977.

Hockett, Robert C. "Finance without Financiers," in *Politics and Society*, Vol. 47, No. 4, 2019, 491-527.

Hulme, Mike. *Why We Disagree About Climate Change: Understanding Controversy, Inaction and Opportunity*. New York: Cambridge University Press, 2009.

Immerwahr, Daniel. *How to Hide an Empire: A History of the Greater United States*. New York: Farrar, Straus, and Giroux, 2019.

Keil, Roger. *Suburban Planet*. Cambridge, UK: Polity, 2018.

Klein, Naomi. *This Changes Everything: Capitalism vs. the Climate*. New York: Simon & Schuster, 2014.

Lamoreaux, Naomi, R. "The Mystery of Property Rights: A US Perspective," *Journal of Economic History*, Vol. 71, No. 2, 2011, 275-306.

Larson, John Lauritz. *Laid Waste! The Culture of Exploitation in Early America*. Philadelphia: University of Pennsylvania Press, 2020.

Latour, Bruno. *Down to Earth: Politics in the New Climatic Regime*. Cambridge, UK: Polity Press, 2018.

Lenten, Timothy M. and Bruno Latour. "Gaia 2.0: Could Humans Add some Level of Self-Awareness to Earth's Self-Regulation?" *Science*. Vol. 361, No. 6407, September 14, 2018, 1066-1068.

Lewis, Simon L. and Mark Maslin. "Defining the Anthropocene." Nature, Volume 519, March 12,2015, 171-180.

Logan, John R. and Harvey L. Molotch. *Urban Fortunes: The Political Economy of Place*. Berkeley: University of California Press, 1987.

Marx, Karl. *Capital*. New York: International Publishers, 1967.

Mazower, Mark. *Governing the World: The History of an Idea*. New York: Penguin, 2014.

McDonough, William and Michael Braungart. *Cradle to Cradle: Remaking the Way we Make Things*. New York: North Point Press, 2002.

Merchant, Carolyn. *The Death of Nature: Women, Ecology, and the Scientific Revolution: A Feminist Reappraisal of the Scientific Revolution*. San Francisco: Harper & Row, 1979.

Merchant, Carolyn. *The Death of Nature: Women, Ecology, and the Scientific Revolution*. San Francisco: Harper & Row, 1980.

Merchant, Carolyn. *Reinventing Eden: The Fate of Nature in Western Culture*. New York: Routledge, 2003.

Michaels, David. *Doubt is Their Product: How Industry's Assault on Science Threatens Your Health*. New York: Oxford University Press, 2008.

Migliavacca, Mirco, et al. "The Three Major Axes of Terrestrial Ecosystem Function," *Nature* Vol. 598, October 21, 2021, 468-472.

Mooney, Chris. *The Republican War on Science*. New York: Basic Books, 2005.

Moore, Jason W. "The Rise of Cheap Nature" in Moore, Jason W. (ed.). *Anthropocene or Capitalocene? Nature, History, and the Crisis of Capitalism*. Oakland: PM Kairos Press, 2016, 78-115.

Morozov, Evgeny. "Digital Socialism? The Calculation Debate in the Age of Big Data," *New Left Review*, March/June, 2019, Vol. 116/117, 33-67.

Network for Greening the Financial System (https://www.ngfs.net/en)

Nordhaus, William. "Climate Change: The Ultimate Challenge for Economics," *American Economic Review*, Vol. 109, No. 6, 2019, 1991-2014.

Omarova, Saule T. "The Finance View of the Corporation: Purpose, Personality, Public Policy." In Elizabeth Pollman and Robert B .Thompson (eds.). *Research Handbook on Corporate Purpose and Personhood*. Cheltenham, UK: Edward Elgar, 2021, 201-221.

Oreskes, Naomi and Erik M. Conway. *Merchants of Doubt: How a Handful of Scientists Obscured the Truth on Issues from Tobacco Smoke to Global Warming*. New York: Bloomsbury Press, 2010.

Ostrom, Elinor. *Governing the Commons: The Evolution of Institutions for Collective Action*. New York: Cambridge University Press, 1990.

Patel, Raj and Jason W. Moore. *A History of the World in Seven Cheap Things*. Oakland: University of California Press, 2017.

Pateman, Carole. *The Sexual Contract*. Stanford: Stanford University Press, 1988.

Pettifor, Anne. *The Case for a Green New Deal*. London: Verso, 2019.

Philippon, Thomas. *The Great Reversal: How America Gave Up on Free Markets*. Cambridge, MA: Harvard University Press, 2019.

Pollin, Robert. *Greening the Global Economy*. Cambridge, MA: MIT Press, 2015.

Poovey, Mary. *A History of the Modern Fact: Problems of Knowledge in the Sciences of Wealth and Society*. Chicago: University of Chicago Press, 1998.

Posner, Richard A. *The Crisis of Capitalist Democracy*. Cambridge, MA: Harvard University Pres, 2010.

Posner, Richard A. *A Failure of Capitalism: The Crisis of '08 and the Descent into Depression*. Cambridge, MA: Harvard University Press, 2011.

Postone, Moishe. *Time, Labor, and Social Domination. A Reinterpretation of Marx's Critical Theory*. New York: Cambridge University Press, 1993.

Prentiss, Mara. *Energy Revolution: The Physics and the Promise of Efficient Technology*. Cambridge, MA: Harvard University Press, 2015.

Rajan, Raghuram G. and Luigi Zingales. *Saving Capitalism from the Capitalists: Unleashing the Power of Financial Markets to Create Wealth and Spread Opportunity*. Princeton, NJ: Princeton University Press, 2004.

Raworth, Kate. *Doughnut Economics: Seven Ways to Think Like a 21st Century Economist*. White River Junction, VT: Chelsea Green, 2017.

Reich, Robert B. *Saving Capitalism: For the Many, not the Few*. New York: Alfred A. Knopf, 2015.

Salzman, James, Genevieve Bennett, Nathaniel Carroll, Allie Goldstein, and Michael Jenkins. "The Global Status and Trends of Payments for Ecosystems Services." *Nature Sustainability*. Vol. I March, 2018, 136-144.

Schiermeier, Quirin. "The Science That Support Climate Lawsuits," *Nature*, Vol. 597, September, 2021, 169-171.

Schwagerl, Christian. *The Anthropocene: The Human Era and How It Shapes our Planet*. Santa Fe: Synergetic Press, 2014.

Sheng, Andrew. "The One-Earth Balance Sheet". Institute for New Economic Thinking, July 23, 2021. https://www.ineteconomics.org/perspectives/blog/the-one-earth-balance-sheet.

Shiller, Robert J. *Narrative Economics: How Stories Go Viral and Drive Major Economic Events*. Princeton, NJ: Princeton University Press, 2019.

Smith, Adam. *An Inquiry into the Nature and Causes of the Wealth of Nations*. New York: The Modern Library, 1994.

Stern, Nicholas. *The Global Deal: Climate Change and the Creation of a New Era of Progress and Prosperity*. New York: Public Affairs, 2009.

Tomba, Massimiliano. *Insurgent Universality: An Alternative Legacy of Modernity*. New York: Oxford University Press, 2019.

Turner, David P. *The Green Marble: Earth System Science and Global Sustainability*. New York: Columbia University Press, 2018.

Vogl, Joseph. *The Ascendancy of Finance*. Cambridge, UK: Polity 2017.

Wilson, Edward O. *Half-Earth: Our Planet's Fight for Life*. New York: Liveright Publishing Corporation, 2016.
Wood, Mary Christina. *Nature's Trust: Environmental Law for a New Ecological Age*. New York: Cambridge University Press, 2014.
Wulf, Andrea. *The Invention of Nature: Alexander Von Humboldt's New World*. New York: Alfred A. Knopf, 2015.
Zingales, Luigi. *A Capitalism for the People: Recapturing the Lost Genius of American Prosperity*. New York: Basic Books, 2012.

Chapter 9
Conclusion and Further Reflections

In conclusion, we will consider some ongoing issues and questions.

In reviewing the human relation to nature and considering alternatives, there are two systems which deserve further examination: capitalism and science.

First, capitalism assumes that the earth is organized by parcels of individual private property, the owners of which have discretion as to its use and purpose. Second, science assumes that the earth is organized by natural systems which can be explored by an objective scientific method. In a way, these two perspectives are like filters between human sense data and immediate experience and abstract knowledge of reality.

Modern philosophy has also encouraged us to understand that both of these filters, each of which seems "true," are human creations and projections. They are "real abstractions" which influence our collective behavior, and so have real material effects.

There are further connections between these two ways of viewing the world. Without the "scientific revolution," there would arguably not have been an "industrial revolution," which inaugurated capitalism in Europe. Both capitalism and science seem to have an inner dynamic, in which "progress" is achieved objectively. Capitalism provides incentives and science initiates discoveries.

The scientific revolution has been part of the narrative of "progress" and Western superiority. Science has also been instrumental in the "military revolution", which then led to the "financial revolution." Global exploration in fifteenth-century Europe was also supported by scientific instruments and methods. Modern "infrastructure" consisted of energy systems (Hughes 1983) and improvement of methods of commodity production. Modern military advances such as nuclear power and aeronautics, as well as spatial exploration, have affected the balance of power among nations.

Industrial systems such as water, electricity, and communications have affected the infrastructure of modern cities and the role of government in providing or managing these services at all levels. Advances in telecommunications have resulted in new forms of "reality," based on cyberspace and simulation of immediate sensations. Coupled with advances in neurophysiology, realistic images and sensations

A. E. Davis, *Whole Earth*, https://doi.org/10.1007/978-3-031-01934-0_9

can be produced by virtual reality headsets and allow entrance into the "metaverse." Will exploration of outer space locate new sources for valuable minerals and possible viable landscapes for human habitat?

The question at present is whether the discovery of climate change (Hulme 2009, 35–70) and the associated advances in ecology will result in another "revolution," as some claim (McDonough and Braungart 1998). Both science and capitalism claim to be "objective," but as conflicts arise, will individual members of both communities begin to speak out? President Trump will declare that climate change is a "hoax," on behalf of capitalists, and James Hansen will testify in Congress and write about "storms" of his grandchildren (Hansen 2010), ringing the alarm about climate change. Alternatively, the challenges to climate science have led to considerable doubt as to the reliability of these findings (Oreskes and Conway 2010).

The basic approach of ecology is based on a holistic view, with complex interconnections over a long time period. By contrast, capitalism emphasizes the short term, with increasing productivity, and increasing speed and scale of production. As capitalism has become the dominant economic system of the earth, it has put pressure on earth's dynamic interconnections.

Economics has developed with an axiomatic paradigm, using the methods of natural science, such as physics (Mirowski 1989). Would a new approach to natural science lead to a new economics? Is it possible to adapt ecology into economics or to reframe economics entirely? Rather than self-interested rational individuals and private property, economics could view the atmosphere, land, and ocean as immense public goods, with new methods of science-based collective management, instead of the military as the classic case of a public good (Davis 2021). Instead of deskilled producers and consumers, there would be a new ecological citizenship, in which each resident understands the unique and common aspects of the regional ecology, compared with others, as well as the common evolutionary heritage of human beings with all living things. There would be a new definition of "work." Rather than commodity production for pay, work would consist of stewardship of each community's region, as well as nurturance of the next generation. There would be a new set of assumptions that humans live in cooperative communities, on earth, which is a fragile planet with the only known life in the universe. The alternative proposals in Chapter 8 above rely on changing social and economic institutions, to provide cohesive relationships for ecological restoration instead of competition for wealth and power.

The proposals above in Chapter 8 also rely on earth system models to provide reliable guidance for future governance mechanisms. Can a realistic view of science provide credible frameworks, in spite of understanding the contingency of modern scientific findings (Perillan 2021; Oreskes 2019; Hulme 2009, 72–107)? The recent award to Syukuro Manabe for his global climate models (Hulme 2009, 56–59) by the Nobel Prize committee in 2021 may mark a new level of recognition.

Can scientific literacy among the general population develop so that there are citizen scientists, sharing observations of the ecosystem in real time and developing new methods for preservation and restoration? Such a reskilling of consumers may go far in stoking the excitement of DIY handy persons, who enjoy constructing new bird feeders and observation stations, or volunteer naturalists in national parks. Rather than see the earth as "vacation" and restoration, it is viewed as an essential life system in which humans participate.

Knowledge, ethical, and philosophical perspectives are also at stake, in judging what are the overarching values for humans (Hulme 2009, 109–140). Rather than separate "objective" science and moral "values," it is important to see that scientific knowledge is "co-produced" with political and economic systems (Jasanoff 2004). In envisioning a human stewardship of the earth, the political implication is a world at peace. Rather than use science to advance military and economic competition, it would be used to restore a resilient global ecology, for human development. Human sciences, natural and social, would be newly integrated, with a common goal.

Carolyn Merchant calls for a "global ecological revolution" in which she includes consciousness (Merchant 2020, 150–156; diagram below from p. 151) (Fig. 9.1).

It is possible that the ecological insights could have the same order of magnitude impact on human culture as did the Copernican revolution and the Darwinian revolution. In both cases, the role of science challenged religious worldviews and led to centuries of debate and disputes. In the context of the twenty-first century,

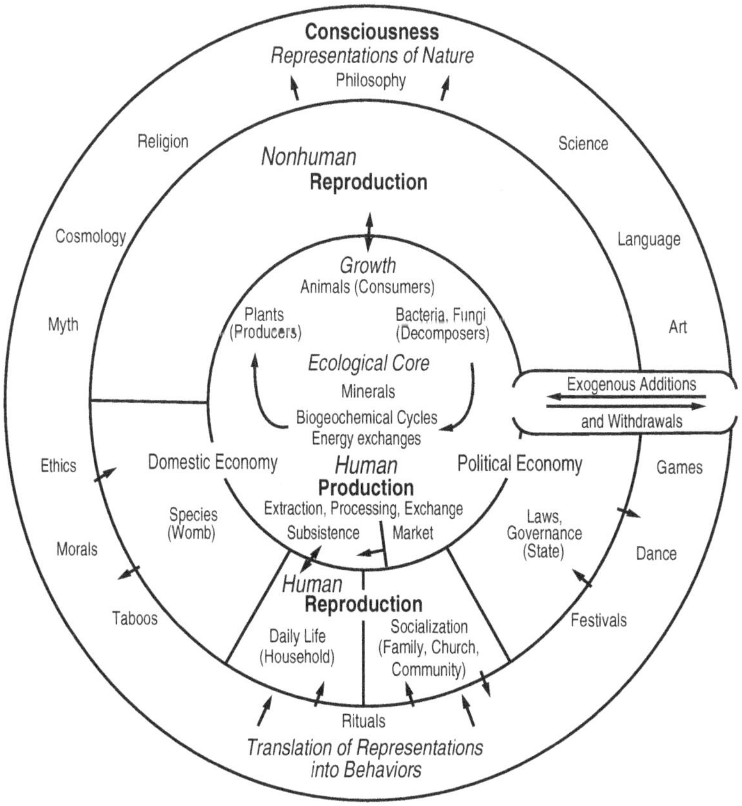

Fig. 9.1 Ecological revolutions diagram

ecological science may challenge the dominance of capitalism, rather than perform as its assistant (Marx 1967, Vol. I, Chap. 15). Rather than see technology as autonomous, with its own internal direction, one would view science as integrated in the social order, guided by common values and commitments (Jasanoff 2004; Jasanoff and Kim 2015).

Governance mechanisms remain a puzzle (Hulme 2009, 285–317; Turner 2018, 181–205), whether market driven, or existing international institutions, or by new global forms of organization, such as a federation of regional ecological communities guided by climate science.

Can the notion of ecological regions inspire a new governance model, of citizen commitment and scientific exploration and application? My personal experience in the Hudson River Valley suggests that potential exists (Davis 2015, 181–192). The panorama of its history, from Henry Hudson the explorer, to manors granted by the crown, to the Erie Canal inspiring infrastructure development in other states, to railroad industrialists like Vanderbilt, to the water system of reservoirs and tunnels, to the rise of the New York port and the world financial center. The art of the Hudson River School recorded the iconic landscapes before industrialization, including Thomas Cole and Frederick Church, as well as a distinctive literature and authors like Washington Irving and his memorable character Rip Van Winkle, the notable architectural styles of mansions, estates, as well as parks and tourist sites in the Catskills before the rise of global air travel. The preservation of the Adirondack region was partly inspired by concerns of water for New York City, with its provisions for "forever wild." Does any region which is "home" to any family have a similar appeal and loyalty? That is, does every region have such a potential for community relationships, stewardship, and scientific study? Can the integration of history and culture with ecology, in which citizens understand and nurture the unique niche and habitat for all its living species, provide a new form of cohesion and collaboration?

I am suggesting the globally federated bioregions can provide a new form of governance, integrating economics, politics, science, and humanities, providing a new form of relation of humans to the earth. Such a "bioregion" could be small enough for interpersonal relations and large enough to represent an ecological niche relevant for global systems. Coordination among such regions for the purpose of human development and ecological resilience could achieve human cooperation at a global scale.

Appendix: Human Relation to the Earth

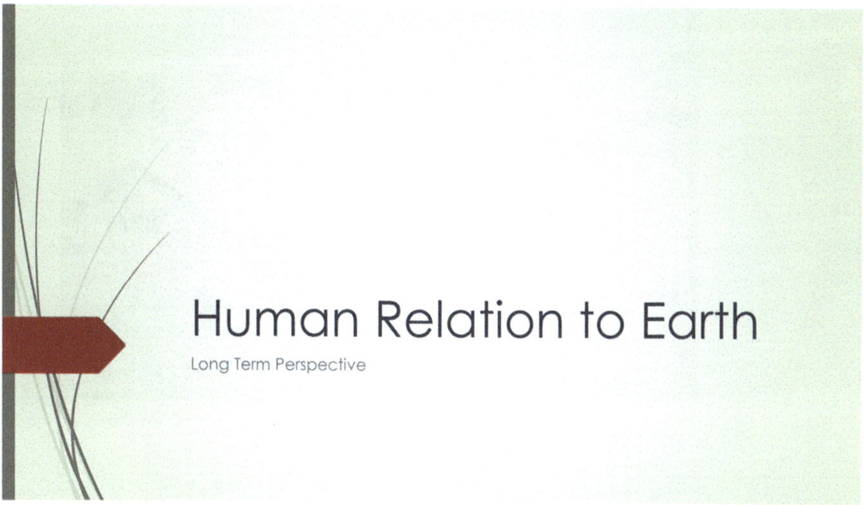

Settled Agriculture

European Exploration

Lockean Narrative

Land = Property

- In the beginning, there were individuals in the state of nature, according to John Locke and Jean Jacques Rousseau
- Those individuals formed a collective, a "social contract," for the purpose of protecting each one's individual private property.
- Money was based on gold, and helped preserve value beyond the "spoilage limit," which would otherwise restrict the role of food stuffs as a literal storage of value.
- The state was no longer considered a "collective," because it was formed by individuals based on consent and the right to rebellion.
- Property and enclosure were viewed as "productive," not the people or the "commons".
- The purpose of land is enclosure for money and financial gain

Land is Resource for Commodity Production

- Agriculture and cash crops
- Fuel for substitution for animal, hydropower, and human labor
- Mobile factories no longer tied to resources
- Extensive development of real estate for housing
- Change in land use and land cover (deforestation)

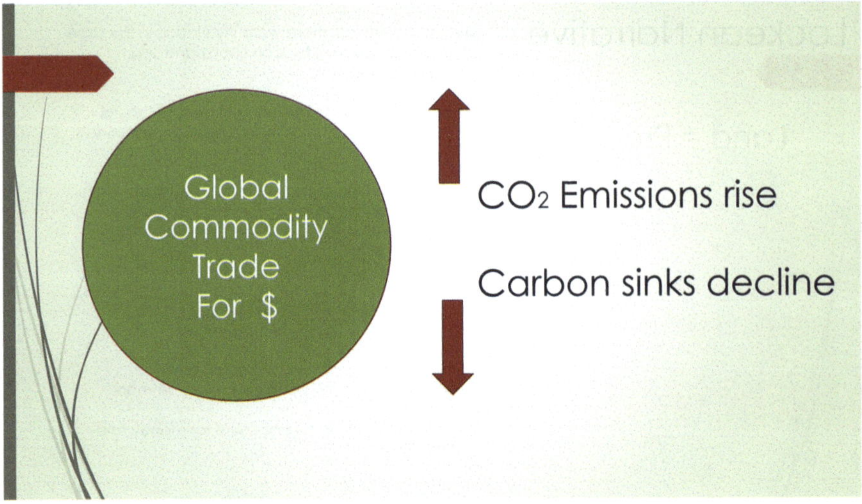
Global
Commodity
Trade
For $
CO2 Emissions rise
Carbon sinks decline

Climate change

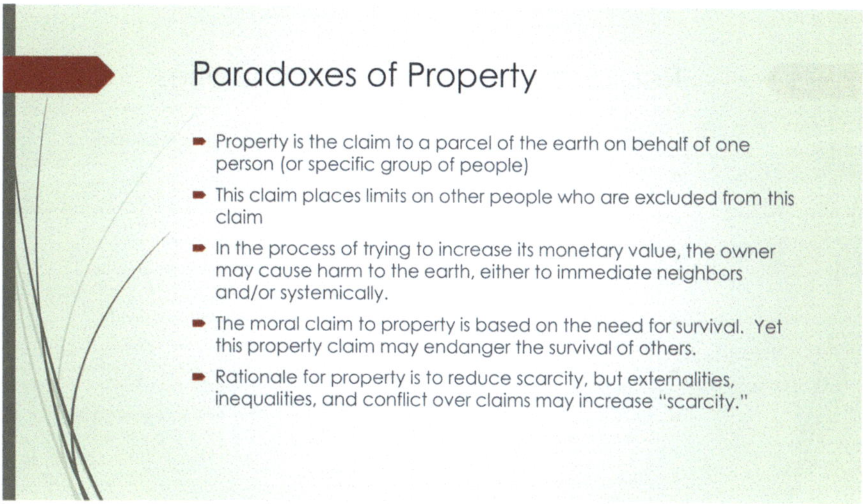
Paradoxes of Property
Property is the claim to a parcel of the earth on behalf of one person (or specific group of people)
This claim places limits on other people who are excluded from this claim
In the process of trying to increase its monetary value, the owner may cause harm to the earth, either to immediate neighbors and/or systemically.
The moral claim to property is based on the need for survival. Yet this property claim may endanger the survival of others.
Rationale for property is to reduce scarcity, but externalities, inequalities, and conflict over claims may increase "scarcity."

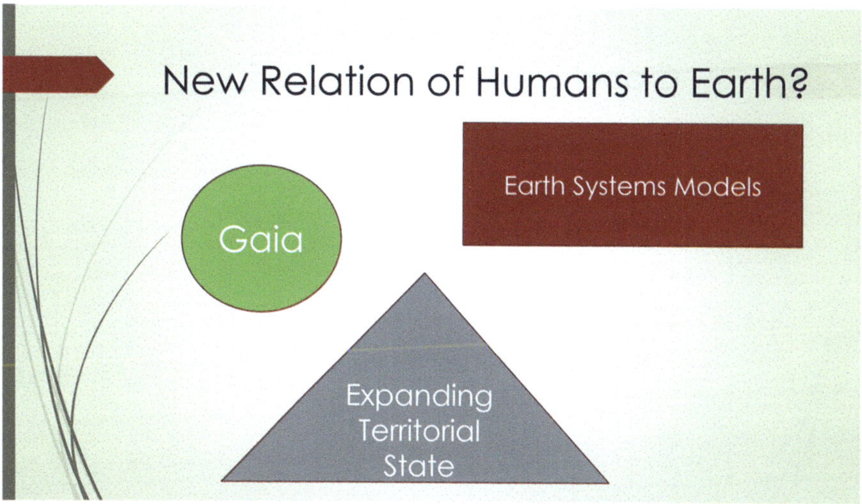
New Relation of Humans to Earth?
Earth Systems Models
Gaia
Expanding Territorial State

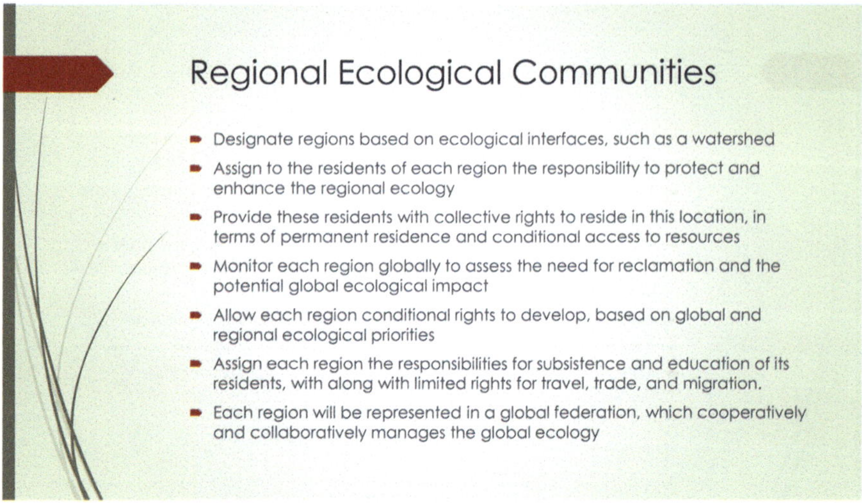
Regional Ecological Communities
Designate regions based on ecological interfaces, such as a watershed
Assign to the residents of each region the responsibility to protect and enhance the regional ecology
Provide these residents with collective rights to reside in this location, in terms of permanent residence and conditional access to resources
Monitor each region globally to assess the need for reclamation and the potential global ecological impact
Allow each region conditional rights to develop, based on global and regional ecological priorities
Assign each region the responsibilities for subsistence and education of its residents, with along with limited rights for travel, trade, and migration.
Each region will be represented in a global federation, which cooperatively and collaboratively manages the global ecology

Global Ecological Citizenship
This new form of human residence on the earth is a new "social ecological compact"
Each person is part of a global collective, with specific regional rights and responsibilities
Permanent residence rights will enhance the growth of communities, with collective ties and meaningful relationships
Ecological foundation of governance will encourage and reward the development, dissemination, and application of scientific knowledge regarding human health, regional ecologies, and global systems.

Bibliography

Arthur, W. Brian. *Complexity and the Economy*. New York: Oxford University Press, 2015.

Davis, Ann E. *The Evolution of the Property Relation: Understanding Paradigms, Debates, Prospects*. New York: Palgrave MacMillan, 2015.

Davis, Ann E. " "It's Humanity, Stupid": Values and the Definition of Public Good." *Journal of Economic Issues*, Vol. LV, No. 2, June 2021, 382-387.

Hansen, James E. *Storms of my Grandchildren: The Truth About the Coming Climate Catastrophe and our last Chance to Save Humanity*. New York: Bloomsbury, 2010.

Hughes, Thomas P. *Networks of Power; Electrification in Western Society, 1880-1930*. Baltimore: Johns Hopkins University Press, 1983.

Hulme, Mike. *Why We Disagree About Climate Change: Understanding Controversy, Inaction and Opportunity*. New York: Cambridge University Press, 2009.

Jasanoff, Sheila. *States of Knowledge: Co-Production of Science and the Social Order*. New York: Routledge, 2004.

Jasanoff, Sheila and Sang-Hyun Kim (eds.). *Dreamscapes of Modernity: Sociotechnical Imaginaries and the Fabrication of Power*. Chicago: University of Chicago Press, 2015.

Marx, Karl. *Capital*. New York: International Publishers, 1967.

McDonough, William and Michael Braungart. "The NEXT Industrial Revolution," *The Atlantic*, Vol. 282, No. 4, October 1998, 82-92.

Merchant, Carolyn. *The Anthropocene and the Humanities: From Climate Change to a New Age of Sustainability*. New Haven: Yale University Press, 2020.

Mirowski, Philip. *More Heat than Light: Economics as Social Physics, Physics as Nature's Economics*. New York: Cambridge University Press, 1989.

Oreskes, Naomi. *Why Trust Science?* Princeton, NJ: Princeton University Press, 2019.

Turner, David P. *The Green Marble: Earth System Science and Global sustainability*. New York: Columbia University Press, 2018.

Oreskes, Naomi and Erik M. Conway. *Merchants of Doubt: How a Handful of Scientists Obscured the Truth on Issues from Tobacco Smoke to Global Warming*. New York: Bloomsbury Press, 2010.

Perillan, Jose G. *Science Between Myth and History: The Quest for Common Ground and Its Importance for Scientific Practice*. New York: Oxford University Press, 2021.

The manufacturer's authorised representative in the EU is Springer Nature Customer Service Centre GmbH, Europaplatz 3, 69115 Heidelberg, Germany. If you have any concerns regarding our products, please contact ProductSafety@springernature.com

Printed and bound by CPI Group (UK) Ltd, Croydon, CR0 4YY
30/09/2026
02225496-0001